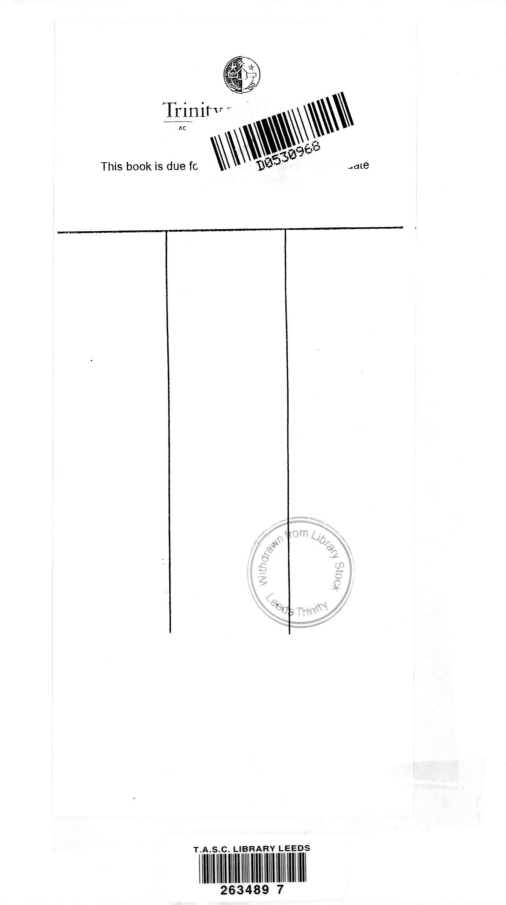

Trinity

This book is due fo

D0530968

Key Thinkers from Critical Theory to Post-Marxism

Simon Tormey and Jules Townshend

SAGE Publications
London • Thousand Oaks • New Delhi

2634897

190.904 TOR

SAGE Publications Ltd
1 Oliver's Yard
55 City Road
London EC1Y 1SP

SAGE Publications Inc.
2455 Teller Road
Thousand Oaks, California 91320

SAGE Publications India Pvt Ltd
B-42, Panchsheel Enclave
Post Box 4109
New Delhi 110 017

British Library Cataloguing in Publication data

A catalogue record for this book is available
from the British Library

ISBN-10 0-7619-6762-1   ISBN-13 978-0-7619-6762-0
ISBN-10 0-7619-6763-X   ISBN-13 978-0-7619-6763-7

Library of Congress Control Number available

Typeset by C&M Digitals (P) Ltd, Chennai, India
Printed in Great Britain by Athenaeum Press, Gateshead
Printed on paper from sustainable resources

Contents

Acknowledgements

This work has been a collaborative product in more ways than one. The ambitions of its authors could not have been fully realised without the help of a number of people. Jules would like to thank Valerie Bryson, Morgan White, Glyn Daly, Simon Malpas and Martin Reynolds. He is also deeply gratified to know that Saoirse, a fully evolved contrarian spirit, has listened to bits of this book and now has a chance to see whether they make any sense. Simon would like to thank Andy Robinson for reading drafts of earlier chapters, and to the many others who have read and critically commented on his work on Heller and Deleuze over the past few years. He also thanks his family for keeping him relatively sane during the long gestation of the book. With regards to the latter, thanks too to the folks at Sage for keeping the faith well after the embers of reasonable expectation had gone out. Simon dedicates his efforts to the many students on his various Masters courses at the University of Nottingham who have rightly demanded clear accounts of the obscure, confusing and jargon-laden theories he struggles to teach, some of which are covered here. Both of us would like to acknowledge that this book is the product of two minds that owe something to the critical spirit of two very special schools: Summerhill and St Christopher's, Letchworth. Long may they thrive as examples of how 'other worlds' are not merely thought, but enacted.

Simon Tormey
Jules Townshend
November 2005

From Critical Theory to
Post-Marxism: An Introduction

This book offers an introduction to and assessment of some of the most influential figures in contemporary critical theory. What separates this treatment from a number of others is that we have selected figures by reference to a key term in debates concerning the legacy of critical thought: 'Post-Marxism'. As will be apparent even to non-expert readers, this presents something of a difficulty. It presumes that there is something stable and known that can be unpacked and studied in the manner of a 'conventional' school of thought, ideology or tradition of theorising. The difficulty here is that the object of study is notoriously elusive, difficult to define and, not least of all, thoroughly contested. Why is this?

At one level Post-Marxism is closely associated with the work of Ernesto Laclau and Chantal Mouffe, and with *Hegemony and Socialist Strategy*, published in 1985 (Laclau and Mouffe, 1985). Many of those working in the field of political and critical theory would recognise this as the key text of Post-Marxism, and for some *Hegemony* evidently remains its *only* text (Geras, 1987; Mouzelis, 1988). It is here that we find the ambition, as implied in the label Post-Marxism, to leave Marx whilst at the same time recognising Marx's importance to the task of shaping a left radical discourse 'after' his disappearance from the scene. Important and influential though the intervention undoubtedly was, those who were prepared either explicitly or implicitly to take up the reins of the 'project' they mapped remain comparatively few. Even those who share its broad remit such as Slavoj Zizek have remained clear of the appellation 'Post-Marxist' – unless applying it to others (Zizek, 1998). 'Post-Marxism' is a label that one pins on others (and has pinned on oneself), as opposed to being a badge of self-identification.

This, however, has not prevented others such as Stuart Sim describing Post-Marxism as a fully-fledged intellectual 'movement' with roots in the emergence of Western Marxism after the bifurcation of Marxism in the period of the Russian Revolution and the collapse of the Second International (Sim, 1998: 1; 2000). Post-Marxism, it is alleged, includes many – perhaps most – of those who are otherwise called 'Marxists', albeit of a heterodox or Western variety such as Gyorgy Lukacs or Antonio Gramsci. So we can move quite quickly from the idea of 'Post-Marxism' as a collaboration between two theorists, to a definition that insists that it is a fully-fledged 'movement' that somehow unites many of the key figures in critical theory. There are nonetheless clear problems with both approaches. The former assumes too readily that the form and nature of the project associated with Laclau and Mouffe is unique or idiosyncratic and thus by extension that it represents a rupture in the 'normal' order of things. It also assumes that a label only has validity when it is self-consciously used as a badge of self-description, which discounts the way in which such 'badges' work. Marx himself once famously declared that he was no 'Marxist', as if with such a gesture he could prevent himself being associated with others who were happy to use the term in self-description. What is more realistic is to note that Laclau and Mouffe are just two amongst a very great number of theorists who have sought in some measure and to some degree to get 'beyond' Marx through a problematisation and supplanting of his work.

On the other hand, we do not think it is useful to think of Post-Marxism as a movement reaching back to the early decades of the twentieth century. This is not the same as saying that heterodox varieties of Marxism and not-quite-Marxisms were not operating over the period. Clearly they were. What it implies is that the specific problematic animating the work of Laclau and Mouffe, namely the calling into question of the validity or relevance of Marxism as a theoretical practice and mobilising ideology, is not the same as that investigated by 'Western' Marxists. Lukacs, Bloch, Gramsci et al. were not motivated by the vision of the exhaustion of Marxism, so much as, to borrow directly from Lukacs, its 'renaissance' or flowering (Lukacs, 1971: 1967 preface). These figures sought the development and elaboration of Marxism, not its supplanting by some other system of thought or some other theoretical standpoint. These are the sentiments of Marxists, not of 'Post-Marxists' however defined. They are the sentiments of the post-'68 generation – not that of the aftermath of 1968. Why, then '1968'? What is significant about this date-signifier for our purposes?

If it is not too dramatic to put it in such terms, 1968 represents the beginning of the 'end' of both Eastern and Western Marxism. With regards to the East, the Prague Spring saw the vanquishing of the notion that the Soviet Union represented the locus of anti-capitalist initiatives and a model for 'toiling masses' around the world. With the entry of Soviet tanks onto the streets of Prague those who had vainly clung onto the myth of the Soviet road to communism were compelled to admit that such a perspective was far-fetched if not an outright lie. Reform communism, the great hope of the pro-Soviet

Western intelligentsia as well as many leftists in the East, had been tried and it had failed – or rather it had been put to the sword by Soviet authorities increasingly impatient with the antics at the periphery of the Communist Bloc. Only the sternest Stalinist would cling onto the rubble of failed hopes and expectations regarding the progressive character of Soviet communism after this point. The Prague Spring thus forced a reappraisal of the Soviet road, but it was a reappraisal without nostalgia for putschist tactics, vanguards, elites or cadres leading the way for the toiling masses.

The year 1968 also gave witness to the Paris *Événements*, which unfolded despite, not because of, the official Communist Party in France (PCF). The PCF was on the contrary exposed as part of the problem to be overcome, not the spark or catalyst for a revolutionary politics. Again organised Marxism was dealt a blow from which in Europe it was never to recover, splitting as it did into various Eurocommunisms, Maoisms, Trotskyisms and Stalinist factions awaiting sometimes belated 'refoundation'. More generally 1968 showed that progressive politics was 'elsewhere' than in Marxist parties or under Marxist leadership. It was 'in the streets', 'under the paving stones', in the new social movements of feminism and environmentalism: everywhere, it seemed, but in the Party. The traditional revolutionary subject, the industrial working class, had transmuted, dissipated, 'died' or just refused to budge. This created what is arguably the central problematic animating left theory and practice since 1968. What or whom was to be the new agent of social change, of critique broadly considered? Despite its heterodoxy, Trotskyism relied on the prospect of a reawakening of revolutionary consciousness in the working class. It too was trapped in a cycle of expectation that developments since the Second World War had increasingly brought into question. There had, after all, been crises, deflation, stagflation, unemployment. Yet none of these phenomena looked remotely like cajoling the working class of the advanced industrial world out of the reformist expectations promoted by social democratic parties and trade unions alike. Worse, the impact of developments in the advertising and marketing of commodities seemed, as a long list of critics such as Herbert Marcuse and Daniel Bell complained, to dull the sense of there being meaningful alternatives to advanced capitalism (Bell, 1960; Marcuse, 1964). Where, then, was the new revolutionary or anti-capitalist subject to come from?

'Post-Marxism' is a response to these crises. It was very evidently the background to Laclau and Mouffe's 'project', as it was for a variety of approaches, theoretical innovations and strategies, all of which shared this desire to 'get beyond' Marxism and Soviet communism. For the purposes of this book, 1968 is thus taken as the lode point around which the discussion takes place. But even if we accept the legitimacy of 1968 as a starting point for thinking about the topic, this still leaves the question of what Post-Marxism is, what animates it, and what its major features or characteristics are, assuming as we will do that there is something more to the term than 'Laclau and Mouffe'. How to proceed?

Given the nature of this book, which is intended to introduce the subject to students and interested readers, we have put off the task of offering an opening definition of 'Post-Marxism', even of a speculative kind. We have preferred instead to use the parameters of the 1968 'moment' as a guide to selecting the thinkers to be examined (Murray and Schuler, 1988). Obviously, we include Laclau and Mouffe since they are happy to call their project 'Post-Marxist'. Thereafter, however, matters are trickier given the resistance of major thinkers and theorists to the 'post' prefix generally and 'Post-Marxism' in particular. We are interested in those who have at one time or other asserted that there is a 'crisis' of Marxism, that 'Marxist' orthodoxy has collapsed, in turn necessitating a thinking through of Marx's work and legacy for reconstituting critique and as a political response to advanced capitalism. In this sense we have assumed that a central element of 'Post-Marxism', however finally defined, is the idea of resting within the orbit of the Marxist problematic, even whilst disavowing Marxism as a basis for renewing critique. We are interested in those figures who remain within touching distance of Marx's thought, not those who have shot off into deep space leaving their Marxism trailing behind them like the tail of a comet. Another way of putting the matter, is to invoke Wittgenstein and state that we are interested in mapping 'family resemblances' between thinkers and theorists who might otherwise seem to have little in common in terms of the tradition of theorising to which they relate, their country of origin, or respective trajectories. Of course, some of these thinkers remain closer to Marx than others. Some are what we term 'strong' Post-Marxists in the sense that they wish to be seen or perceived as working within the Marxian problematic. Others are 'weak' Post-Marxists in the sense that they self-consciously see themselves as working against orthodox Marxism however defined. The uniting theme of 'Post-Marxism' is nonetheless the idea of posing a direct challenge to orthodoxy, as opposed to an attempt to refine or hone it.

In asserting such a task we are at the same time querying the claim made above: for example, that Post-Marxism can be identified as a 'movement', whether intellectual or political. This seems to us to be stretching the point, not least 'politically'. We are not here discussing work that has an 'organic' connection to social struggles in the manner of Lenin's connection to Russian Social Democracy or Gramsci's connection to the PCI (Italian Communist Party). Indeed one of the characteristics of Post-Marxian thought is its distance, whether intended or not, from the actual struggle of parties, movements and social groups. 'Post-Marxism' is, with some notable exceptions, an intellectual and academic 'practice', as opposed to a revolutionary one. Nor are we claiming that Post-Marxism is an 'ideology' considered either as a unified vision or set of beliefs concerning the origin and possible fate of modern society, or a tradition of thought with clear lines of affiliation, sympathy or cross-fertilisation between major figures. The 'connections' between the figures considered here are much less tangible, much more elusive and difficult to trace than either of these suggestions allow. On the other hand, we do think that there are resemblances of a theoretically and sometimes politically significant kind – enough at least to fill the otherwise the mysterious signifier 'Post-Marxism'.

As we shall see, there is rich variety of Post-Marxisms on offer, but what characterises all of them is the belief that there can be no simple 'return' to Marx. The working assumption of all of these figures is that in one way or another there is something deeply problematical about Marx and Marxism's claims to be *the* theory of human emancipation. Their emancipatory concerns led them to *problematise* core Marxist concepts. They can be briefly itemised as follows:

- *Marx's theory of history.* Post-Marxists implicitly or explicitly see Marx's view of the historical process as a historical teleology (history-as-goal) or as 'grand narrative' (Lyotard). This is an approach that seemingly proves that 'history' is on the side of the working class, that demonstrates that capitalism will ultimately fail, and that unites the 'facts' of historical development with the values of the 'good' communist society. They question Marxist historical explanation, framed in terms of productive forces coming into conflict with production relations, with the economic base determining the political, legal, ideological and cultural 'superstructure'.
- *Marx's account of the revolutionary subject.* Post-Marxists see the above approach as a form of historical determinism that insists on the centrality of the Party as the locus for all resistance to capitalism. It posits the Party as a kind of repository of theoretical knowledge and thus belittles every other agent as prey to 'spontaneous' and untutored urges.
- *Marx's account of ethics.* Linked to this determinism is the denial of the importance of human agency and ethical deliberation. At best Marxism offers an overly rationalistic and narrow view of human motivation. Marxists presume that workers will inevitably unite to overcome capitalist exploitation as a result of their growing material immiseration (see especially *The Communist Manifesto*). By contrast Post-Marxists assert that human beings (male and female) are driven by a multiplicity of passions, conscious and unconscious.
- *Marxism and positivism.* Marxism is based on a positivist methodology that privileges scientific knowledge over other forms of knowledge, ranging from ethics and aesthetics to 'experience'. It privileges the 'knowing' Marxist Party as representing the most progressive force (the working class) in history, and ultimately privileges the struggles of (often male)

workers over other forms of struggle against oppression and exploitation. This is because it privileges capitalist 'productive' labour over other kinds of labour (such as reproductive). Further, it prioritises one kind of identity (class), over other kinds of identity, which are often deemed to be forms of 'false-consciousness'. Struggles around identity and subjectivity are all in this sense 'secondary' and derivative of the main struggle: that of 'the workers'.

- *Vanguardism and intellectuals.* Marx is ambivalent about the role of radical intellectuals in the emancipatory process, in that he is clear that the Party cannot be separate from the more general struggle to overthrow capitalism, but also posits the party and thus intellectuals as showing 'the line of march'. Marxists have been prone to place themselves at the centre of the emancipatory universe, and have become deeply authoritarian when in power.

- *The problem of democracy.* Whatever the *Communist Manifesto* had said about 'winning the battle of democracy', Marxist political practice has only paid lip-service to such an aspiration. How could emancipatory theory become genuinely democratic and accommodate differences of values and identities? How in particular could we be sure that our communist future was genuinely democratic, open and plural? The evidence from Marxist practice was hardly encouraging in this respect, and of course Post-Marxists made much of the shortcomings of 'actually existing socialism' in this regard.

As we shall see, there were other elements of the Marxist approach that were problematised; but the key point is that post-Marxists were not prepared to search for Marxist answers. These problematisations, however, were not merely because of 'objective' political reasons, such as the failure of the Soviet Union to deliver what it promised, or of the Western working class's reluctance to reveal clear signs of revolutionary consciousness, or as a result of the emergence of New Social Movements. They also stemmed from important intellectual developments, especially in the emergence of what became known as 'post-structuralism' with its accent on the constitutive character of difference, slippage and the unconscious. Here the focus was on issues of meaning and subjectivity and the symbolic world, and the problematic relation between language and the representation of subjectivity. All this seemed a far cry from classical Marxist concerns with explanations of the objective social and material world.

This still leaves the question of selection. Who qualifies as 'Post-Marxist' on our minimal reading of the term? Here again a note of caution is required. Our concern in this book has not been with comprehensiveness. Rather our selection has been guided by a desire to draw out the implications of the crisis to which 'Post-Marxism' speaks. Within the selection there are some theorists whose entire output seems to merit coverage; in other cases it might be just one intervention or set of essays that seems to make linkage to the concerns articulated here. We begin with a number of figures closely associated with the events of 1968 and in particular the Paris uprising. These include Cornelius Castoriadis, Jean-François Lyotard and the writing partnership 'Deleuze and Guattari'.

Castoriadis was associated most readily with the *Socialisme ou Barbarie* group that developed a novel post-Trotskyist analysis of both capitalism and Soviet communism. The other members of the group included Lyotard and Claude Lefort, both of whom were to develop important 'Post-Marxisms' of their own. Castoriadis developed a fiercely critical account of Marxism in all its dimensions, yet retained an uncompromisingly radical politics. Indeed on his terms Marxism was not radical enough, it being wedded to an authoritarian and anachronistic account of the possibilities and potentialities of ordinary people to develop forms of self-management. Marxism remained paternalistic and bureaucratic in its responses to organic revolutionary action and therefore had to be combated in order to keep radical hopes and energies alive. Castoriadis's Post-Marxism is a robust challenge to Marxism itself, which he argued had become debased by the Bolsheviks to the extent of being an obstacle to the development of truly radical forms of political practice. Castoriadis's forte was the polemical essay, sometimes written under one of his pseudonyms. But he also wrote a number of longer pieces that demonstrate the full power of his critique. These include *The Imaginary Institution of Society*, which forms the centrepiece of the analysis presented here (Castoriadis, 1987).

In the second chapter we look at the work of Gilles Deleuze and Felix Guattari, responsible for the two-volume *Capitalism and Schizophrenia*, arguably the most important theoretical intervention to come out of 1968 (Deleuze and Guattari, 1984; 1988). Intriguingly Deleuze and Guattari insisted throughout their careers that they were 'Marxists' (Thoburn, 2003: 1–4). Yet, as even a cursory inspection of their work reveals, this is not a Marxism that many 'Marxists' would recognise or be sympathetic towards. Their work represents a complex amalgam of a variety of different streams and currents from vitalism and existentialism, to chaos theory and psychoanalysis. A perhaps more accurate way of putting the matter is that they generated a highly original synthetic approach, drawing on all manner of theoretical traditions and genres, the creative arts – as well as from Marx's own work. One reason for including them here is that at one level their work is very clearly a literal rendering of 'Post-Marxism'. It retains something 'Marxist', not least in terms of the underlying or animating principle: the critique of capitalism in all its forms and manifestations. But it also clearly leaves a certain kind of Marxism 'behind'. This would be the Marxism of many of the Marxists they criticised: a hermetically sealed orthodoxy immune to criticism, development or revision. As with Castoriadis, the end result is an approach which breaks in tangible ways from the politics of Lenin and his followers, seeking to harness imagination and desire in the service of an emancipatory politics. One of the points in common here is thus the challenge to Marxism as a conservative or hidebound doctrine. Like Castoriadis, Deleuze and Guattari perceived the need to 'break through' Marxism, or rather the Marxism of the Party or self-appointed vanguard in search of an unmediated or immanent radicalism to which an earlier generation of anarchists spoke.

In the third chapter we consider the work of Lyotard, perhaps the most notorious of the so-called postmodernists and one attacked by Castoriadis and Guattari, among many others. Lyotard's importance is perhaps more philosophical and theoretical than political. It was Lyotard who developed one of the key themes that underpins the postmodern 'moment', which is in turn one of the key elements of Post-Marxism. This is the notion of Marxism as a meta-narrative or 'totalising' account of the nature of the historical process and thus as a philosophy that 'eliminated' human contingency and responsibility. Lyotard in his later work called for a kind of politics that avoided what he came to call the *differend*, a stand-off that left no alternative but the transcendence of the system, of the totality from which it arose (Lyotard, 1988). Such a starting point reeked to Lyotard of revolutionism and an almost adolescent disdain for acting in the here and now to ameliorate and improve the present. On his terms this was not so much a reconciliation with liberal-capitalism, as a recognition of the dangers that lurked in the demand to make the totality 'presentable'. The welfare state had many problems; but to Lyotard it was preferable to the likely outcome of revolutionary romanticism.

We then come in Chapter 4 to the Post-Marxism of the 'Post-Marxists', Laclau and Mouffe. Their Post-Marxism was one built from the legacy of Louis Althusser, along with Sartre, perhaps the dominant figure of the Marxist scene in the France of the 1960s. Althusser was in turn strongly influenced by the work of Jacques Lacan, a key interpreter of Freudian psychoanalysis. As opposed, for example, to the theories of flow and abundance of Deleuze and Guattari, the Lacanian–Althusserian approach stresses the centrality of 'lack' and 'antagonism' as an element in the constitution of social reality and indeed the human condition itself (Stavrakakis, 1999: Ch. 1). Laclau and Mouffe's approach similarly places lack at the heart of politics, and in particular the fruitlessness of the project to unify subject and object, language and world in some overarching or total moment of transcendence. The universal is in this sense always contested; the point is to radicalise the nature of the contest so that different visions and identities can come to take part in what the otherwise narrowly circumscribed vision of political life permitted under liberal-capitalism.

In the next chapter we consider one of the key exchanges in the period after 1968. This is between and within feminisms – some Marxist or 'socialist', others much less obviously informed by Marx's work. As we note in this chapter, the relationship between Marxism and feminism is sometimes characterised as a marriage albeit of an 'unhappy' kind. Both present radical critiques of liberal-capitalism and both have been capable of mobilising social movements behind different visions of how the world should be remade in the name of human liberation. The Post-Marxian element has been supplied by those who believe that there is in both the elements of a shared response to the contemporary crisis of Marxism and feminism. The recognition of the unavailability, epistemologically, philosophically and politically, of a 'true' standpoint on the position of women's oppression has led to a proliferation of radical feminisms of a 'Post-Marxian' kind: all manner of standpoint feminisms, resistance feminisms, materialist feminisms. Our aim in this chapter has been to map these different responses and suggest ways in which the evolution of a Post-Marxian form of critique can be productive in terms of developing feminist critiques.

At the same time that Laclau and Mouffe were developing their own Post-Marxism, Agnes Heller was developing a position that in terms of its underlying critique of Marxism and its politics was in many ways similar. Heller came, however, from a *humanist* Marxist background as opposed to the *anti-humanist* position of Althusser and his followers (Tormey, 2001: intro.). Heller's critique also mapped closely onto certain contentions mapped by Castoriadis and Lyotard. Like the former, Heller's own politics were initially derived from the experience of the 1956 Hungarian uprising with which she herself was directly involved. This meant a politics of self-management, of councils and direct democracy. Nonetheless, her belief in the virtues of extending democratic practice to all areas of existence barely survived her experience of life in actually existing democracy (Heller left Hungary for Australia in 1976). Indeed a facet of the 'postmodern political condition' which she closely documented was an increased pessimism as to the prospects for the transcendence of modernity and liberal-capitalism via democratic self-governance. Instead, like Lyotard, she increasingly reconciled herself to the extant openness and contingency she perceived in liberal-democracy. This in turn led to the assertion that there are no foundational beliefs or doctrines preventing the moulding and re-elaboration of society along lines dictated by citizens operating within a context of existing democratic deliberation and political freedom. Of course, this was a long way from the model of the Hungarian uprising. But Heller's point concerned the long-range capacity of democracy to adapt and change with new times. Democracy had in effect become 'radical democracy' and in turn the very ground of universalisation of the values of justice and equality which Marxists themselves upheld.

Heller was influenced in her earlier work by Habermas, some of whose recent work we consider in Chapter 7. Habermas is rarely labelled a Post-Marxist, but again we are invoking the notion of Post-Marxism as an orbit within which a theorist works as opposed to a new orthodoxy or school for which theorists sign up. One of the greatest thinkers of the past four decades, Habermas's entire output can be thought of in terms of a meditation on the relevance and significance of Marx's work. Indeed, Habermas once thought of his own contribution as the attempt at revitalising historical materialism. His work is not iconoclastic so much as inventive and experimental. His relationship to Marx has been as the patient student unpacking and remoulding concepts and positions in ways that he hoped would improve on the original. Up to a point. In more recent work Habermas too has clearly 'left' Marx for a position that can meaningfully be described as Post-Marxist. This is bound up with his defence of constitutionalism, the development of a form of politics that respects and builds upon the creation of the public sphere, in turn the subject for one of his earliest works. This too shows a major Post-Marxist preoccupation. Marx, so it is argued, gave too little thought to the nature of the public sphere, in effect relegating it to bourgeois civil society and thus as something to be transcended rather than incorporated into his thinking on future possibilities. Habermas's contribution is thus in the form of a rethinking of the legacy of democratic theory, held by many of these figures to be a crucial lost dimension of Marx's thought.

The last major figure we consider is Jacques Derrida. Derrida is best known for having elaborated the contours of deconstruction and 'post-structuralism' in response to the crisis of the 'human sciences' at the end of the 1960s. Most commonly thought of as a philosopher and literary theorist, Derrida produced a startling intervention into debates on the future of radical theory in his *Specters of Marx*. An elusive, demanding work of great power and creativity, *Specters* announced Derrida as a major theorist of Post-Marxism, that is as one prepared to announce the importance of Marx even whilst adapting and moulding Marx in the name of a 'New International,' as he called his desired vehicle for emancipatory politics. Derrida's contribution was key not only for what it signalled – the continuing significance of Marx – but also for what it seemed to portend: the emergence of a diffuse, almost spectral anti-capitalist movement of a perhaps 'Post-Marxian' kind. At one level Derrida foresaw one of the key problematics of the new century: how to keep the spirit of Marx alive without succumbing either to nostalgia for lost times or to the passivity of a position that insists on waiting for the return of the spectre. We have to live with and without Marx – we have to live with and for the spirit of Marx – a very Post-Marxian gesture as we shall see (Derrida, 1994).

This leaves us to reassert that what we are presenting is not and could not be a definitive or comprehensive account of Post-Marxian thought. As we noted above, such a goal would confuse what for us Post-Marxism is: a diffuse pattern of interlocking and interrelated thoughts, prescriptions and criticisms. It would also be to undermine the sense that each of the thinkers here has an original contribution to make. For this latter reason we have sought to make each of the chapters largely self-standing, recognising that there will be many who are less interested perhaps in the story of 'Post-Marxism' than the particular contribution a given thinker has made to the development of critique in his or her own right. We also recognise that there are many thinkers and theorists who might have been considered here, but who for various reasons were not. Indeed it would be possible to assemble an alternative book on 'Post-Marxism' including the likes of André Gorz, Jean Baudrillard, Slavoj Zizek and Claude Lefort, a variety of green post-Marxisms (John Bellamy-Foster, James O'Conner) and heterodox quasi-Marxisms (Frederic Jameson, David Harvey, Ellen Meiksins Wood). Such figures can be considered in similar terms to those being looked at here, that is as theorists who remain within the orbit of Marxism and the mode of critique represented by it. What we hope, however, is that the reader will begin to see the connections between thinkers who might not otherwise be thought of in the same theoretical or political 'space', and go on (if needs be) to discover these other theorists for themselves.

Finally we should also add, perhaps paradoxically, that any discussion of the nature and meaning of 'Post-Marxism' will serve to highlight what seems to us to be an obvious point which may otherwise be overlooked in discussions of fashionable figures: Marx's own work is at one level affirmed – if only in 'spectral' terms – by Post-Marxism, if not by 'post' critique more generally. The need to disavow or get 'beyond' Marx is at the same time the need to *reread* Marx, to *rethink* Marx and to keep continually in motion the question of Marx's relevance for us as inhabitants of a world that remains – according to those who defend it as well as those who criticise it – unambiguously and triumphantly capitalist. As long as there is capitalism, then there will, we think, be a need to reread the greatest theorist *of* capitalism and capitalism's possible 'after'. In this sense we do not see the emergence of Post-Marxism as signifying the 'death' or 'end' of Marxism. Far from it: as seems obvious we are at some level still in Marx's 'time'. The challenge for Post-Marxism is the same as that for any self-consciously radical current of thought, i.e. to show that the modifications, rereadings and critiques it offers improve on Marx's appreciation of capitalism and the forms of struggle, contestation and resistance able to be mobilised against it.

Sources and Further Reading

Bell, D. (1960) *The End of Ideology*, Cambridge, MA: Harvard University Press.
Castoriadis, C. (1987) *The Imaginary Institution of Society*, trans. K. Blamey, Cambridge: Polity Press.

Deleuze, G. and Guattari, F. (1984) *Anti-Oedipus: Capitalism and Schizophrenia*, London: Athlone Press.

Deleuze, G. and Guattari, F. (1988) *A Thousand Plateaus: Capitalism and Schizophrenia*, London: Athlone Press.

Derrida, J. (1994) *Specters of Marx: The State of the Debt, the Work of Mourning, and the New International*, trans. P. Kamuf, London: Routledge.

Geras, N. (1987) 'Post-Marxism', *New Left Review*, 163: 40–82.

Laclau, E. and Mouffe, C. (1985) *Hegemony and Socialist Strategy: Towards a Radical Democratic Politics*, London: Verso.

Lukacs, G. (1971) *History and Class Consciousness*, trans. R. Livingstone, London: Merlin.

Lyotard, J.-F. (1988) *The Differend: Phrases in Dispute*, trans. G. v. d. Abbeele, Manchester: Manchester University Press.

Marcuse, H. (1964) *One Dimensional Man*, London: Sphere Books.

McLennan, G. (1996) 'Post-Marxism and the "Four Sins" of Modernist Theorizing', *New Left Review*, 218: 53–74.

Mouzelis, N. (1988) 'Marxism or Post-Marxism?', *New Left Review*, 167: 107–23.

Murray, P. and Schuler, J.A. (1988) 'Post-Marxism in a French Context', *History of European Ideas*, 9: 321–34.

Sim, S. (ed.) (1998) *Post-Marxism: A Reader*, Edinburgh: Edinburgh University Press.

Sim, S. (2000) *Post-Marxism: An Intellectual History*, London: Routledge.

Stavrakakis, Y. (1999) *Lacan and the Political*, London: Routledge.

Thoburn, N. (2003) *Deleuze, Marx and Politics*, London: Routledge.

Tormey, S. (2001) *Agnes Heller: Socialism, Autonomy and the Postmodern*, Manchester: Manchester University Press.

Zizek, S. (1998) 'Psychoanalysis in Post-Marxism: The Case of Alain Badiou', *South Atlantic Quarterly*, 97: 235–62.

1

Cornelius Castoriadis: Magmas and Marxism

[W]e have arrived at the point where we have to choose between remaining Marxist and remaining revolutionaries, between faithfulness to a doctrine that, for a long time now, has ceased to fuel either reflection or action, and faithfulness to the project of a radical change of society, which demands that we first understand what we want to change and that we identify what in society truly challenges this society and is struggling against its present form. (Castoriadis, 1987: 14)

Cornelius Castoriadis would have been horrified to be regarded as a 'Post-Marxist' on any definition of the term. As he made clear in a number of essays towards the end of his life, 'post' theory meant resignation, despair, impotence (Castoriadis, 1997: 32ff.). It meant accepting the given, the limitations of the critical imagination and capitulation in the face of superior ideological forces. Castoriadis was, by contrast, a self-styled militant, temperamentally, theoretically and most of all politically. This in turn meant being hostile to ideas that are complicit in the continuation of hierarchy and subordination, whether under the aegis of capitalists or communists. Nevertheless there is an important sense in which Castoriadis shares, if not the political conclusions, then certainly the basic premise that animates others considered in this book. This is to say that he considered Marxism the major intellectual, theoretical and political project of his age, but also the major obstacle to the development of forms of critique and political engagement that could advance the project of creating an 'autonomous' society. This in turn meant having to engage continuously with the works of Marx, with the regimes founded by Marxists, with the efforts of Marxist groups to form the vanguard of revolutionary change. Marxism was not something he could leave behind; he could not 'escape' Marxism, except perhaps for those moments towards the latter part of his life when he was attacking the other great orthodoxy of the day, Lacanianism. Castoriadis's radicalism was formed in and against Marxism, and it is from this point of view that it can be termed 'Post-Marxist'. Quite apart from the possible family resemblance to others considered in this volume, consideration of Castoriadis's unduly neglected work is also pressing from the point of view of those who remain sceptical about the development of a Post- or non-Marxist, yet radical politics. Unlike some of those considered here, Castoriadis did not give up Marxism to embrace liberalism or liberal-democracy. Rather he divested himself of Marxism in order to remain radical. Whether his work succeeds on these terms is another matter. But the point is that the thrust of Castoriadis's rejection of Marxism stemmed from the view that the problem with Marxism was not that it was too radical, but rather not radical enough.

Castoriadis was born in Constantinople in 1922, though his family emigrated shortly afterwards to Athens where he was to remain until after the Second World War. Caught up in the radical left politics that flared during the war, he joined the powerful Greek Communist Party, but almost immediately had his doubts about its fidelity to the emancipation of the working class. Identifying initially with Trotskyism, Castoriadis quickly abandoned even that heterodox tendency for a libertarian communism that had something in common with the other great heterodox movement of the 1940s and 1950s, the Johnson–Forrest tendency. The young Castoriadis was passionate in his commitment to emancipation. Unusually, he was equally passionate in his hostility towards the Soviet Union, and the efforts of other radicals to accommodate the USSR within their own definitions of 'progressive' regimes. Castoriadis's own group, *Socialisme ou Barbarie* [SOB], which broke from the Fourth International in 1948, was to be defined by this hostility to communist rule wherever it reared its head. SOB, which also counted among its number Claude Lefort and Jean-François Lyotard, was to be a persistent thorn in the side of communist parties across the industrialised world in the 1950s and 1960s. Castoriadis himself produced a constant stream of articles and analyses sometimes under the pseudonyms, 'Paul Cardan' or 'Pierre Chaulieu' (Castoriadis, 1988a; 1988b; 1993). Many of these pieces were directed against the efforts of the USSR to impose its dismal vision of socialism on its 'sphere of influence'.

Despite or because of the penetrating nature of its critique, SOB was dissolved in 1967 by its members, though many of its key terms and ideas were to be influential in the 1968 events in Paris, perhaps the quintessential 'anti-bureaucratic' revolt of the post-war period. In 1970 Castoriadis retired from his senior post as an analyst at the OECD, devoting himself to psychoanalytic theory and practice and the displacement of the baleful influence of Lacan in particular. The culmination of this critique was the original and highly demanding essay that makes up the core of *The Imaginary Institution of Society* (published alongside the earlier piece 'Marxism and Revolutionary Theory'). Up to his death in 1997, Castoriadis remained a forceful intellectual presence at conferences and colloquia around the world, where his robust defence of 'self-management' and 'the self-instituting society' served as a challenge to the baroque abstractions of rival approaches and thinkers. He was a prolific essayist, and in later years the concrete analyses of the travails of communism were conjoined and greatly enriched by many wide-ranging essays on a variety of topics. Many of these are collected in *Crossroads in the Labyrinth*, *World in Fragments*, and *Politics, Philosophy, Autonomy*. A further volume of otherwise unpublished articles and shorter pieces was collected in *The Castoriadis Reader* (Curtis, 1997), and a further set of essays written towards the end of his life appeared under the title *The Rising Tide of (In)Significancy* containing reflections with the same vigorous and militant spirit that marked his work of the 1940s. The aim of this chapter is to give an overview of Castoriadis's contribution together with an indication of its utility for emancipatory politics.

Rationalisation, bureaucracy and self-management

As already mentioned Castoriadis's position was informed by his hostility to what Marxism had become at the hands of the 'Marxists', more specifically the Bolsheviks. In his view the promise of Marx's work had been betrayed by Marxism in practice. The critique of Marxism thus moved from the concrete analysis of the forms and modalities of Marxism as a governing doctrine towards a critique of the theoretical and political premises of Marx's work itself. Several themes are relevant in this early critique. The first and most obvious is Castoriadis's characterisation of both capitalist and communist regimes as 'bureaucratic' thereby extending the Trotskyist critique of the USSR to advanced society as such. Castoriadis had studied the work of Max Weber extensively (he was one of the first translators of Weber's work into Greek), and evidently took from him the correlation drawn between the process of modernisation and bureaucratisation, that is the proliferation of structures to maintain and administer social reproduction. This in turn necessitated a growing army of administrators, functionaries and bureaucrats to manage processes and operations on a scale that Marx could barely imagine.

As for Weber, so for Castoriadis such development equated to the suffocation of initiative and creativity in an 'iron cage' of instrumental rationality. The great difference is that whereas Weber's analysis tended towards fatalism with respect to such developments, Castoriadis's analysis remained critical and indeed optimistic, agreeing as he did with Marx's analysis of the exhaustion of capitalism as a social system and the necessity for its over-coming due to the alienation it engendered (Castoriadis, 1988a: 101; 1988b: 92–3). Bureaucratisation was not in his view an insurmountable process that denuded humanity of the capacity to manage itself. It was a historically situated practice of domination like any other. On the other hand, it was one little understood by Marxists who clung obstinately to a mode of analysis that was, as far as Castoriadis was concerned, becomingly increasingly irrel-evant. Marxism was a discourse of class polarisation, of industrial produc-tion and growing immiseration. Bureaucratisation under both capitalist and communist systems challenged these simplistic conclusions, and pointed to the necessity for a new analysis that broke with rather than developed Marxian categories.

Castoriadis documented the ways in which Marxian class analysis was being rendered defunct by the division of the world into those who manage and run the bureaucracy and those who are required to conform to its edicts. The former he termed 'the directors', the latter 'the executants' (Castoriadis, 1988a: 9), thereby echoing the 'post-class' analysis of James Burnham in *The Managerial Revolution*. To Castoriadis, the problem with class analysis is that it confounded 'class interest' with self-organisation, to disastrous effect. In the USSR a group claiming to act in the interests of the working class (the Bolsheviks) had taken power; yet the idea that this move equated with the working class taking power was clearly a fiction. Not only had the Bolsheviks eliminated the very institutions and organisations set up by the working class to manage their own affairs, namely the Soviets, but they had in effect placed themselves in an unchallengeable position – and all in the name of the working class. The feudal order had been replaced by a bureau-cratic order run in the *interests* of the working class, but not of course *by* the working class. This 'substitutionism' mirrored the operation of the capital-ist elites in the West, who under cover of elite-dominated 'democratic' insti-tutions were able to promote themselves as 'representatives' of the people whilst at the same time ensuring that the working class remained subject to bureaucratically exercised control. In this sense Marxism had become an alibi for the disenfranchisement of the working class, rather than the means for its emancipation. The representative claim that underpinned the bour-geois revolution was mirrored in the vanguardism of a Leninist-inflected Marxism.

The line developed by Castoriadis in his early essays echoes the critique developed by Bakunin in his critique of Marx (Bakunin, 1872). It also chimes with that of Georges Sorel who in his essay 'The Decomposition of Marxism' had argued that Marxism had become an ideology of a theocratic kind (Sorel, 1968). As with Bakunin's critique, a persistent theme in the work of the early Castoriadis is that the self-organisation of the working class must be *both* the means *and* the end of the revolutionary transformation of society. Any attempt to annex the will or activity of the working class to a party or movement separate from that class must be opposed. The working class cannot be represented; it cannot be 'made present' in terms of its own interests or some objective will conforming to the objective 'line of march' or deep-lying historical tendencies. Emancipation has to be *self*-emancipation, and management in a socialist society has to be *self*-management. Any other understanding would of necessity lead to the separation of those who manage from those who are managed and thus to the rebirth of bureaucracy. As Castoriadis makes clear in *On the Content of Socialism*, 'the realization of socialism on the proletariat's behalf by any part or bureaucracy whatsoever is an absurdity, a contradiction in terms, a square circle, an underwater bird; socialism is nothing but the masses' conscious and perpetual self-managerial activity' (Castoriadis, 1988a: 297). Castoriadis thus remained true to the self-understanding of the founders of the First International of which Marx himself was the leading member. Yet, whereas Bakunin was discussing forms of organisation that were largely embryonic in the middle to late nineteenth century (mass workers parties, large-scale bureaucratisation of public and private institutions etc.), Castoriadis was able to give close consideration to the ways in which such organisations were able to generate new forms of resistance and new sources of hope.

In terms of resistance, a theme of Castoriadis's writings on bureaucracy was the self-contradiction inherent in the effort to maintain optimum conditions within the constraints of an artificially imposed hierarchy. What becomes evident to Castoriadis is that the new forms of work being generated under modern conditions placed a premium on quasi-autonomous action and creativity, as opposed to the exercise of 'muscle' that characterised the work of earlier periods (Castoriadis, 1988a: 298–9; 1988b: 172–81). More was required of people in industrial settings: more initiative, more responsibility and ingenuity. At the same time, however, bureaucratic control became evermore hierarchical and distant, as new levels of command management were added to the old. In this sense Castoriadis went against the grain of the received wisdom which insisted that modernity affirmed the necessity for increased division of labour and thus to increased subordination, hierarchy and differentiation of input and reward. In his characteristically optimistic view bureaucratisation was a mere cover for the annexing of political and economic power to a new elite. If modernisation carried with it an imperative it was a tendency to *generalise* economic functions and involve the worker to an ever greater degree in key tasks and processes. Ironically such ideas were to become staples of management-speak in the 1970s and 1980s with its talk of 'flat hierarchies' and 'flexible' working practices. Unlike the management gurus, however, Castoriadis took seriously the possibility of, indeed necessity for, generalised self-management and thus the elimination of any kind of hierarchy or differentiation between members of a given collective. From this point of view his account of justice tends at this point to endorse Proudhon's conclusions from *What is Property?* and the view that in a self-managed society there would be little rationale for differentiation of pay (Castoriadis, 1993: 207–15). Since the allocation of tasks and functions would be decided on an egalitarian and democratic basis as opposed to the basis of the market, each and every contribution would be deserving of equal remuneration. Why should those performing one set of tasks not be paid as much as those performing another when in the view of the community each is equally necessary for the well-being of the whole?

Castoriadis's views on the irrationalities of bureaucratic rule were apparently confirmed by the events of 1956 (Castoriadis, 1988b: 57–89; 1993: 250–71). To the left's surprise, communism was overthrown in Hungary by the largely spontaneous and unplanned energies of a wide section of the population. Councils were created, decision-making popularised and new procedures instituted that guaranteed widespread participation in all areas of social and economic functioning. Here was a vindication of Castoriadis's position, one he was never slow to refer to when sceptics doubted the possibility for the kind of self-organisation to which he was dedicated. Hungary announced certain truisms as far as Castoriadis was concerned. The first was the sheer unpredictability of human action, the way it defies pattern or logic. 'Hungary 1956' should not have happened. For communists, it was inconceivable that workers should rebel against a workers' state. For liberals, those rebelling against communism should have rushed into the construction of constitutional arrangements safeguarding those individuals' liberties and rights so rudely taken away in the communist putsch. The fact that 'Hungary' did take place confirmed a basic fact about human action: we create the world and thus we are able to transform our world into a radically different world. The onset of 'crisis' does not make for a transformative or radical politics; radical activity by ordinary men and women did.

Secondly, hierarchy and subordination are not more rational under modern conditions as many a pessimistic commentator asserted: they are less so. We should be able to see more clearly than our forebears the mystical basis for elite rule in whatever guise, and thus that whatever obstacles there are to self-management are supported and sustained by human action – not by 'necessity' however interpreted. There is no reason why ordinary people cannot be free, which for Castoriadis equates to managing society unaided by priests, monarchs or communist party officials. It is not building new systems that are the key to developing autonomy as a collective project, but participating in processes in which society is reproduced. No amount of tinkering with democratic institutions will make them better if the end product is the *representation* of people's needs and interests as opposed to the direct *participation* of people in the self-management of society. In this sense representation is opposed to autonomy. What the Hungarians seemed clearly to grasp on Castoriadis's reading is the moment a group annexes governance to something external to self-activity autonomy itself is alienated. In this sense Castoriadis fully endorsed the Bakuninist critique not only of bureaucracy, but of 'statism' more generally. The problem was not merely a set of institutions suspended above the social, but the abdication of political creation as a collective activity, as opposed to an activity undertaken by the few whether in trade unions, political parties or society more generally.

The end of Marxism

In his early work Castoriadis's analysis of contemporary politics is the source of his disappointment with Marxism. Marxism fails in practice, if not in theory. He still evidently hoped, however, that the radical and autonomist politics to which he was attached would re-emerge phoenix-like from organised revolutionary politics to which he himself was dedicated until the disbanding of SOB. From the late 1950s onwards these expectations are progressively displaced in his deepening critique of Marxism. The latter comes increasingly to be regarded by Castoriadis, not merely as a project that failed, but as a position fully implicated in the horrors of twentieth-century despotism. Marxism thus has to be combated not only as a practice, but also as a theory. The major theoretical attack was launched in the work of the late 1950s and in particular in the essay 'Modern Capitalism and Revolution' (1959). The critique culminates in 'Marxism and Revolutionary Theory' written in 1964. Castoriadis's analysis of Marxism is a dense and complicated one operating on a range of levels. Yet there are certain core notions which were to form the basis of his revolt against what he now termed 'a collective irrational belief' (Castoriadis, 1988b: 331). The main props of his attack were as follows.

1   As an economic theory Marxism had become redundant. The analysis of the major trends and tendencies of capitalist production were wrong empirically, and this in turn highlighted its weakness in theoretical terms (Castoriadis, 1988b: 226–308). In particular Marx had been wrong about the 'contradictory' nature of capitalism. Capitalism is certainly antagonistic in the sense that it is characterised by the struggle between the haves and have-nots. But the idea that capitalism is marked by some fundamental flaw which *necessitates* its supersession by a higher or superior kind of economic organisation is flawed. Capitalism is not ·doomed. Far from it: capitalism demonstrates great capacity to survive periodic crises through the extension of markets and the generation of new needs and thus new

products to satisfy those needs. Capitalism is prone to crises and recessions, but these are relatively minor disturbances considered from the point of view of the system as a whole. Nor does decolonialisation signal the crisis of the market, as widely predicted by Marxists. Rather it presages the deeper integration of all parts of the world into the global capitalist market, in turn aiding expansion and accumulation.

2   Marxism was wrong about the *nature* of the struggles that marked advanced capitalism. In other words it was wrong on sociological grounds. The struggle between the bourgeoisie and the proletariat documented by Marx had given way to the struggle between those who direct society and those who are directed, a division that does not correspond to that between exploiter and exploited in classical class analysis. It is impossible to identify strata on the basis of the ownership and control of the means of production. Everyone works, everyone earns, everyone is employed, everyone has the same need structure, even if the ability to meet it varies enormously. The overt class struggles of the past had given way to sporadic resistances to bureaucratic control (1936, 1953, 1956, 1968), serving as a reminder of the deep human desire for autonomy and collective self-management. These ruptures did not, in Castoriadis's view have a class character, but on the contrary demonstrated the human as opposed to class character of resistance. Indeed, the working class was 'dying' as a meaningful political subject to be replaced by indistinct or diverse patterns of affiliation and identity expressing themselves as new social movements and resistance against specific injustices.

3   Marxism was trapped within the same circle of expectations that underpinned Enlightenment thought generally: the notion that politics is primarily a realm of technique (*technē*) emitting of rational, theoretically driven 'solutions' (Castoriadis, 1987: 71–84). Such an outlook had proved devastating to the nascent workers' movement in Russia, encouraging the Bolsheviks to snuff out embryonic institutions of self-management in the name of 'scientific' leadership and planning. This substitution of the direct participatory impulse with the cynical schemes of the Bolsheviks was in Castoriadis's view directly attributable to Marx having fetishised the realm of *theoria* over that of *praxis*, of theory over practice, and thus of representatives and planners over the wishes, needs and activities of ordinary people. The outcome was a hyper-extension of the very bureaucratic logic that a genuinely revolutionary politics should aim at transcending.

At the heart of Castoriadis's critique lay a perhaps even more profound objection, one that was to resurface in his critique of Lacan in his work of the late 1960s and 1970s. This was directed against the determinism of Marx's approach, one which by definition posited the moving force of history in 'productive forces' thereby reducing contingent human action to a mere epiphenomenon of the historical process. Marx had famously described the terms of historical progression when he noted in the *1859 Preface* that 'just as the handloom gave us feudalism, so steam power gave us capitalism', appearing to signal that technology determined the character of the society that followed. Where Marx saw the operation of the hidden hand of technological advance operating to construct the social, Castoriadis saw the creation of distinct worlds by the express and intentional action of individuals acting in groups as well as individually. Where Marx sees the world in class terms, documenting the rise and fall of aggregate social forces, Castoriadis increasingly comes to see history as the outcome of contingent choices and variables. As he asserts, '[t]here is no longer a general explanation of history, but an explanation of history in terms of history' (Castoriadis, 1987: 152). In short, where Marx subjects history to the overarching logic of production, Castoriadis urges us to see history as a series of interlocking yet distinct events shaped by and for the actors within. In other words, human life is a field of radical contingency and openness. As he argues:

> Nothing in any society whatsoever ... exists that is not at one and the same time the inconceivable presence of what is no longer and the just as inconceivable imminence of what is not yet ... The actual existence of the social is always intentionally dislocated or, constituted in itself by what is outside of itself. (Castoriadis, 1987: 219)

Nothing determines, nothing inheres; there are no 'axioms' or rules of social progression. There is only social creation and that creation is an intentional articulation of possibility. The base does not 'determine' the superstructure; the superstructure determines the superstructure.

From Marx to Lacan: from self-management to self-institution

The rejection of all determination and necessity for understanding human action still left the vexed matter of accounting for why people act in the way they do. Why do societies and cultures have one kind of character and not another? The question was key not only in theoretical and philosophical terms, but also in political terms. Marxism's failure to provide an adequate basis for the analysis of social action, of motivation and desire, left a gaping hole at the heart of revolutionary theory – one that struck Lyotard, Deleuze and Guattari in similar terms. Each of these theorists wanted to understand why and how it is that people decide to overthrow domination. What is it that lies behind the demand for radical change? How is it that people who seem to be fully integrated into social reality can suddenly and 'spontaneously' turn their backs on it and revolt?

In a sense at the core of Castoriadis's approach lay a simple proposition: we are the authors of our own actions. We know what we are doing and why we are doing it. There is no mystery as such to 'explaining' action. However, Castoriadis knew that behind this disarmingly straightforward observation lay a further difficulty: the origin of 'action' itself. Action, or the desire to act, comes from 'somewhere'. In the absence of any other possible 'location' that somewhere had to be located in the unconscious, a site of possibility that becomes increasingly important in his writings from the mid-1960s onwards.

Yet there were further obstacles to be overcome. Just as left radical thought and practice was dominated by Marxism, so psychoanalytic theory had increasingly become dominated by Lacanian approaches, with deleterious consequences for critique and the possibility of a radical politics. The issue of how to reformulate radical politics on a psychoanalytic reading acquired even greater moment as, with the failure of the 1968 upheaval, thinkers such as Lyotard, Deleuze and Guattari invested heavily in various iterations of a desire-based analysis. In Castoriadis's view 'desire' reeked of obscurantism and a complicity with the given that was every bit as powerful as the Lacanian paradigm it sought to displace. 'The unconscious' had to be reconfigured so as to prevent it becoming hostage to conservative forces. Much of Castoriadis's work of the 1970s onwards can be read as a response to the problematic of how to reconnect the unconscious back to the politics of emancipation. In this sense the operation evokes the efforts of an earlier generation of left radicals such as Wilhelm Reich, Herbert Marcuse and Erich Fromm who wished to explore the potential of the unconscious for emancipatory purposes. As for them, so for Castoriadis the unconscious was key to establishing the basis for human action, for potential and possibility. If the unconscious was ultimately the mainspring for social action, it had to be remodelled as a source of radical energies as opposed to a source of inertia and social conservatism.

Castoriadis had grappled with the idea of how exactly to counter the threat posed by the Lacanian reading of the unconscious throughout his writings of the 1960s. Lacan had posited 'lack' as the basis of reading the development of subjectivity. The infant lacks the mother's breast and this lack shapes the development of the infant's relationship to the outside. Language also 'lacks' in the sense that the sign only stands in for, but can never come to be that which is signified. Language is in its very structure witness to the more general alienation of human existence. From here it is but a short step to an account that stresses the dislocated and antagonistic character of individual and social life generally: the unavailability of the Real, the object of desire and the impossibility of a society perfectly 'transparent' to itself, meaning one that realises the unity of subject and object lying at the heart of the post-Kantian vision of emancipation. This characterisation of dislocation is nevertheless largely accepted by Castoriadis. 'Transparency' and 'universality' are indeed the false idols of political theorising. We will never be 'beyond' the political, or 'beyond' justice in the manner suggested by Marx in particular. The individual will always be separate and 'apart' from the social. We will always experience needs, wants and desires as our own, not as part of some collective agent (Castoriadis, 1987: 114, 119). There will always be a gap between the I and the We. The job of the theorist is not therefore to eliminate the gap or to pretend it is not there (Marx); nor, however, is it to fetishise the gap so that alienation is built into the very definition of the social (Lacan). It is to emphasise the ineliminability of the particular and the universal, individual and the social, and thus the necessity for using whatever creative possibilities exist to augment, enhance and promote the possibility of collective self-understanding and self-definition. Where Castoriadis's account departs from the Lacanian account is in his insistence on the centrality of phantasy and the imagination to signification, and by extension the possibility of radically transforming social life in accordance with new conceptualisations of reality. How does this work?

On the Lacanian schema, and indeed in structuralist and post-structuralist accounts more generally, the subject is inserted into the symbolic order. We learn language and in doing so become social subjects. This in turn presupposes that language is something that pre-exists the subject. It is not the subject that creates language; it is language that shapes and creates the subject. The problem in Castoriadis's view is that such an account mirrors the Marxian operation with regard to production in situating the construction of subjectivity outside the subject herself. For Marx production is always-already present. For Lacanians language is always-already posited. Yet this implies that it is impossible to describe language as a *human* institution at all. Such an operation is, he argues, self-defeating. How can something so palpably human be said to lie outside or beyond the human itself?

In Castoriadis's view such a starting point is flawed theoretically, and defeatist politically. In political terms it means that we are compelled to accept as inevitable the kinds of social arrangement that he was so critical of, namely those based on hierarchy and subordination. Hierarchy is after all more or less a constant in human society, and to the structuralist this indicates that there is something innate (structural) in the pattern of human interactions that makes it rational from the point of social reproduction. 'History' is a process of determination by forces that are exterior to human understanding or meaning. Human society is a product, not something that produces. Language reflects the world; it does not create it.

In Castoriadis's view it is only by recuperating signification within human activity that we can begin to make sense of it analytically. Here the key role of the (radical) imagination generally. The unconscious is a source of reality, but a source that has a protean, shifting and unknowable character, one in other words that is *determining*, not *determined*. What he wanted to avoid was the sense of some static space or place where symbolic creation is said to lie. The unconscious cannot be regarded on such reductive terms, but is much better characterised as something molten, protean, shifting and unpredictable – yet still creative. Castoriadis's metaphor for describing some-thing primordial and creative is the 'magma'. The 'magma' is his solution to the problem of origin, of newness. It provides the answer to the question: where does meaning or reality come from? As Castoriadis notes:

> [t]he psyche is a forming, which exists in and through what it forms and how it forms; it is *Bildung* and *Einbildung*, formation and imagination. It is the rad-ical imagination that makes a 'first' representation arise out of a nothingness of representation, that is to say, out of nothing. (Castoriadis, 1987: 283)

Just as the earth's core is something lying beneath the surface of the visible and known, so the unconscious magma is something unknown and unknow-able in its detail (Castoriadis, 1987: 343). All the same we know it is there, and we know it cannot be located in any other space/place. The magma is a mysterious, creative space that is nonetheless 'productive', in this case productive of meaning.

In social theoretical terms the importance of the magma to Castoriadis's later work cannot be underestimated. It is the launch pad for the attack on any and all species of determinism and fatalism, whether materialist or psychoanalytic in character. Societies, Castoriadis wants to say, are the cre-ations of those who live within them, as opposed to the effect of historical forces or of any other force working from outside society itself. 'Society, like any automata, defines its universe of discourse ... The institution of society is the institution of the world of significations, which is obviously a creation as such, and a specific one in each case' (Castoriadis, 1987: 234–5). Such a view puts him at odds, not merely with Marx and Lacan, but with what he terms in *The Imaginary Institution of Society* 'identitary-ensemblist' thought: all thought that seeks to explain individual and social creation in something outside of the individual and the society of which she is a part. In his view, philosophy seeks to denude reality of its specifically human dimension, that is the dimension of creativity and contingency. It seeks to create a source of reality in something outside or beyond the 'making/doing' of society itself, principally in the 'self occultation of the world through the generation of gods' (Castoriadis, 1991: 133).

Castoriadis's operation will, we can note, mirror that of Deleuze and others who criticised the Platonic insistence on an extra-social origin of real-ity. As he asserts, 'reality is socially instituted' (Castoriadis, 1987: 262). The problem is, we have allowed it to be instituted for us and not by us. If it is us who really create the world, then the attempt to annex signification to something outside of the community or society is an act of alienation of that which constitutes our humanity. It denies us that which at one level is the very essence of our humanity: our capacity to create reality and to alter it continually in conformity with altered or diverse conceptions of the world. What thus becomes evident is the degree to which the idea of the link between imagination and social creation becomes the key to his analysis of domination and in turn the key to his renewal of the 'project of autonomy'.

Autonomy, radical imagination and the magma

Having 'located' the process of signification, Castoriadis re-theorises social antagonism as the struggle over the process of signification itself. Why are societies characterised by certain forms of hierarchy and domination and not others? To this question Castoriadis unequivocally answers: because elites are able to articulate a view of the world that supports and sustains such relations. The reason for any particular configuration of social classes has nothing to do with the relations of production, or any other exogenous factor. It is located in the particular conception of the world that a given group of individuals uses to justify access to privilege, wealth and power. It thus follows that a change to that set of meanings produces a change to the basic matrix of understandings about how individuals relate to each other. An acceptance of the term 'woman' as referring to a 'human being' – as opposed to an appendage of 'man' – has revolutionary consequences. That such changes are tied to given historical and social developments does not for Castoriadis change the basic point: that changing the meaning of words, the pattern of social significations is at the heart of social transformation itself.

In this analysis, which forms the bedrock of Castoriadis's work of the 1980s, the project of autonomy comes to be redefined in ways that take it well beyond the more classically left libertarian positions of the work of the 1950s and early 1960s. Self-management, as the physical divesting of elites in the name of popular participation, is augmented by the project of the recuperation of the process of signification itself. Unless the process of meaning-production is taken off elites, then vested interests will always be able to redefine terms in such ways as to justify their own exalted position and the division of the world more generally in terms of 'haves' and 'have-nots'. This might suggest an attachment to a Gramscian strategy of engagement with the underlying 'common sense' that justifies and sustains particular hegemonic projects. Such an interpretation of Castoriadis would, however, seem to be mistaken. Castoriadis's approach goes much 'further' than Gramsci's account, being premised upon a different account of the function of language. Whereas Gramsci's position concerns the 'war of position' between competing conceptions of the world, for Castoriadis the issue concerns the recuperation of the process whereby meaning is produced. It is not enough to contest dominant meanings so as to create a new 'common sense', a new bedrock of understandings constituting a hegemonic world view. We have to recover the process as well as the space of meaning creation.

In view of the above it is little surprise to find that the model of a 'self-instaurating' community to which he leaned in later writings was that of the Athenian *polis* (Castoriadis, 1991; 1997). Here citizens gathered in an *agora* or space the openness of which literally and figuratively meant the possibility of a collective *autopoeisis* – or self-creation. In the *polis*, what was 'just' was what the community acting together felt to be just, more accurately defined as 'just'. The key point for Castoriadis is that this process of definition, revision and creation was one held in permanence, not in some one-off moment of inauguration or foundation. The *polis* is not an inaugurating event in the manner of liberal democratic revolutionary moments such as the English Glorious Revolution or the American Declaration of Independence. Nor was it some essentially fictive or mythological 'moment' of the sort described by Social Contract theorists such as Hobbes and Locke. What Castoriadis means is a process of continual creation and re-creation by the entire community, one going beyond the definition of 'self-management' to which Castoriadis was wedded in the early writings, which is to say beyond the allocation of tasks and decisions by the community as a whole. It means that the community actively and self-consciously takes part in the *definition* of the just, the good, equality and so forth. The community is here giving law to itself. As Castoriadis describes it, this is collective governance as *'poiesis'*: the continual creation of a common world of meanings and understandings. To participate in the life of the *polis* is on this reading to take part in the creation of the very fabric of social reality itself.

Social constructionism as 'making/doing'

Castoriadis's later work attempts to fuse two otherwise unconnected propositions: first, that reality is socially constructed, and secondly, that social construction can be described as an active process in which all are encouraged to participate. It is this notion of individual as active in relation to the system of signification that leads Castoriadis to be so critical of the dominant philosophical paradigms which have with few exceptions (on his reading) insisted that the subject is essentially passive in relation to signification/representation and thus that some foundation has to be found for a necessity that remains outside the 'making/doing' of conscious subjects. This sense of the passivity of the subject is in his view only a reflection of the contingent, social-historical 'realities' that have for centuries posited the construction of meaning either as beyond the grasp of the temporal altogether (as 'God'-given or in the form of Natural Law etc.) or as the task of some specific class or group of 'far-sighted' individuals to perform.

Here then the origin of Castoriadis's critique of Marxism as attempting to define 'making/doing' or *praxis* in relation to the historically constituted role of the proletariat – for which we read the Party. Marxism arrogates the definition of the world to revolutionary *praxis*, but that *praxis* is itself defined in relation to material conditions thereby excluding those who by virtue of their class identity cannot be described as 'proletarian'. What should be an activity shared in common becomes the basis for excluding the many from the process whereby the social is reimagined and redefined.

The libertarian sentiments underpinning the argument seem to be unarguable. The creation of social signification cannot, according to Castoriadis, be posited as a 'task' that only some are qualified to carry out, but rather the ontological expression of what it is to be human. We create our world – or rather we *recreate* our world – whereas we *should* be creating it, self-consciously with others, *collectively* in a process of 'objective reflexivity' (1987: 266). We should create the world because the world is a human creation and we are human. Moreover, creation should be on the basis of the 'radical imaginary' as opposed to the dominant imaginaries that have hitherto determined human life. Reality should be governed by 'phantasy' and novelty, not the 'dead weight' of human history, tradition and consensus, received truths and the 'wisdom of the ages'. The radical imaginary would thus recuperate or 'recover' that which rightly belongs to us: our capacity to shape social signification through the expression of our 'madness', the 'uncontrollable other' or 'primordial' 'eidetic' properties lurking within the psyche (Castoriadis, 1987: 299). In doing so it would render the world subject to those who compose the world; it would overcome the alienation of ourselves from the world – 'the concealment of the being of society from its own egos, covering over its essential temporality' (Castoriadis, 1987: 327).

'Hitherto existing history' thus becomes the history of concealment of the world from the subjects of the world. With 'the revolution' comes the democratisation and universalisation of 'making/doing' and with it the overcoming of representation as the alienation of the power of instauration. Thus it is the ontologically rooted nature of 'genesis' that provides the normative validity for the critique of heteronomy and the pursuit of autonomy in social life. We should participate in the creation/re-creation of the world because we (i.e. each one of us) are the authors of the world even if we have been convinced by those with an interest in denying our ontological essence that the world is created 'elsewhere'. Denying this common ownership of the world is to deny what, for Castoriadis, it is to be human. We need to recover 'the world' in order to recover our humanity.

Castoriadis and the project of autonomy

The key element of Castoriadis's later critique and recasting of the project of autonomy is the suggestion that the symbolic order is something to which we relate either 'passively' or 'actively'. As we noted, this goes beyond the usual premise of social constructionism of the kind associated with the later Wittgenstein. The latter view equates to the notion that the world or reality is constructed in and through language and is thus shared by the members of a given linguistic community, as opposed to humanity on the one hand or the solipsistic individual on the other. Such a conception does not usually carry the implication that the subject is 'active' in the construction of reality itself, self-consciously adding to the otherwise sedimented framework of meanings she inherits in the process of socialisation. This is particularly so in 'anti-essentialist' accounts, of which Lacanianism is one kind. As neo-Lacanians have argued, Castoriadis's position appears to embrace a Cartesian position in which the subject is posited as prior to social reality and thus as author of her own world (Zizek, 1999: 24; Stavrakakis, 2002). This would in turn render Castoriadis's politics *existentialist* – focused on the embrace of possibility and creativity of individual existence, as opposed to one that invokes the collective. But Castoriadis is insistent that this notion of the subject as passive in relation to the construction of social signification is a result of the subject being prevented or excluded from so doing by the unequal distribution of power. Heteronymous individuals passively imbibe meaning; autonomous individuals actively create it. Given the centrality of this argument to Castoriadis's later politics, it is perhaps worth pausing here to gauge the degree to which such an account represents an advance on those it seeks to displace.

Notwithstanding the degree to which such an account departs from anti-essentialist variants of social constructionism, it might still be argued that Castoriadis is inclined to conflate two issues: the issue of how meaning is generated and that of how and under what circumstances dominant meanings can be challenged and overturned. What he appears to be arguing is that if society could define for itself its own understanding of the world then this would constitute a kind of autonomy or self-rule. This seems on face value a curious position to hold. Let us consider one of Castoriadis's own examples, which concerns colour terms (Castoriadis, 1997: 337–8). Castoriadis notes that colours do not lie in the world; they are created or constructed by 'us'. But should noting that colour concepts are a human creation lead us to suppose that it is important for us to *participate* in their creation – in this example in defining the term 'red'? It is difficult at face value to see why this should be the case. Disagreements about how words are applied are witness to the fact that language is replete with nuance, incongruity and slippage. No amount of active participation in the definition of terms will alter the fact that such disagreements are part and parcel of membership of a linguistic community (*'you think it's purple, I think it's mauve'*). Such disputes also indicate that there is some known or fixed point of meaning of words. We know what mauve 'normally' means; our argument is over whether the object being described conforms to that meaning. That stability of the sign is provided not through the active generation of a consensus, but rather through habits and conventions of usage within a given linguistic community.

Castoriadis seems to be on firmer ground when he focuses, as he frequently does, on the recuperation of *contested* terms such as 'justice' or 'equality' or 'democracy'. Here we can see clearly why one might want to be a part of the deliberations concerning the meaning of concepts. Someone who is concerned about the injustice of the world will want to be involved in discussion over how a more just world can be created. Yet even here the issue concerns less the generation of new or different meanings than the expression of preferences for one conception of the just over another. What is at stake here is less the *meaning* of the term itself, which since Aristotle has equated to the proposition that 'equals should be treated equally'. The difficulty lies with the implementation or application of one vision of justice over another. Even if we collectively agree to implement justice as Model A (for example, distribution of goods according to the maxim 'to each according to their needs'), justice as Models B, C and D do not become any less 'meaningful'. The concept of justice remains contestable as a concept – and will remain so as long as there are people who are attached to a different conception of how we should live.

Assuming this to be the case, what is at stake in discussions over justice is less the *meaning* of the term – certainly not in any absolute or final sense – than the way in which the term is to be defined and implemented. In modern plural societies there are a variety of possible models of justice that could find validity. The question facing any given community is which should be chosen as the basis for ordering social affairs, distributing goods and so forth. What is important or significant for a community to determine is how justice is to be *implemented*. There are many possible meanings of justice and this will remain the case as long as people disagree on what kind of world they wish to live in, what kinds of norm they wish to live by, who deserves what. This is what is meant by political argument. Given that Castoriadis anticipates that such disagreements will continue and indeed flourish under conditions of autonomy, we can anticipate that 'justice' will remain a contestable and contested term. At the same time what is key to autonomy here is evidently the reappropriation of the *power* to implement different conceptions of justice from those who have annexed it in the service of some or other elite. What is at stake is who has the right or capacity to determine what model of justice applies in any given setting. It is possible that this is what Castoriadis implies, notwithstanding the discussion of the recuperation of the process of social signification that forms the basis of, for example, the central essay in *The Imaginary Institution of Society*. There are enough indications in the later essays to suggest that what he is most concerned about is the recuperation of the power of creating or 'instaurating' law. But in this case it would be difficult to identify what his approach adds to radical democratic theory. It would repeat the demand found in left radical thought and practice from the Levellers onwards, i.e. that communities are able to govern themselves without the 'help' of intermediaries, representatives or the enlightened. The suspicion remains, however, that Castoriadis is committed to a much stronger reading of autonomy than this, one that does indeed entail the positing of meaning creation as an active and collective process.

What is also eye-catching from the point of view of the development of his later work is Castoriadis's understanding of the 'social' posited as a relatively homogenous linguistic community. The frequent evocation of the Athenian *polis* in his later work is significant, for here we see how the 'social' overlaps with the 'community' to the point where they are treated as equivalents. From this point of view to talk about the recuperation of social signification as a communal activity has a plausible ring to it. The *polis* was a tightly-knit group of citizens defined in terms of a given *ethnos* backed by the exclusion of outsiders or 'metics'. The 'social' was the 'community' in this instance, just as the community was 'the social'.

What remains to be asked is the extent to which such a model has validity under modern conditions. A feature of modernity is hybridity, transnationality and increasing diversity, particularly in 'world cities' such as Toronto, Paris or New York. Here we find a multitude of languages, ethnicities, understandings and conceptions of the world. On a Castoriadian view such communities would be autonomous in so far as each member is involved in the generation of a common symbolic understanding with which each would presumably be expected to identify, as per the *polis*. Yet, for example, the experience of diaspora and exile is commonly marked by a heightened sense of the particular identity 'under threat' and thus the necessity for preserving an attachment to the 'local' meanings and understandings 'left behind' in the process of migration. Under modern or 'cosmopolitan' conditions the community is not a homogenous linguistic and cultural entity, but rather a complex mix of different and competing identities, with different languages, different customs, morals and religions, all jostling against each other in the same space. If we are looking for examples from Antiquity to illustrate the dilemmas and possibilities of autonomy under modern conditions the relevant model would not be the Athenian city-state, but the Tower of Babel.

Castoriadis's politics can in this sense be read as nostalgic for a world that modernity itself effaces. It asks us to think of ourselves as subjects whose fate or destiny is bound up with others sharing the same communal identity at the moment when under intensifying pressure of transnational forces such identities become progressively more difficult to generate or maintain. If modernity is characterised by anything it is, as commentators such as Homi Bhabha and Arjun Appadurai assert, surely the multiplication and dislocation of identities, a process that puts in question the ideal of a world of shared interaction in the generation of social signification (Bhabha, 1994; Appadurai, 1996). In social spaces where perhaps hundreds of ethnicities and languages co-mingle and wash into each other, the call for a social space in which meaning can be generated on a collective basis has limited relevance, and can even be read as a threat to the validity of hybrid or otherwise uncertain identities and subjectivities, as well as the discrete identities found in metropolitan spaces. The suggestion that everyone should participate in the construction of a shared framework of meanings might imply the inferiority of such identities and more generally of minority demands to maintain a distance from the majority – however defined. Minorities may be less concerned about the generation of shared meanings and more concerned about the generation of mechanisms in which a multiplying plurality can proliferate on its own terms rather than be cajoled into some overarching process of symbolic self-creation.

Castoriadis and Post-Marxism

Notwithstanding his withering assault on postmodernism and indeed every other major intellectual trend and tendency of the times, Castoriadis's own critique of Marx overlaps in significant ways with the work of those he harshly dismisses, if indirectly ('the postmodernists'). We can mention here the emphasis on the contingency and openness of the historical process and thus the fruitless as well as totalising effort to make the historical conform to some autotelic process of predestination. Such a conception was advanced by Castoriadis at the moment that Lyotard was developing an almost identical critique of Hegelian-Marxism in his *The Postmodern Condition*. The assault on the basis of what he terms 'identitary-enslembist' thought that added philosophical depth to what had started as political critique mirrors to a startling degree the critique advanced by Deleuze in *Difference and Repetition*. The abandonment of class analysis in favour of more diffuse identities and new social movements anticipates the critique of a narrowly class-based analysis and the opening up of political space to participation and direct involvement as opposed to representation of needs and interests. Such a conception of the changing political subject will be the enduring legacy of the work of Laclau and Mouffe. None of which is to say that Castoriadis was not an original thinker. It is merely to note that Castoriadis shares in often striking ways the concern with the recuperation of contingency, possibility and creativity from both structuralism and Marxian orthodoxy. What he retained was, on the one hand, the militancy of the self-consciously organic intellectual and, on the other, a keen sense not only of critique's political dimension but also of its radical and even revolutionary potential.

Notwithstanding the above, what is less certain is whether the particular model to which he himself was attached, namely the devolved decentralised self-instaurating 'council' is one that maintains the relevance it once held for a generation of militants, particularly to the many French ex-communists, Situationists, Maoists and autonomists who drew inspiration from it. There is perhaps a sepia-tinted quality to the major refrain of Castoriadis's politics, namely the commitment to communal self-management read either as the obliteration of bureaucracy as in its early iteration or as the communal-collective recuperation of the kind embodied in his view in the Greek *polis*. The critique of bureaucracy comes up against the sheer complexity of modern life, whether it be in terms of the increasing specialisation of knowledges and competences or the explosion of productive capacity on a global scale. Castoriadis's evocation of a face-to-face community working through the allocation of collective tasks belongs to the world of Godwin and William Morris, not that of transnational flows of production, people, the media, language and indeed politics itself. Too bad for hyper-modernity we may think; but the point is Castoriadis did not see self-management as a step *away* from modernity. Far from it: as he made clear in, for example, the *On the Content of Socialism* essays, he saw self-management as a way to *overcome* the paradoxes and inconveniences of an increasingly bureaucratised as well as an increasingly industrialised world. There was no suggestion then that we would be forced to give up advanced production which he, like Marx, regarded as socialism's birthright. Castoriadis was committed to the reappropriation of social and economic power from the elites back to the working class, not the dissipation of advanced production and the return to 'simpler' ways of living. The problem is that modernity has outstripped not only the commune, but also the nation as the site of production. Castoriadis's vision lost touch with modernity – or rather with what 'modernity' had come to mean: increased specialisation, the internationalisation of production and the transnationalisation of once 'local' problems whether they be of resource allocation, environmental degradation or the development of advanced infrastructure, such as transportation or water supply. 'Localisation' is one answer to such issues, but many of today's localisers argue that such a demand can only be meaningful in the context of a recognition of the unsustainable nature of modern production and exchange, an argument that barely features in Castoriadis's treatment of the subject.

We should also recall that the critique of 'bureaucracy' was a major refrain of political discourse towards the end of the 1970s; but it was one annexed by the political right, as part of the neo-liberal revolution. 'Bureaucracy', whether public or private, was the very object of the critique associated with Milton Friedman and Friedrich von Hayek, both of whom shared in surprising ways the critique articulated by Castoriadis of the suffocating tendencies of bureaucratisation. The 1980s and 1990s were to witness an unparalleled stripping back on grounds of cost of anything and everything that hampered competitive 'advantage'. By the end of the century it was not 'bureaucracy' that threatened the project of collective self-management, but the return of the more ruthless *laissez-faire* instrumentalism of the Imperial Age. Perhaps Marx had been right after all: the law of value could not be bucked, even by 'bureaucrats' zealous to maintain their own position. It was not the bureaucratisation of public life that inspired the anti-capitalist protests of the new century, but rather the assault on 'the commons' and the submission of both private and public life to the law of value. If Castoriadis's analysis of bureaucracy implies that capitalist accumulation has become steadily more 'comfortable' and non-antagonistic, then these developments and the resistance to them suggest that his analysis placed too much faith in the acuity of Weber's vision.

As far as the later work is concerned, the attempt to bolster the claims of the *polis* as the form of autonomy has an anachronistic aspect to it – as is perhaps intended. Here the difficulty is more immediately theoretical in kind. It lies in the view that since reality is socially constructed, society should recuperate the power to generate meanings for itself. This is to understand the world as composed of relatively homogenous linguistic communities occupying a given geographical space with a given collective identity. 'All' that is required to produce autonomy is in this sense to gather all language users in one 'place' and allow them to reappropriate the 'making/ doing' of their own social reality. As well as the analytical and theoretical objections already raised against such a vision, of perhaps greater pertinence is the endangered basis of the set of expectations giving rise to the model. Castoriadis's suggestion depends on the identification of some fixed and stable aggregate, not in this case that of 'people', 'class' or 'nation', but rather 'society'. Yet far from being a stable ontological reality, society is under modern conditions a conceptual aggregate whose validity and utility for social analysis is itself increasingly in question. Far from being homogenous linguistically discrete entities, contemporary societies are increasingly marked by diversification and heterogeneity, by the proliferation of minorities, with an ever-fragmenting repertoire of local and particularistic forms of signification. It is not in 'society' that we engage in 'making/doing' but in the various and overlapping groups with which we identify. There is of course a 'society', but the ability to equate 'the social' with relatively homogenous ethnic, linguistic, cultural and religious collectivities is increasingly in question. So too is the project of the recuperation of 'social signification' as we proliferate ever-diversifying forms of communication, identification and socialisation.

What then of the project of autonomy? Notwithstanding the discussion above, it is clear that Castoriadis's legacy is important in terms of antici-pating in forceful and politically informed ways many of the trends and tendencies of post-Marxian thought and practice: the necessity to think past determination on the level of theoretical abstraction or political engage-ment; the openness and contingency of history and social creation and thus the availability of other ways of living; the impossibility of representation and thus the necessity for participation and direct involvement in those matters that dictate the terms and conditions of our existence. Such matters remain key questions for our times, as he maintained throughout his life. Castoriadis was to political conservatism whether of the left or the right what Wittgenstein might have been to philosophical conservatism: a herald proclaiming the possibility, indeed necessity, of 'other worlds'. To Wittgenstein these other worlds reminded us of the contingency and creativity of social life and the availability of other ways of living; to Castoriadis they are reminders that the horrors and wastefulness of contemporary existence whether capital-ist or communist were not 'written in the stars' but could, with collective action, be overcome. In his relentless critique of determination, of positivism and structuralism, Castoriadis affirmed the creativity of human action, and thus the availability of other ways of living. His outlook was comprehensively validated with respect to communism, the collapse of which was one of his great satisfactions. It is in the process of being validated with respect to the proliferation of alternative social spaces, social forums and 'horizontal' polit-ical forms that pose a challenge to the dead weight of inherited radical polit-ical practice. These attempts at recuperation of making/doing may not have been directly inspired by Castoriadis, but they give witness to the concerns at the core of his life and work.

Summary

- *Castoriadis's aim*: develop a radical libertarian theory to complement a politics built on the centrality of participation and communal-collective autonomy over bureaucracy and centralisation. This necessitates a critique of Marxist theory and politics that in privileging theory over practice leads to a vanguardism that repeats rather than undermines the bureaucratic tendencies of modernity.

- *Background*: early break from orthodox Marxism leading to Trotskyism and then more heterodox radicalism. Founder member of *Socialisme ou Barbarie* which counted amongst its members Claude Lefort and Jean-François Lyotard. Developed critique of the bureaucratic tendencies of both communism and capitalism, positing self-management and the development of workers' councils as the object of critique. Whilst influenced by Weber, Castoriadis maintained the possibility of overcoming the extreme division of labour and alienation of working conditions through communal participation and equal remuneration.
- Analysis apparently confirmed by the Hungarian uprising of 1956, which represented a rejection of both communism and liberal-democracy. The idea of spontaneous and unpredictable autonomous action becomes a core element of his critique of deterministic politics of the kind associated with orthodox Marxism.
- Development of critique of Marxism along a number of lines: economic theory disproved by increasing capitalist expansion and the development of new needs; critique of sociological projection of increasing class struggle and polarisation of advanced society; critique of the idea of politics as a set of technical skills; rejection of all forms of necessity and determination.
- Critique of Marxism and structuralism conjoined by critique of Lacanian theory which had gained in influence in France in the 1960s. Developed an account of the unconscious as 'magma' to challenge 'desire'-based accounts of Deleuze and Guattari, Lyotard etc. Centrality of the radical imaginary and phantasy as constitutive of human creativity. Emphasis on the possibility of 'newness', and innovation as at the heart of the human condition.
- Development of a politics of the social imaginary and the idea of autonomy as the recuperation of the process of social signification.
- Normative theorising turns on the idea of reconstituting community and society as self-creating – model of the *polis* assumes significance as a precursor for the idea of self-governance as self-definition or self-rule.

Assessment

- *Strengths*: restated the libertarian critique of Marxism associated with the council communists (Pannekoek; Mattick) and the left wing of European revolutionary socialism (Korsch; Luxemburg), i.e. Bolshevism as a form of vanguardism; placed participation and communal deliberation at the heart of critique; recalled the centrality of human invention and creativity as being at the heart of the human condition.

- *Weaknesses*: difficulty in reconciling modernisation with self-management and workers' councils (transnationalisation of production; division of labour; problem of incentives); critique of bureaucracy becomes a critique of social democratic 'organised' capitalism itself supplanted by neo-liberal restructuring from the late 1970s; emphasis on the constitutive character of 'society' and 'community' can sound nostalgic and/or exclusionary within the context of complex, diverse modern societies.

Sources and Further Reading

Appadurai, A. (1996) 'Disjuncture and Difference in the Global Cultural Economy', in A. Appadurai (ed.), *Modernity at Large*, Minneapolis: University of Minnesota Press, pp. 27–47.

Bakunin, M. (1872) 'Marxism, Freedom and the State', various editions. Available at http://www.Marxists.org/.

Bhabha, H. (1994) *The Location of Culture*, London: Routledge.

Breckman, W. (1998) 'Cornelius Castoriadis Contra Postmodernism: Beyond the "French Ideology"', *French Politics and Society*, 16(2): 30–42.

Castoriadis, C. (1984) *Crossroads in the Labyrinth*, trans. K. Soper and M.H. Ryle, Cambridge, MA.: MIT Press.

Castoriadis, C. (1987) *The Imaginary Institution of Society*, trans. K. Blamey, Cambridge: Polity Press.

Castoriadis, C. (1988a) *Cornelius Castoriadis, Political and Social Writings*, Vol. 1, trans. D.A. Curtis, Minneapolis: University of Minnesota Press.

Castoriadis, C. (1988b) *Cornelius Castoriadis, Political and Social Writings*, Vol. 2, trans. D.A. Curtis, Minneapolis: University of Minnesota Press.

Castoriadis, C. (1991) *Philosophy, Politics, Autonomy: Essays in Political Philosophy*, Oxford: Oxford University Press.

Castoriadis, C. (1993) *Cornelius Castoriadis, Political and Social Writings*, Vol. 3, trans. D.A. Curtis, Minneapolis: University of Minnesota Press.

Castoriadis, C. (1997) *World in Fragments: Writings on Politics, Society, Psychoanalysis, and the Imagination*, trans. D.A. Curtis, Stanford, CA: Stanford University Press.

Castoriadis, C. (2003) *The Rising Tide of (In)Significance (The Big Sleep)*, available at http://www.notbored.org/cornelius-castoriadis.html [accessed January 2004].

Clark, J. (2002) 'Cornelius Castoriadis: Thinking about Political Theory', *Capitalism, Nature, Socialism*, 13(49): 67–74.

Curtis, D.A. (1997) *The Castoriadis Reader*, Blackwell Readers, Cambridge, MA: Blackwell.

Dews, P. (2002) 'Imagination and the Symbolic: Castoriadis and Lacan', *Constellations*, 9: 516–21.

Fotopoulos, T. (1998) 'Castoriadis and the Democratic Tradition', *Democracy and Nature* 4(1): 157–63.

Howard, D. and Pacom, D. (1998) 'Autonomy – The Legacy of the Enlightenment: A Dialogue with Castoriadis', *Thesis Eleven*, 52: 83–102.

Ojeili, C. (2001) 'Post-Marxism with Substance: Castoriadis and the Autonomy Project', *New Political Science*, 23(2): 225–40.

Sorel, G. (1968) 'The Decomposition of Marxism', in I. Horowitz (ed.), *Radicalism and the Revolt Against Reason*, Carbondale, IL: Southern Illinois University Press.

Stavrakakis, Y. (2002) 'Creativity and its Limits: Encounters with Social Constructionism and the Political in Castoriadis and Lacan', *Constellations,* 9: 522–39.

Urribarri, F. (2002) 'Castoriadis: The Radical Imagination and the Post-Lacanian Unconscious', *Thesis Eleven*, 71: 40–51.

Zerilli, L.M.G. (2002) 'Castoriadis, Arendt, and the Problem of the New', *Constellations*, 9: 540–53.

Zizek, S. (1999) *The Ticklish Subject: The Absent Centre of Political Ontology*, London: Verso.

2

Deleuze and Guattari: Rethinking Materialism

[S]ocial machines make a habit of feeding on the contradictions they give rise to, on the crises they provoke, on the anxieties they engender, and on the infernal operations they regenerate. Capitalism has learned this, and has ceased doubting itself, while even socialists have abandoned belief in the possibility of capitalism's natural death by attrition. No one has ever died from contradictions. And the more it breaks down, the more it schizophrenizes, the better it works, the American way. (Deleuze and Guattari, 1984: 151)

Gilles Deleuze and (Pierre-)Felix Guattari were both *militants* who fully supported the uprising of May 1968. Though very different characters with different intellectual interests as well as different perspectives on a number of key issues, they formed a formidable writing team, 'Deleuze and Guattari', which delivered two seminal works, *Anti-Oedipus* and *A Thousand Plateaus*, as well as a number of less well-known works including *Kafka: Toward a Minor Literature* and *What is Philosophy?* Both Deleuze and Guattari were insistent that they were 'materialists' and 'Marxists' (Deleuze, 1995). Guattari also explicitly rejected the label 'postmodern' often attributed to them (Genosko, 1996). Yet for many commentators Deleuze and Guattari are the embodiment of postmodernism in their embrace of a 'relativistic' epistemology combined with a celebration of difference, multiplicity and indeterminacy (Callinicos, 1989; Best and Kellner, 1991; Sarap, 1993). There is also an explicit and frequently acknowledged attachment to Nietzsche, the mere mention of whose name is enough to convince many of the irrationalist, 'postmodern' character of what follows.

Yet their work has been highly influential for contemporary debates on the possibilities of resistance to neo-liberal globalisation and the development of anti-capitalist alternatives. Michael Hardt and Antonio Negri's collaborative works *Empire* and *Multitude* draw heavily from their work. This is true both in terms of an analysis of the neo-liberal 'Empire' itself and, to a more questionable extent, in terms of the prescriptions they draw up for a counter-empire ('exile', 'flight'). We could also mention in this regard, the work of Arjun Appadurai, whose essay on the character of globalisation borrows heavily from their conceptual apparatus (Appadurai, 1996). More generally, contemporary anti-capitalist literature is replete with terms borrowed consciously or unconsciously from their work. The concepts of the 'rhizome', 'deterritorialisation', of 'nomadism' and the 'multitude' – to name a few – have become part of the vocabulary of contemporary politics and left activism. This is particularly so in France where Deleuze and Guattari's work has been central to the revitalisation of radical political thought and activity, one marked by the range of journals and newsletters such as *Chimères*, *Multitude* and *Recherches* that carry their distinctive imprimatur. Deleuze and Guattari's work has also been highly influential in feminist debates, as for example in the work of Elizabeth Grosz, Rosi Braidotti and Dorothea Olkowski (Braidotti, 1994; Grosz, 1994; Olkowski, 1999). In sum, their work has been an important resource for rethinking not only the theory but also the practice of radical politics 'after' Marx.

Despite the familiarity of the partnership, Deleuze and Guattari were very different characters with quite distinct intellectual agendas. Guattari, born in 1930, was a psychiatrist and political activist who helped set up the Clinique de la Borde at Courcheverny near Paris, an experimental psychiatric unit that implemented some of the more heretical ideas of the 'anti-psychiatry' movement associated in the anglophone world with figures such as R.D. Laing, David Cooper and Robert Castel (Deleuze and Guattari, 1984 [1972]). A persistent theme of Guattari's work is the necessity for challenging the expectations and assumptions of conventional psychiatry and psychoanalysis which set up a model of 'normal' human activity counterposed to a subnormal or schizoid subject unable to be integrated into conventional to social relations. In an echo of Foucault's work on 'madness', Guattari regarded such distinctions as essentially 'political', equating normality with conformity to the status quo. Guattari was always insistent on the underlying reality of psychic or unconscious structures and thus of the need to examine the manner by which unconscious forces would be harnessed in the cause of the 'workers' struggle'. It was this problematic that underpinned the first major work of collaboration, *Anti-Oedipus*. Beyond his collaborations with Deleuze, Guattari's forte was the essay, some of which are collected in the neglected *Molecular Revolution*, a collection that spans his work of the 1960s and 1970s. A number of other important essays are collected in *The Guattari Reader* edited by Gary Genosko, who has also written an advanced introduction to Guattari's work (Genosko, 2002). Guattari also collaborated with Negri on *Communists Like Us*, and reflecting his 'green' turn towards the end of his life wrote *The Three Ecologies*, an attempt to marry his political commitments to ecological themes (Guattari and Negri, 1990; Guattari, 2000).

Deleuze, born in 1925, built his early reputation through a series of original and contentious readings of key figures in the philosophical canon: Hume (*Empiricism and Subjectivity*); Spinoza (*Spinoza: Practical Philosophy*), Nietzsche (*Nietzsche and Philosophy*), Leibniz (*The Fold*) and Kant (*Kant's Critical Philosophy*). As well as being important critical studies, there is a common theme or *problematique* running through them, giving us some idea of Deleuze's political as well as philosophical orientation. What becomes evident is Deleuze's hostility to all forms of 'transcendentalism', which equates to the search for the 'true' or 'underlying' structure of reality or being. Deleuze was in this particular sense animated by a similar suspicion to that found in Castoriadis's critique of 'identitary-ensemblist' thought. This is the view that the philosophical enterprise could be divided between those who thought that some special key or code was needed by which to read the inner meaning or essence of the world and those who thought of the world as immediately accessible, as in empiricist approaches. The political ramifications were quite clear to Deleuze, as they were to Castoriadis. What is intriguing is that Deleuze challenges the view long held that empiricism is an innately conservative doctrine that tends to support and sustain the status quo and thus that it is transcendental philosophies that are 'revolutionary'. The Deleuzian project as it developed in the works such as *Difference and Repetition* and *The Logic of Sense* sought to reverse these propositions. In such fashion it was to be a 'superior empiricism' that was to be regarded as revolutionary, and the dominant transcendentalist – for which read elitist and exclusionary – approach which was to be cast in reactionary light. *A Thousand Plateaus* was perhaps the ultimate expression of this philosophico-political manifesto, though Deleuze continued in his other works to hone and refine his position.

Anti-Oedipus: 'desire is revolutionary'

As mentioned above Deleuze and Guattari collaborated on a number of key works. It is generally acknowledged, however, that the most important of these is the two-volume *Capitalism and Schizophrenia*. For the purposes of explicating the key features of Deleuze and Guattari's contribution we will concentrate on these texts beginning with *Anti-Oedipus*. We will also stick rather closer to explication here than in other chapters, since without some account of the two projects and the concepts associated with them, it will be difficult for the reader to make much headway in assessing the contribution of Deleuze and Guattari to critical thought and practice generally.

Thinking about the context giving rise to the work it is evident that *Anti-Oedipus* can be read as a direct response to the key issue that animated French radical intellectuals in the wake of 1968. To put the matter in the terms with which the issue was expressed, why is it that people often desire their own enslavement as opposed to liberation? Marxian answers to the question attribute causal primacy to material factors, so that any answer to such questions had to take account of prevailing material conditions. People would rebel because economic conditions make rebellion 'rational' or necessary; an answer has to be found to the 'riddle' confronting them. On the other hand, Marx himself took seriously the vexatious nature of the 'subjective' problem of the 'how and why' of rebellion, and his political writings in particular are fascinating analyses of the issue generally. He certainly saw nothing mechanical about the relationship between economic crisis and the emergence of a widespread revolutionary consciousness, even if certain correlations could be detected. The problematic in the France of 1968 was that those who initiated the uprising were largely middle-class students, not the working class, the 'subject' of the Marxian schema. Here was a rebellion built not on class 'interests' but on the desire for a different world from the one people found themselves in.

How the argument develops in *Anti-Oedipus* is that desire cannot be regarded as a mere 'effect' of the superstructure, something that reflects a governing logic or ideology. Desire should be regarded as in some sense primary and constitutive – part of the 'base' in turn underpinning consciousness. In this sense desire is a cause and not an effect. It is itself constitutive of the social world. Changes in desire in turn produce changes in that world. The existing system survives therefore not because desire reflects the governing order, but because the governing order shapes desires in ways that are affirmative of it. We are made to want our repression instead of our liberation.

In trying to make the case Deleuze and Guattari trod on the toes of not one but three orthodoxies or 'transcendentalisms'. As well as the tacit critique of 'official' Marxism, the text is explicitly anti-Freudian and anti-Lacanian in structure as well. With regard to psychoanalytic orthodoxies, the title of the book *Anti-Oedipus* gives us a sense of the argument to be pursued. In their view Freudian psychology was fixated with the Oedipal triangle reducing the dramas and intensities of feeling to a 'theatrical' battle between Subject, Father and Mother (Deleuze and Guattari, 1984: 55). The search for the meaning of human life had, according to Freud, been resolved in favour of this primordial tussle with Father for the attentions of Mother. What was implied was that there was no outside or beyond of this disabling *ménage à trois*. We are doomed to suffer, doomed to be disappointed, doomed to have our deepest needs and desires channelled and rechannelled into this never ending cycle of competition which could only be made bearable with the help of the Analyst as 'interpreter' of the struggle – as the one who could *represent* what it *means*. Freud drew notoriously conservative conclusions from his observations of the struggle, seeing human civilisation as a history of the containment of the dark urges lurking beneath the surface of conscious existence (Freud, 1973). The best we could hope for, he argued, was a relatively 'civilised' existence in which the sublimation of our deepest and most destructive impulses made daily life possible and bearable for the majority, though a neurotic minority are unable to subject themselves to the rigours and disciplines needed to cope.

With regard to Lacan, the dominant figure in the French Freudian renaissance, the prospect for an emancipatory reading of the potential of 'unlocking' the unconscious looked even bleaker. As we have already noted, for Lacan the subject is marked by 'lack' – not just lack of the mother, but of the Thing, whether it be personal, sexual or linguistic. 'Desire' is in this sense read as stemming from lack, and could not be made sense of in any other way. We desire things that we do not have, and as soon as we have them we desire something else. In an echo of Hobbes, lack and scarcity are thus seen as constitutive of subjectivity and social life more generally, rather than as contingent, historically situated facts, as Marx argued. We struggle for things we do not have, objects we cannot possess, goals that escape us, meaning that lies beyond us. Human life is alienated, and antagonistic, and the sooner we realise this – with help from the Analyst of course – the better able we will be to cope with it. Society too is like this, in the sense that there can be no resolution of antagonism or alienation at the level of social life. Utopias might give witness to the need for reconciliation; but this reconciliation or 'fullness' always eludes us (Stavrakakis, 1999).

Anti-Oedipus repudiates this approach, offering in its place a different animating principle for understanding human subjectivity and thus a different reading of its 'potential'. What Deleuze and Guattari proposed is a rereading of the structure of desire on the basis of a 'vitalist' reading of the kind associated with Nietzsche, Bergson and Reich – or, to put the matter differently, from the point of view of an autonomous life force as opposed to an underlying 'drama' mediated and shaped by the specificities of human needs and wants. Reference to Nietzsche may well be useful at this point.

To Nietzsche, the 'will-to-power' characterises life generally, not just human life. All life strives to keep itself in being, and it is this striving that he terms 'the will-to-power'. In the hands of Deleuze and Guattari, will-to-power translates as 'desire'. In this sense desire is anterior to 'lack' in the Lacanian sense, where it is lack that creates desire (Deleuze and Guattari, 1984: 26). Here desire is, on the contrary, constitutive of the subject and social life more generally. Thus, like Nietzsche they want to avoid the notion that it is the subject herself who 'creates', who 'desires'. This is getting matters back to front, and loses the specificity of the claim they are making in *Anti-Oedipus*. Desire is the element from which 'molar' subjects such as the 'individual' and 'society' are created and recreated. This in turn echoes Nietzsche's analysis in *The Genealogy of Morals* where the subject is famously rendered an 'effect' of the cause: 'will-to-power' (Nietzsche, 1956: §13).

Reinforcing the point, they write, notoriously, in terms of 'desiring production' or 'machinic desire' rather than 'desire' as such. Behind – or within – the subject lies a 'material' process of production that creates subjectivity. In this sense desire cannot be reduced to something outside of itself, but is itself constitutive and primordial. The 'machinic' quality of desire, that desire connects and is connected to things, reinforces the sense that 'the individual' is itself produced and producing, as opposed to the figure of liberal theory: a fully formed autonomous entity. As Deleuze and Guattari put it, instead of the model of the theatre with the subject acting out the Oedipal drama, the subject is merely one kind of 'factory' producing 'flows' of varying intensity and form (Deleuze and Guattari, 1984: 1). It is, we can note, in this highly idiosyncratic sense that their analysis is 'materialist'. For Deleuze and Guattari 'materialism' means the primacy of 'production' over the individual or social domains of existence, though at the same time they dissolve the sense in which the 'individual' and the 'social' are in any meaningful sense differentiated from the economic, as they are in Marx's materialism. They are aspects of the singular 'socius' or body to which these elements all belong. The identification of the analysis as 'materialist' is nonetheless important in that they claim to provide a *refinement* of Marx's analysis of the process by which capitalism becomes 'machinic' and 'abstract', obliterating the distinctions and hierarchies of production in favour of a complete integration of labour into production.

Here also is a clue to their account of resistance, for as Deleuze and Guattari put it, 'desire is revolutionary' (Deleuze and Guattari, 1984: 116). This is to say that desire exceeds and outstrips that which can be desired. It is 'desiring-production' that is inventive and creative, not the system of social production which is merely parasitic upon the latter (Deleuze and Guattari, 1984: 36). This is signalled in the continued creativity we see in the domains of art and science in particular, both of which are tolerated forms of 'creativity' in the capitalist socius (Deleuze and Guattari, 1984: 378). Desiring production is not derivative or 'representative' of something outside of itself, such as the Oedipal triangle or 'lack' more generally, but is rather fully creative and autonomous. It is, however, the very fluidity and plenitude of desire that creates the necessity for class and state repression, and for the ceaseless channelling of desire into socially reinforcing behaviour, such as consumerism.

Here they are happy to endorse the earlier conclusions of Wilhelm Reich. Without the creation of the necessary 'libidinal investments', society would explode under the force of desire (Deleuze and Guattari, 1984: 118). Thus desire is continually made to turn in on itself, to become reactive, instead of becoming active and affirmative of life. For capitalism to 'work' we have to desire our own repression and by extension the repression of those who will not or cannot conform to the logic of capitalist reproduction. This is just one example of 'micro-fascism', a channelling of desires and suppressed feelings in ways that support and sustain repression rather than overcoming it (Deleuze and Guattari, 1984: 104–5). However, as they make clear, all social structures require this shaping, funnelling and blocking of desire, in turn reinforcing the divisions, classes and stratifications of a given social order. 'Fascist desire' is not the 'same' as capitalist desire; but it operates in similar fashion, encouraging modes of identification with reference to 'out-groups' and 'minorities' that need to be suppressed in order to maintain the whole. The operation of a society requires that we want it to operate and this in turn means replicating and identifying with the 'micro-fascisms' without which it would collapse.

Anti-Oedipus and the end of ideology

One of the key points that emerges in their analysis is the necessity for abandoning the Marxian theory of ideology as 'false consciousness', and thus of oppression as the operation of class interests that are in some way hidden from view (Deleuze and Guattari, 1984: 104). Class interests do not explain why it is that people accept a given state of affairs. This would be to ignore the role that desire plays in repression. Desire is active, not passive, in systems of oppression. Oppressors must 'convince' the subject of the 'desirability' of a given state of affairs, rather than rely on mere acquiescence or 'silence', which is a much weaker basis for social governance. Here their analysis complements the cultural Marxism of figures such as Antonio Gramsci. The latter argued that the struggle for political control was a struggle for 'hegemony', which in turn is seen as a positive commitment on behalf of the ruled to the ruling class. Thus the problem is not that people are duped into thinking that fascism (for example) is in their class interests; it is that the fascists are able to get people to want fascism at a deep enough level to sustain a fascist political order. One can condemn the means that were used by the fascists in order to promote itself, the mythology, pageantry, symbolism etc., but this only reinforces the point, which is that the fascists understood that they had to get people to *want* fascist rule if they were to establish an effective political and social order.

Looking at the matter from the point of view of revolutionary struggles, Deleuze and Guattari insist that it is not enough for revolutionaries merely to assert that they understand human need better than the fascists; they have to challenge fascism (and capitalism) on the ground of desire itself.

What is noticeable, then, is how irrelevant class and by extension 'class consciousness' becomes in their definition of capitalism (Deleuze and Guattari, 1984: 252–3). From the point of view of value there is only one class: the bourgeois. In an echo of Marcuse's analysis in *One Dimensional Man* they assert that

> there are no longer any masters, but only slaves commanding other slaves; there is no longer any need to burden the animal from the outside, it shoulders its own burden. Not that man is ever the slave of technical machines; he is rather the slave of the social machine. (Deleuze and Guattari, 1984: 254)

From this point of view the 'revolutionary' impulse is not a quality 'possessed' by a distinct class, but is – as we have seen – internal to desiring production, and thus something that lies within every 'subject'. The middle-class student was from this point of view just as potentially revolutionary as a worker in the mines of eastern France. Both are created under a regime of desiring production that in turn creates its own revolutionary subject: the 'schizo-revolutionary' of May 1968.

Here of course is another departure from 'official' Marxism and from the Leninist theory of the Party as articulated in *What is to be Done?*. For Deleuze and Guattari, as for Castoriadis, 'class consciousness' is a cover for the elaboration of a strategy in which 'representatives' of the oppressed are able to substitute themselves and their interests for those of the latter who in turn are said to be able to develop only a 'trade union consciousness'. A properly revolutionary politics cannot be built on such 'micro-fascisms', but on the recognition that as a facet of desire itself, we are all potentially at least 'revolutionaries' (Deleuze and Guattari, 1984: 344). In place of the revolutionary party, with its hierarchies of professional cadres they follow Sartre's analysis in *The Critique of Dialectical Reason* in positing revolution as an active creation of 'subject groups' (Sartre's 'groups-in-fusion') as opposed to '*subjected* groups' ('pledge groups'). Subject groups are flat, horizontal groups of like-minded individuals united by bonds of affect, affinity and alliance, as opposed to loyalty to a particular person or set of texts (Deleuze and Guattari, 1984: 348). The schizo-revolutionary gesture is one of 'fleeing from' preconceived projects, entities and visions (Deleuze and Guattari, 1984: 277, 286). They thus proposed a rethinking of the party as a necessarily contingent, temporary and shifting 'crystallisation' for ends and purposes that are themselves constantly reviewed and reviewable. This is a politics of participation and direct involvement by those who desired change, not representation and the abstraction of power in the interests of an ossified or 'molar' subject ('the working class').

The significance of the shift in the sense of 'materialism' to desiring-production is felt in other ways too. One of the unstated conclusions drawn in *Anti-Oedipus* is that a revolutionary politics has to be looked at less like a means to an end, than as an end in itself. This is to say that the object of revolution cannot be seen in terms of the creation of a different regime of social-production. To recall, desire is *itself* revolutionary, creating its own excess that exceeds whatever it is that could be produced to satisfy it. Desire as we have seen is not produced by 'lack', but rather the other way around (Deleuze and Guattari, 1984: 26–7). So from this point of view, creating a system in which all lack (as 'needs') could be satisfied would not 'realise' or consummate 'the revolution', as Marx and many anarchists argued it would. There is no resting place for desire and thus there can be no 'end' to the revolutionary process as such. Liberation is always a 'liberation from' the constraints of social life, social production, social morality. Indeed, if liberation is to have any meaning at all it is in terms of the generation of greater intensities, as opposed to the realisation of some settled norm or blueprint. Such intensities cannot be legislated for, they cannot be produced by changing the system of distribution, or by reconfiguring power in ways that seem more 'just' or rational. To Deleuze and Guattari intensity can only be measured with reference to what they term the 'body without organs' (Deleuze and Guattari, 1984: 328–9). Such a body would be freed from the obstacles and blockages that create the neurotic, sanitised subject of contemporary life. It would revel in its own existence, and the existence of others similarly freed from the neurotic form of life represented by 'capitalism'. It would quite literally be an escape, a fleeing from the axiom of capitalism (value, profit, the commodity). The 'new earth' (Deleuze and Guattari, 1984: 382) would be one in which it is not just the capitalist axiom but any and all axioms that are resisted and thus where the social body remains unencoded, flowing, contingent.

A Thousand Plateaus: from desire to multiplicity

To move from *Anti-Oedipus* published in 1972 to *A Thousand Plateaus* published in 1980 seems at first to be catapulted into a radically different conceptual project. Not only is the form of the latter very different to that of the former, we are confronted at every turn with a battery of new terms and reformulations that make it at first difficult to imagine that the work has very much to do with *Anti-Oedipus*. What, however, does become immediately noticeable is that the transposition of the object of critique from 'desiring production' to 'multiplicities', of how it is that entities combine and recombine. We move from an analysis whose primary focus is the subject and subjectivisation (the coming-to-be of subjects – whether individual or group) to the analysis of combination and recombination of complex pluralities – though the distinction is less clearly cut than this image allows.

'Schizo-analysis' moves towards the search for a 'nomadic' outside of the hierarchies and asymmetries of contemporary existence.

Before attempting to unpack some of the key arguments we need to say something about the form of the work. One of the bemusing aspects of *A Thousand Plateaus* is the mode of presentation. *Anti-Oedipus* is not a 'conventional' work in most respects, but it does present an argument in a recognisably linear narrative with what can be taken for a beginning, a middle and an end. As the title implied, however, *A Thousand Plateaus* presents its 'findings' in terms of layers or 'plateaus'. The intention is that readers are able to read the plateaus in any order one chooses, to skip plateaus if they fail to 'say' something to the reader, and in all other respects to use them as seems appropriate. Each plateau comes with a date of an event or occurrence that in some sense illustrates or marks the appearance of the particular intensity to be found within. Thus 'Plateau 3' is called '10,000 BC: "The Geology of Morals" (Who does the Earth Think it is?)', 'Plateau 4' is 'November 20, 1923: Postulates of Linguistics', and so on. There is no 'whole', no totality and certainly no 'story' that could be retold in some unproblematical way – which is precisely the point. A perhaps more useful way of rendering the matter is to note that each plateau presents an exposition and/or demonstration of a concept or group of concepts (majoritarianism/minoritarianism; smooth/striated etc.), which together represent something like a system of thought – or perhaps an 'anti-system'. The presentation in this sense mirrors the intention of the authors to counterpose the linearity and unity of occidental thought with the 'rhizomatic' alternative they hope to displace it with. So what exactly is one to make of the text? What can we divine by way of core themes, if not core arguments?

What becomes apparent is that *A Thousand Plateaus* presents a dazzling critique of Western rationalism, and with it the various props and devices which have been used to maintain the 'statist' practices that emerge from and are sustained by it. As we noted above, if it is possible to isolate a particular thematic or problem within the text then this would be the question of how it is that 'multiplicities' come to be combined or configured in particular ways. For Deleuze and Guattari, multiplicities – whether composed of people, of musical notes, of animals or atoms – can be arranged in one of two ways. They can be arranged either asymmetrically or symmetrically, in hierarchical or non-hierarchical terms. Hierarchies or asymmetries require some principle of origin, some mode of differentiation by which to arrange the various points/atoms/people in ways that allow the hierarchy to be maintained. It is the search for this point of origin, this basic principle by which order can be imposed on the multiplicity, that Deleuze and Guattari term 'arborescent' (or 'arboreal') thought. A 'seed' is 'planted' which then grows tree-like, establishing all the basic connections between the multiple elements governed by thought. Arborescent thought in this sense equates to the search for a 'governing' principle by which to think thought itself.

Deleuze and Guattari refer here and elsewhere to the 'Cartesian' moment as being one such example. 'I think, therefore I am'. Once it is possible to trace the origin of thought in thought itself, then in a sense all else follows: it is to thought itself that we must look for the basis of understanding. But the Cartesian moment is, as the analysis in *A Thousand Plateaus* makes clear, just one 'moment' among many similar moments. Indeed, as the dates of the plateau suggest, they read civilisation as the history of moments of a similar kind: moments in which 'seeds' are 'planted'. Each moment implies its own regime, its own 'order' that is not only abstract or philosophical, but directly 'political' in the sense that each legitimates a particular conception of how multiplicity should be perceived, how elements should relate to each other, how the unity of any given system is to be maintained and reinforced. 'Arborescence' concerns thought and also the mechanisms by which order is created (Deleuze and Guattari, 1988: 16). *A Thousand Plateaus* can be read as a set of successive attempts to undermine the view that there is no 'outside' or 'beyond' of 'arborescence' and thus of 'order' more generally. In asserting the connection between the regime of truth and order, they echo not just Nietzsche, but of course Foucault whose analyses they share up to this point. But here the similarity tends to fade. Deleuze and Guattari are insistent that there is indeed a genuine 'outside', as opposed to the fragments, glimpses or moments of hope associated with the Nietzschean perspective.

Resting with the vegetal analogy, they contrast arborescence as an organising principle with the figure of the 'rhizome' (Deleuze and Guattari, 1988: intro.). A rhizome is a kind of plant that grows underground, and is hidden from view. It shoots roots outwards, randomly and without 'logic' or 'sense' rather than in terms of a predictable pattern or hierarchy. The root is thus a 'line of flight', an 'escape' as opposed to the branches of the tree which are supported by the trunk. Here we can hear the echo of *Anti-Oedipus* and the idea of desiring-production as, optimally, an unhampered molecular 'flow'. The rhizome is a direct analogue for desiring production in that it embraces the principle of embodying flow as 'escape' or 'flight'. Here it is the flow of thought, of music, of art, of science, of nature. So what, for example, would rhizomatic thought be like? In a sense, thought that disrupts the creation of order, that disrupts 'foundation' around some 'truth' or point of origin. It is thought that remains molecular, that is fluid, mobile and unhampered. From this point of view they see Nietzsche (for example) as a quintessentially rhizomatic thinker: a thinker who disrupts, as opposed to laying the basis for order and rationality. Deleuze and Guattari want to establish that there are two different forms of combination or multiplicity, one rhizomatic, the other arborescent; one that is 'immanent' to a multiplicity itself, and another that is subject to an external 'principle' that domesticates it, rules it, creates and recreates it in conformity to the transcendental point of origin – that acts as 'a General', as they put it (Deleuze and Guattari, 1988: 21). Understanding this core distinction facilitates not only following the arguments of the various plateaus, but also getting a clearer sense of the political dimension of Deleuze and Guattari's work. How then does the arborescent/rhizomatic distinction play out in terms of the latter?

Trees and rhizomes; generals and nomads

Arborescent forms of thought give rise to arborescent forms of organisation. The point of origin or first principle allows multiplicity to be 'segmented', organised and delineated in accordance with a 'valid' molar principle. A segmented multiplicity occupies 'striated' space, meaning space that has been organised into discrete units that interweave in a predictable or 'rational' fashion (Deleuze and Guattari, 1988: 474ff.). This is contrasted with forms of multiplicity that are, like the rhizome, open, flowing and 'deterritorialising'. In place of striated, segmented space there is 'smooth' space, a space without boundary, linearity, edges. But what does all this mean? Imagine a typical school playground. Before the whistle goes for class, the children run round in a free-flowing, spontaneous fashion, each child following his or her own inclinations. Some want to run, some want to talk to others, others want to wander by themselves. The impression we get is of a blur of random activity, a constant weaving and interweaving of discrete 'molecules'. But then the whistle goes: the children are made to line-up in neat queues waiting to be called to their classrooms. The free-flow of bodies is transformed into lines, into 'segments' obeying a particular 'logic'. The 'smooth' space of play has been transformed into the 'striated' space of organisation, rank and rationality. 'Molecular' flow has given way to 'molar' segmentation – organisation around a transcendent or 'normatively valid' principle.

The example is overly simplistic, but what it is intended to illustrate is that, despite the apparently abstract and analytical manner in which the terms emerge, the question of agency is a very real one – though the immediately 'political' character of the analysis sometimes has to be searched for according to the context. Striated space is space that has been *created* by someone or something, whether it be a logic, an argument or a practice. There is an intervention in the 'anarchic' flow imposing 'order' on the multiplicity, order which itself obeys a particular logic or principle. The school 'needs' to be organised, it needs to be regulated in accordance with known and fixed principles, and all this is signalled in the whistle. Of course the school is a mere microcosm of the ultimate 'apparatus of capture': the state.

It is the state that imposes and maintains striated space, 'transcendence', 'territoriality', 'overcoding' and 'majoritarianism'. All of which is to say that within a given territorial space the state functions through axiomatising social life, making it conform to a certain principle or 'truth', whether that be of the market, of theocratic belief, of an ideology. The axiom 'overcodes' everything within; it makes everything obey its own logic, and that which does not is regarded as a threat to it. The state is 'majoritarian': it stands for and 'represents' that which is dominant, that which is 'true' or rational. It is in this sense that the state is regarded as an 'apparatus of capture'. The 'multiple' is captured, annexed, trapped in a space or territory over which it has, despite the contractarian rhetoric of contemporary liberal states, minimal control.

If arborescence underpins the apparatus of capture and the creation of striated space, then rhizomatic thought and activity underpins what they term the 'nomadic war machine' which in turn creates smooth space. Smooth space is space without structure or organisation, without foundations, pre-existing or always-already known rules and principles. The smoothness here should not be thought of in tactile terms so much as a description of space without contours, or rigid boundaries. Deleuze and Guattari suggest as an analogy the sea – though of course even the sea is now territorialised by international treaty (Deleuze and Guattari, 1988: 479). But think of the sea as it was perceived in medieval times, that is the 'high seas': a lawless, rule-less, infinite space traversed by those who hold no allegiance to anyone but the band or 'pack' of which they are a member. That the sea was portrayed as a 'dangerous' place illustrates the logic of capture under which states operate: smooth space will always appear 'threatening' and 'lawless' precisely because it has not been 'captured' and annexed to known and fixed principles. But of course to those who wish to escape the despotic overcoding and majoritarianism of the state, smooth space appears like a haven of safety.

Smooth space is not therefore a geophysical attribute of a given territory, as the term might intuitively suggest. The 'smoothness' of the sea or the desert is not an innate quality, but rather the effect of a particular relationship between people. Where the terms and conditions that unite people are 'immanent' to that group we see a nomadic multiplicity, as opposed to a set of relations organised by something like a state or authority that lies outside those terms and conditions. Since 'nomadic' multiplicity does not capture space, it becomes a deterritorialising force, a force that counters and overcomes that which captures – the state. This is what intrigues Deleuze and Guattari about nomads and nomadism. The latter describes a form of multiplicity, or combinatory dynamic. By contrast with 'sedentary' peoples whose relations to others are determined by fixed and known rules guaranteed and enforced by the state, nomads interact with others on their own terms. Nomadic combination is without 'force of law'. Quoting Arnold

Toynbee, they observe that nomads do not have to move to be regarded as nomads (Deleuze and Guattari, 1988: 381). What makes them nomads is that combination with others is not based on law or coercion, but on practices that are contingent, flowing, negotiable. The nomadic war machine is 'immanent' to itself. It disavows in its very being the logic of territoriality, coding and majoritarianism. Nomads are 'minor', which is to say that they embody the logic of the rhizome: of escape, flight, flux, flow, never 'stopping', even when they do not 'move'.

A distinction that emerges here (and one that will become the focal point of the critique articulated in *Kafka*) is that between 'minoritarianism' and 'majoritarianism'. As we have noted, the apparatus of capture is one that proceeds via the assertion of the validity of what is termed a denumerable set, that is a set with a molar identity that can as it were be 'counted' (and counted upon). 'The majority' is a denumerable set in that it represents the figure 'more than 50 per cent'. When we hear a politician say that 'the majority wants *x*' this rules out the rationality or desirability of other outcomes, possibilities or end states. Statist politics operates via the mobilisation of denumerable sets whether it be 'the majority' or 'the black community' or 'youth'. Similarly, radical politics has traditionally operated via the mobilisation of different sets, 'the working class', being the classic formula. This operation ('majoritarianism') is in their view a silencing not only of those who remain outside the set, but of those who lie *within*, those who are 'represented' in the claim articulated. It is one that transforms *molecular* flow into the stasis of a *molar* subject position to which one is subject.

One of the most persistent themes in the work of Deleuze and Guattari is the insistence that a revolutionary politics is and must be 'minor'. This means accepting that 'the people are not present'; there is no 'people'. There are only 'singularities'. A singularity that is unable to speak for itself is not a singularity, but only part of a set. As they state in Plateau 13, 'ours is becoming the age of minorities' and by extension of singularities (Deleuze and Guattari, 1988: 469). Whatever purchase molar identities once had is in the process of dissipation, not least due to the deterritorialising effect of capitalism itself ('all that is solid melts into air'). As we noted with respect to *Anti-Oedipus*, 'the working class' has no reality for Deleuze and Guattari, displaced as it is by the class of 'slaves'. It follows that there is no working-class 'subject' as such, merely those who fall outside the logic of identity itself, which may in numerical terms be *the vast majority*. When they invoke 'the proletariat' it is in the sense of a non-denumerable and hence molecular set, 'the outside' or 'margin' (Deleuze and Guattari, 1988: 472). As they put it, the proletariat is the 'becoming-revolutionary' of all minorities rather than the crystallisation of the working class via the transformation of class consciousness. This in turn necessitates a reorientation of the kind signalled in *Anti-Oedipus* away from the revolutionary group as apparatus of capture or state-in-waiting, towards a multiplicity of 'war machines' which could maintain and embody 'the pure becoming of minorities' (Deleuze and Guattari, 1988: 471). A revolutionary strategy cannot affirm the identity of one or other oppressed groups, but rather has to 'become everybody/everything' that is minoritarian. It is to adopt the stance of the 'universal' figure thereby dissolving the axiom of identity and identities altogether.

Where then does this analysis leave critique? What is the politics of *Capitalism and Schizophrenia* considered in the round? To say that what they offer is 'anarchistic' is a truism. What is more interesting perhaps to note is the *way* in which what they are offering is rendered. What is stressed at all times is the necessity for flight, for flow, for escape. This differentiates their thought strongly from classical anarchism, which like its rival ideologies, often sought to construct an image of a future Good Life as a contrast to capitalist modernity. *Capitalism and Schizophrenia* can be read as a rejection of the narrative construction of other worlds based on 'insight' into human rationality, need or nature. It is this mode of theorising to which they are objecting in their delineation of rhizomatic as opposed to arborescent forms of thought. The point is to escape from fixed or permanent 'constructions', however well-meaning or rational they may seem. It is to stop thinking that the voice of the Philosopher or the Analyst can 'represent' complex and multiple singularities. In particular it is a move away from the notion of space as something to be 'captured'. They seek an escape from the suffocating character of spatial thought, and the insistence that it is the task of philosophy to legislate. The point is to reject thought that insists that we have to construct boxes, that systems have to be created, that 'justice', 'equality', 'democracy' emit of some universal or transcendent definition. Life, they want to argue, is 'outside' the box. It is flight *from* normative and utopian schemas, no matter how 'just' they may seem. It is anarchy – but not as we 'know' it.

Nomadism and/or Marxism?

As should be apparent even from this abbreviated account, *A Thousand Plateaus* is an important complement to *Anti-Oedipus*, helping us to see more clearly the import of ideas that would otherwise have remained suggestive or undeveloped from the earlier work. What may still be useful to discuss is the degree to which their self-description as 'Marxists' is merely a provocation or something more substantial. What in short is 'Marxist' in Deleuze and Guattari's 'Marxism'?

To classical Marxists such as Ebert and Callinicos the suggestion that Deleuze and Guattari's analysis is Marxist is absurd. To begin with an obvious point, despite the insistence on the 'materialist' nature of their analysis, this is, as far as Marxist critics are concerned, a materialism that seems a long way from the reassuringly 'scientific' analysis of objective macro-economic developments of the form we get in *Capital*. This equates to the charge that they abandon the 'primacy' of production in social and histori-cal development thereby in turn abandoning the necessity for the close study of economic trends and tendencies as a basis for elaborating a mean-ingful resistance to the dominant class. In effect 'materialism' is turned on its head so that instead of referring to the 'objective' process of production that in turn creates and shapes social life, it refers to an ahistorical or pri-mordial 'force' that shapes production and subjectivity, collapsing the two into the category of 'desiring production'. It is from this point of view that Callinicos and Ebert regard Deleuze and Guattari's work as a form of 'irra-tionalism' or 'ludic' vitalism that reduces reality to ontological categories rather than the objective economic categories that are the *sine qua non* of any authentically Marxist analysis. Ebert, in particular, spares little in her assault on the pair accusing them of constructing an 'alibi' for the bourgeois class. In displacing 'production' with a discursively driven approach, they reduce analysis to a ludic post-materialist theory the effect of which is to ignore the needs and interests of the global poor (Ebert, 1996). Zizek echoes Ebert in arguing that the project of 'multiplicity' is a cover for global capital-ism where 'lifestyle' differences are held up as evidence of the possibility of self-definition and self-creation (Zizek, 2004).

We could add to the charge sheet by noting that a 'Marxism' that rejects *inter alia* the theory of ideology as 'false consciousness'; that displaces the analysis of class struggle in favour of a 'schizo-analysis' in which it is non-denumerable 'multitudes' who compose the subject of analysis; that denies the desirability or the necessity for a revolutionary Party, either in the transformation of capitalism or in the 'transition' between capitalism and communism; that turns its back on dialectics in favour of a self-declared 'empiricism' (albeit of a 'superior' form); that displaces production for 'need' with 'nomadic distribution' and communism with 'crowned anar-chy' would be a 'Marxism' deeply foreign to many of those who have gone under its banner. Why not simply accept that this is an 'ex-Marxism', if not a 'non-Marxism'?

The question is an acute one because what is implicit in the query is whether a heterodox position of this kind can still articulate an oppositional politics. This seems an odd point to make, until one remembers that when theorists get called 'postmodern' it is assumed that what they are criticising is 'modernity' or the Enlightenment 'project', in turn equating to the idea of the availability of a better, more emancipated world. Yet the notion that Deleuze and Guattari are turning their backs on the Enlightenment and thereby dissolving the idea of a better world, that consequently we are unable to find a politics, radical or otherwise, is curious. This is not the same as argu-ing that what they offer is necessarily compelling or useful, or that it is better than the competing anti-capitalisms on offer, including more orthodox visions of Marxism. It is merely to note that they frame their own project in terms of the necessity for overcoming capitalism, and they do so on terms that are familiar to Marxists. One of the suggestions in *Anti-Oedipus* is that it is only with an acceleration or a full working-out of capitalism that a 'post-capitalist' order could be contemplated. As Deleuze and Guattari ask:

> But which is the revolutionary path? Is there one? – To withdraw from the world market, as Samir Amin advises Third World countries to do, in a curious revival of the fascist 'economic solution'? Or might it be to go in the opposite direction? To go still further, that is in the movement of the market, of decoding and deterritorialisation? (Deleuze and Guattari, 1984: 239)

Here, in other words, they seem to share some of Marx's wariness towards anti-modernists and romantic anti-capitalists who argue that the revolutionary transcendence of capitalism could have been effected at any stage in the evolution of modern society. As we noted above, Deleuze and Guattari see capitalism as a process of revolutionary 'deterritorialisation' that prepares the way for alternatives to traditional society. It is a crushing process that transforms and undermines all 'transcendentalisms' and archaicisms in the extension of the law of value. Capitalism is pure 'flow' washing away everything that presents an obstacle to its own progression. From this point of view there is no possible accommodation with capitalism. As they state often enough, 'reformism', social democracy, even socialism affirm capitalism because they represent the attempt to live within the law of value. Only a complete break with value and the capitalist axiomatic will permit the generation of meaningful alternatives (Deleuze and Guattari, 1984: 373).

These are sentiments of a classically Marxist kind. They also suggest that they may well be closer to Marx than many of the other thinkers we consider at least in terms of invoking a *narrative* of revolution. The narrative is not teleological; but we are confronted in passages like these with the idea of having to break through capitalism to reach the 'other side'. The complicating element here is that by contrast the analysis of *A Thousand Plateaus* suggests that there is in effect *always* an outside of capitalism, or indeed any other axiom of social life – the nomadic 'smooth' space that forms the counterpoint of the analysis there. Another way of putting the same point would be to ask whether the actualisation of the latter is necessarily post-capitalist, or whether the trope of smooth space represents a valid reference point of an ahistorical kind. The analysis in *Anti-Oedipus* would point towards the necessity for overcoming capitalism as a prelude to the creation of a post-representative space, whereas the analysis of *A Thousand Plateaus* seems to point in the opposite direction, i.e. towards the ideal of nomadism as a figurative and historical practice that is 'always' with us.

The uncertainty or 'undecidable' nature of the analysis would seem to suggest that revolutionary theory or strategy is itself undecidable or ambivalent, in turn creating serious issues to be confronted at the level of social movements and practice. Should radicals sit back and wait for the full 'deterritorialising' force of capitalism to take its course; or should they set their face against any kind of accommodation with capitalism in order to accentuate the necessity for a 'break'? That one could be posing such questions illustrates one of the elusive qualities of Deleuze and Guattari's approach. Yet at the same time it is one that mirrors the dilemmas faced by Marxists over the previous two centuries. A certain historical teleology is a key component of historical materialism, and without it Marxists would argue that revolutionary theory loses its foundation in the analysis of the trends and tendencies of any given social horizon. But Marx was equally insistent that revolutions are not made by crises, but by individuals acting together in common cause ('Men make their own history ...'). What if that common cause is pursued before 'the time is ripe'? Here in microcosm the dilemmas that are utterly familiar to students of Marxism in action. When to act? When to act legitimately and with prospect of success? Act too 'early' and revolutionary praxis becomes 'ultra-left' voluntarism, one that is always searching for the revolutionary 'outside' and thus discounting the need to build opposition in a concerted fashion as opposed to one that relies on the spontaneous and thus fleeting energies of today's *enragés*.

On the other hand, if desire really is 'revolutionary' or capable of exploding extant structures and boundaries then it would be inconsistent not to be looking for an 'outside' for fear of affirming capitalism as opposed to confronting it. The answers to such questions would, however, seem to be concrete or 'micro-political' issues rather than ones that can be resolved by reference to causal determinants lying beyond desire itself. They are questions concerning the nature and form of the 'molecular' forces at work in any given setting. Capitalism may appear solid, indeed 'natural', in one location and be teetering on the brink of fundamental crisis in another. In one place or at one moment to act against 'capitalism' will appear ludicrous in the extreme, at another wholly rational and indeed necessary on these terms. In 1989 Fukuyama can write of the triumph of liberal-capitalism to be followed within a decade by the eruption of a global 'anti-capitalist' movement that made his sentiments seem bizarrely inappropriate. Such perhaps are the modalities of 'schizo-analysis' and the 'question of capitalism'. But on the other hand, they show how their account of desire renders 'history' contingent and open in a way that is familiar to other writers considered here, not least Castoriadis. It is in turn one more manifestation of the 1968 'effect'. The desire to overturn capitalism can come from anywhere and be lodged in anything. Economic 'crisis' may enter the equation, but it does not of itself determine it.

Towards a new (anti-)politics?

What of the 'after' of capitalism? Here Deleuze and Guattari's critics differ only to the extent that they are determined to demonstrate the degree to which their 'vision' differs from that of Marx. We have heard from Ebert and Zizek, both of whom insist that their approach serves to sustain rather than undermine capitalism. To Laclau, on the other hand, their radicalism is a new form of 'nihilism', celebrating with Nietzsche the impossibility of a better world, and thus of the necessity for the reduction of politics to the narcissistic pursuit of an individual 'aesthetic' existence (Laclau, 1996). To Best and Kellner, their approach is by contrast *too* redolent of Marxism, being essentially 'productivist' in character and thus wedded to an essentialist 'imaginary' of alienation from some core ontological model of the non-alienated self (Best and Kellner, 1991: 106–7). That we can get such different assessment shows that we need to think past the question of their relation to Marxism and on to the issue of what *kind* of politics is on offer here.

As should be clear from the brief account of *A Thousand Plateaus* in particular, their concerns are obviously libertarian in character, even if their libertarianism is that associated in Leninist terms with the 'infantile' disorder of 'Left-wing communism'. This is to say their analysis concerns the preservation and enhancement of autonomous thought and action as an end in itself. That which excludes, subordinates or oppresses the singular is rejected irrespective of whether some 'greater good' is likely to be produced by it. Their approach is thus resolutely anti-utilitarian. Indeed, it is anti-utilitarian to the extent that they reject many celebrated 'anti-utilitarian' positions (most noticeably Kant's) as too compromised by the requirement that such a position has to be grounded in a transcendental or foundational principle, such as the principle of autonomy itself. On their reading a 'principle' of autonomy cannot by definition be 'autonomous' as it implies that autonomy is obedience to a law, rather than something embodied or practised. Autonomy is 'flight', or becoming minor, and is thus the condition of those who have turned their face against 'principles' and legislations, which for Deleuze and Guattari are invariably majoritarian and exclusionary.

Their approach also means that they have an innate suspicion, frequently aired, of the idea that a libertarian form of life has to be crystallised or 'grounded' in institutions or organisations. Thus they are notoriously wary of 'organised' politics generally, seeing resistance as 'lines of flight', a much more spontaneous and fluid notion than that implied in the language of parties, if not of 'movements'. This is not to say that they think that politics is impossible *per se*. Rather they argue that there is a frequent – if not permanent – danger of the emergence of 'micro-fascisms' in any attempt to 'organise' or 'institutionalise' that 'crystallisation' of a 'becoming-minor' they see as the basis for a revolutionary politics.

For Deleuze and Guattari smooth space cannot be created by institutional fiat or constitutional act. It is not legislated for or enshrined in 'fundamental principles' that are then preserved or upheld by judicial apparatuses. It is a mode of being with others, not a set of laws, norms or regulations that are enacted and upheld. In this sense the revolutionary body, the nomadic war machine, is both the means and end of revolutionary practice. It does not so much create and maintain smooth space like a gardener maintains a lawn; rather smoothness is the *effect* of nomadic combination. Nomadism is not a system of governance, but a form of combination, a form of multiplicity, in which what happens to any given group remains 'immanent' to that group. Moreover, there is no appeal to what 'the majority', actual or fictive wants. 'Nomadic' assemblages are minoritarian: they are constructed by reference to the particular, specific needs, wants and desires of each singularity. What should be acknowledged therefore is that Deleuze and Guattari's critique goes well beyond the more utopian moments encountered in orthodox and heterodox Marxism, such as that of Castoriadis. They reject permanent, standing structures no matter how 'democratic' or participatory in structure. Smooth space is not obviously 'democratic' space, nor space that has been rendered more 'transparent' or 'accountable'. It is space that exhibits a *complete* lack of segmentation or striation, of hierarchy and 'organisation', even of a 'popularly' run or 'auto-poietic' kind. 'Radical democracy' of the kind described by many Post-Marxists may well be radical at one level; but it will never be radical enough for Deleuze and Guattari.

Such an observation in turn leads to lively controversy (see, for example, Patton, 2000; Protevi, 2001; Thoburn, 2003). The question is often posed as to whether there is in fact a 'politics' in their work, that is, whether there are resources not merely for the *critique* of governance, but for creating a different *kind* of governance – one that might be germane to our lives in modern or perhaps postmodern times. To put the matter bluntly, what is the object of their critique: a world *without* government or a world with more democratic and egalitarian government than at present? Is this an *anti*-political politics or a politics that at one level represents the full working out of the narrative of the Enlightenment, one pointing towards 'immanent' self-governance?

That such a fundamental question can be posed (politics *or* anti-politics) shows the ambiguous nature of the analysis offered, and beyond that the difficulty of making it 'work'. Both positions bring their own problems. If the object is the dissolution of governance and governed spaces then there may be a danger of what has been termed the 'tyranny of structurelessness' (Freeman, 1970). If there are no rules or procedures for governing relations between individuals then it is not difficult to imagine that outcomes and decisions will become distorted in favour of the strong, the well organised or the most vocal, leaving minorities powerless and without means of making themselves heard. The continual references to nomadic and barbarian hordes in their work may have a certain rhetorical appeal, but historically such forms of 'collectivity' are hardly noted for tolerance, openness and inclusivity of the kind that many associate with a progressive politics. Nor are they noted for their ability to maintain complex, diverse or industrialised societies.

Should we therefore conclude that a 'nomadic' politics is not merely figuratively pre-modern but *actually* pre-modern? If so, then this would of course undermine the claim referred to earlier that what is on offer is a quasi-Marxian position that sees the traversing of capitalism as a necessary prelude to the generalisation of smooth or nomadic space. If, on the other hand, such a perspective is intended to complement modernity and industrial production then we need to be able to see how modern society could operate on such a basis. With Deleuze and Guattari we learn a lot about what a 'smooth' world will *not* be ('over-coded', 'axiomatised', 'isomorphic' etc.). What becomes more difficult is to imagine how collectives might organise themselves without lapsing into 'sedentary' ways. Will there be markets? Will there be commodity production, divisions of labour, work? If not, how (for example) is production to be organised in such a fashion that it does not immediately proliferate markets, accumulation, the division of labour? To invoke 'nomadism' is of course a provocation; but is it *just* a provocation – or is there some substantive critique of capitalist modernity behind it that encourages us to imagine the availability of a post-capitalist modernity – or post-capitalist modernities?

It may be, on the other hand, that the object is a form of democratic governance or 'immanent structuring' (Protevi, 2001: 192). In this case we still need to know how this will differ from existing forms of democratic governance. Deleuze, for example, was struck by the difference between jurisprudence and constitutional law – the former rendering the nature and indeed form of law contingent on immediate 'immanent' conceptions of the just.[1] The British system of justice would seem on this reading to fully conform to such a model of immanent structuring, even more so given that it is Parliament that is the repository of sovereign power, in turn implying that there is no block to legislation and re-legislation on terms dictated by the people (or rather their representatives) as there is in constitutional systems. Is this to say, by extension, that the UK 'constitution' can be regarded as providing the basis for an immanently structuring social order? If so, we need to ask what is particularly radical about such an account. Does it not simply echo Burke's defence of 'the rights of Englishmen' as opposed to the abstract 'Rights of Man' outlined by Tom Paine and Enlightenment progressives? Burke's point was that social orders need to develop in accordance with their own needs, wants, habits and prejudices – as opposed to the 'transcendental' imperatives dreamed up by the Men of Reason. In the terms being used here, they need to be 'immanently structuring'. As Paine later argued, in Burke's hand this is code for elite rule untrammelled by considerations relating to the needs of 'Everyman'; yet as the example of Burke highlights, there is nothing particularly radical about the idea of social orders governing themselves in accordance with 'immanent' needs and preferences as opposed to 'transcendental' or 'universalist' ones. What we need to know is *whose* needs and preferences are to form the basis for such an evaluation and *how* they are to be translated into policies and decisions. One searches in vain in Deleuze and Guattari's work for a democratic theory supplying answers to such questions, or even suggestive models of the kind we see in the work of others considered here.

In their defence, however, it might be argued that to pose such questions and to demand models is to remain within the very imaginary that their work is designed to unsettle. Political theory is a question of thinking about how we get from where we are now to some other place. How do we imagine that our world could be reconfigured in a way that is more just or democratic? It is this way of conceiving the role of political theory that, arguably, is the *object* of the critique offered by Deleuze and Guattari. Foucault is surely justified on this view in arguing that what they offer is less a political theory than an *ethics* that has as part of its objective the transformation of 'the political' into an ongoing and permanent war against 'fascism' in all its guises and manifestations (Foucault, in Deleuze and Guattari, 1984: xii). It is for this reason that the 'politics' on offer seems to be thin and underdeveloped. For Deleuze and Guattari there is an outside of hierarchy and subordination and thus of 'rulers and ruled'. But to maintain such an outside requires a practice of the self in relation to others and in relation to the categories of representation that have traditionally been the mechanism of democratic governance. In this sense the figure of the 'nomad' or the schizoid subject is not itself an unattainable figure. As sympathetic commentators such as Todd May and Saul Newman point out, it is like Max Stirner's insurgent self-owned 'ego', which is to say an image of rebellion in 'everyday life' (May, 1994; Newman, 2001). Or to put it in Deleuze and Guattari's own terms, it is an image of permanent war on the stasis of representation, of roles, of authentic 'being', whether individual or collective.

From this point of view Deleuze and Guattari are not political theorists: they do not have firm answers to questions such as 'who gets what?' What they ask us to consider is what is the basis of the 'deciding'? Is this deciding for others; or is it deciding *between* others. Is it deciding on the basis of a system of hierarchy that allots the task of decision-making to one class, one caste, one group – or is deciding a function of and immanent to groups and collectives? Deleuze and Guattari ask *us* to decide whether this is political theorising. If it is, they are political theorists; if not then they are antipolitical theorists, that is theorists whose *raison d'être* can only be understood in terms of the overturning of politics and all it 'represents'.

In terms of Post-Marxism, this will as we shall see create something of a difficulty. Post-Marxism can at one level be viewed as the response of radicals to the lack of a developed democratic theory in Marx, and in terms of the wider problem of substitutionism and vanguardism to which Marxist political practice was, they thought, prone. The answer, according to many thinkers considered here, is either to radicalise existing democracy, or to generate normatively valid models that will in turn highlight the deficiencies of current democratic theory and practice. With Deleuze and Guattari, on the other hand, we see something quite different: the thinking beyond or 'after' of democracy and all systems of governance. Yet the grounds of this move are clearly in sympathy with many of the themes that are otherwise articulated amongst those we consider: the rejection of determinism and transcendentalism in all its forms; the suspicion of politics as 'theory-led' and thus as an intellectual practice as opposed to a practice stemming from individual and collective desire; the stress on the historicity and contingency of human action. It is on this basis that we think the Post-Marxist label may well be valid in describing their contribution even whilst, at another level, it problematises the equation of Post-Marxism with 'radical democracy'.

Summary

- *Their aim*: initially to interrogate the reasons for the events of May 1968 which they held refuted the basis of both orthodox Marxian and structuralist accounts of social action. This lead to the development of a new 'materialism' based on the analysis of desire (*Anti-Oedipus*) and an examination of the basis of collective combination and recombination (*A Thousand Plateaus*). More generally they aimed to generate a superior account of social reality and historical development and, by extension, a new politics built on the figures of the schizo-revolutionary and the nomad.
- *Background*: abandonment of the dichotomy between 'base' and 'superstructure' and seeing production as a continuous 'machinic' process between the individual and the social. This in turn necessitated overcoming the Lacanian insistence on the split in the subject, and the subject's alienation from the social.
- Critique of Marxian account of ideology and 'false consciousness' on the grounds that desire is active, not passive, even in systems of repression (people desire their own repression).
- Revision of the theory of the party on the basis of Sartre's analysis of revolutionary groups. Stress on the necessity for avoiding 'micro-fascisms' and the 'pledge group' mentality associated with Marxian sectarianism.
- Notion of revolution as a continuous process of confronting blocks and obstacles to the liberation of desire. Need for break with orthodox model of the militant in favour of the 'schizo-revolutionary'.
- *A Thousand Plateaus*: radical revision to form as well as content of earlier work. Argument presented as non-linear 'plateaus' of varying intensity,

developing a range of new concepts and arguments. Focus on possible forms of interaction and 'multiplicity' – more generally a critique of Western rationalism including Marxism. Transcendentalism attacked and supplanted by 'rhizomatic' forms of thought, action and organisation.

- Contrast between 'smooth space' and 'striated space' intended to demonstrate the possibility of radically reconstructing social life along 'nomadic' lines, i.e. avoiding 'capturing' space by subjecting it to 'overcoding' by the imposition of an 'axiom'. Critique of capitalism develops as a critique of 'isomorphy' imposed by the axiom of the law of value, necessitating a nomadic 'deterritorialisation'.
- Revolutionary machine reconfigured as 'nomadic war machine' – a rhizomatic 'assemblage' of a pack-like kind that evades capture.
- Key distinction between 'majoritarian' and 'minoritarian' politics. Critique of politics that builds from the positing of an imagined fixed identity (e.g. class), in favour of one that sees each singularity as distinct or 'minor'.

Assessment

- *Strengths*: conceptual innovations helped to reinvigorate debates over the nature of 'materialism' and the place of 'ontology' in social and historical explanation. Sought to develop a fundamentally libertarian account of both transformative politics and 'post-capitalism'. Re-emphasised the role of creativity and possibility in human action, and thus the possibility of theorising radically different ways of living and acting.
- *Weaknesses*: the dazzling array of concepts and neologisms can hinder understanding, particularly by those who are supposed to be the target audience. Lack of clarity in relation to certain key questions: the relation between resistance and social organisation; the applicability of the model of 'nomadism' to contemporary politics; whether there is a political theory in their work – or a resistance against incorporation into the 'political', however defined.

Sources and Further Reading

Appadurai, A. (1996) 'Disjuncture and Difference in the Global Cultural Economy', in A. Appadurai (ed.), *Modernity at Large*, Minneapolis: University of Minnesota Press, pp. 27–47.

Best, S. and Kellner, D. (1991) *Postmodern Theory: Critical Interrogations*, New York: Guilford Press.

Braidotti, R. (1994) *Nomadic Subjects: Embodiment and Sexual Difference in Contemporary Feminist Theory*, New York: Columbia University Press.

Callinicos, A. (1989) *Against Postmodernism: A Marxist Critique*, Cambridge: Polity Press.

Deleuze, G. (1995) *Negotiations, 1972–1990*, New York: Columbia University Press.

Deleuze, G. and Guattari, F. (1984) *Anti-Oedipus: Capitalism and Schizophrenia*, London: Athlone.

Deleuze, G. and Guattari, F. (1986) *Kafka: Towards a Minor Literature*, Minneapolis: University of Minnesota Press.

Deleuze, G. and Guattari, F. (1988) *A Thousand Plateaus: Capitalism and Schizophrenia*, London: Athlone.

Deleuze, G. and Guattari, F. (1994) *What is Philosophy?* London: Verso.

Ebert, T.L. (1996) *Ludic Feminism and After: Postmodernism, Desire and Labor in Late Capitalism*, Ann Arbor, MI: University of Michigan Press.

Freeman, J. (1970) 'The Tyranny of Structurelessness'. Available at www.jofreeman. com/joreen/tyranny.

Freud, S. (1973) *Civilization and its Discontents*, London: Hogarth Press.

Genosko, G. (ed.) (1996) *The Guattari Reader*, Oxford: Blackwell.

Genosko, G. (2002) *Felix Guattari: An Aberrant Introduction*, London: Continuum.

Goodchild, P. (1996) *Deleuze and Guattari: An Introduction to the Politics of Desire*, London: Sage.

Grosz, E.A. (1994) *Volatile Bodies: Towards a Corporeal Feminism*, Bloomington, IN: Indiana University Press.

Guattari, F. (2000) *The Three Ecologies*, London: Continuum.

Guattari, F. and Negri, A. (1990) *Communists Like Us: New Spaces of Liberty, New Lines of Alliance*, trans. M. Ryan, New York: Semiotext(e).

Holland, E. (1999) *Deleuze and Guattari's Anti-Oedipus: Introduction to Schizoanalysis*, London: Routledge.

Laclau, E. (1996) *Emancipation(s)*, London: Verso.

Marks, J. (1998) *Gilles Deleuze: Vitalism and Multiplicity*, London: Pluto.

May, T. (1994) *The Political Theory of Poststructural Anarchism*, Pennsylvania: Penn State University Press.

Newman, S. (2001) *From Bakunin to Lacan: Anti-Authoritarianism and the Dislocation of Power*, Oxford: Lexington Books.

Nietzsche, F. (1956) *The Genealogy of Morals*, London: Anchor Press.

Olkowski, D. (1999) *Gilles Deleuze and the Ruin of Representation*, Berkeley, CA: University of California Press.

Patton, P. (2000) *Deleuze and the Political*, London: Routledge.

Protevi, J. (2001) *Political Physics*, London: Athlone.

Sarap, M. (1993) *An Introductory Guide to Post-Structuralism and Postmodernism*, London: Harvester Wheatsheaf.

Sartre, J.-P. (1976) *The Critique of Dialectical Reason*, Vol. 1, London: Verso.

Stavrakakis, Y. (1999) *Lacan and the Political*, London: Routledge.

Thoburn, N. (2003) *Deleuze, Marx and Politics*, London: Routledge.

Zizek, S. (2004) *Organs without Bodies: On Deleuze and Consequences*, London: Routledge.

Endnote

[1] The clearest statement of this kind is offered in response to the 'G comme Gauche' section of the 'Abecedaire' interviews filmed with Claire Parnet. Deleuze complains about the left's fascination with the 'rights of man' which he regards as 'abstract' and irrelevant to progressive struggles. As he explains, 'fighting for freedom is to engage in jurisprudence', meaning to change specific laws, practices, procedures – not to invoke one conception of law against another. For an English transcript of the interviews see http://www.langlab.wayne.edu/CStivale/D-G/.

3

Jean-François Lyotard: From Combat to Conversation

The nineteenth and twentieth centuries have given us as much terror as we can take. We have paid a high enough price for the nostalgia of the whole and the one, for the reconciliation of the concept and the sensible, of the transparent and the communicable experience. Under the general demand for slackening and for appeasement, we can hear the mutterings of the desire for a return of terror, for the realization of the fantasy to seize reality. The answer is: Let us wage a war on totality; let us be witnesses to the unrepresentable; let us activate the differences and save the honour of the name. (Lyotard, 1984: 82)

As we noted in the last chapter, the events of 1968 were seminal in the rethinking of Marxism as a valid oppositional paradigm and as a strategy for advancing resistance to capitalism. We also noted in considering the work of Deleuze and Guattari how they wished to modify or supplant aspects of 'Marxism' from within – hence their willingness to maintain an affiliation with Marxism and indeed the 'workers' struggle' whilst at the same time suggesting new and iconoclastic pathways from Marxism – or at least the official Marxism of the PCF. This explains too their hostility to their being labelled 'postmodern' even whilst others were inferring that the analysis announced in *Capitalism and Schizophrenia* was the very embodiment of the 'postmodern' in theory and practice. The position of Jean-François Lyotard is somewhat different. Although in many respects he shared Deleuze and Guattari's analysis of the 'failure' of organised Marxism, he embraced the 'postmodern' label, producing the key text of the 'pomo' canon, *The Postmodern Condition*, as well as numerous other works defending, exploring and illustrating the concept (Lyotard, 1984; 1993c; 1997: 42). On the other hand, as the more sympathetic commentators note, Lyotard never lost his 'oppositional' stance (Dews, 1987; Williams, 2000). This is to say he criticised capitalism and late modern society generally, and indeed proposed strategies for resisting the meta-narrative of capitalist expansion. In this respect we might regard his project as true to a certain spirit of Marxism. Of course to Marxists the suggestion is absurd, as indeed it was to Guattari and Castoriadis who themselves attacked the 'complacency' and 'passivity' of postmodern approaches (Genosko, 1996: 109ff.; Castoriadis, 1997: 32ff.). What we explore in this chapter is, nonetheless, a Post-Marxism that is unapologetic about the necessity for 'leaving Marx' in the name of advancing critical thought and action.

Lyotard was born in Versailles, France, in 1924 and studied in Paris before taking up a variety of teaching posts including stints in Algeria and at the Universities of Paris and Nanterre. It was the experience in Algeria in particular that radicalised the young Lyotard and encouraged him to become an activist in the ferment that was French left radical politics. In 1954 he joined Cornelius Castoriadis and Claude Lefort in the *Socialisme ou Barbarie* group. However, after various disagreements Lyotard left the group in 1963 and aligned himself with the *Mouvement du 22 Mars* which was to be closely associated with the May 1968 uprisings in Nanterre where Lyotard was a teacher. In the aftermath of 1968 he moved to the University of Vincennes where he was to produce some of his most startling and iconoclastic work, including most notably *Libidinal Economy* (Lyotard, 1993a). It was, however, during the late 1970s and early 1980s that he secured his global 'celebrity' with the more sober and measured analyses such as *The Postmodern Condition, The Differend* and *Just Gaming*. Towards the end of his life Lyotard joined that small band of intellectuals whose omniscience seemed to transcend the limitations of time and place. As well as continuing to write prodigiously he held a number of visiting positions in North America, and remained to his death in 1998 a model of a certain kind of intellectual *engagé*, an infuriatingly 'singular' thinker who seemed to embody the vicissitudes of 'postmodern' thought, at once 'radical' and iconoclastic, yet also coolly 'realistic' when it came to the assessment of prospects for far-reaching change to the status quo.

Early years: desire, art, self

Given the nature of Lyotard's political attachments in the 1950s and 1960s it comes as somewhat of a surprise to find that, discounting his political journalism (collected in *Political Writings*), his early work of this period seems barely 'political' in the sense of manifesting an obvious critique of the given; but this is arguably too narrow a definition of the term 'political', as the work of an earlier generation of cultural critics would suggest (Walter Benjamin, Georgy Lukacs, Theodor Adorno). If 'politics' is broadened to include the notion of the potential of the aesthetic or 'figural' as a form of resistance then what becomes apparent is that his entire *oeuvre* is intensely political, signalling as it does how and under what conditions critique and resistance can take place. If there is a single thread running through Lyotard's work then this would be the centrality of the aesthetic over language and the 'word', and thus the centrality of art to strategies of resistance. This might not sound particularly 'confrontational' or indeed political a stance until it is remembered the extent to which the Bolsheviks, for example, were preoccupied with just such questions in the period of war Communism and beyond. Indeed the hijacking of 'cultural production' under Stalin in the service of 'socialist realism' demonstrates the centrality of art to politics and vice versa.

In his first major work, *La Phenomenologie* (*Phenomenology*) published in 1954, Lyotard had, unfashionably, defended the notion associated with the work of Merleau-Ponty that perception cannot be reduced to language or symbolisation, that there is a layer of reality prior to symbolisation and thus only accessible in some extra-linguistic fashion (Lyotard, 1991a). This is not the same as the Lacanian view with which it has a tendency to be reduced, i.e. that the Real is constructed via a 'failure' of language. The 'reality' that Lyotard was interested in was not an absence or 'lack' which could be construed through the gap between language and the world it seeks to 'represent'. Rather he was interested in exploring the space between the perception of something and its symbolisation, the implication being that there were things we could perceive but not articulate: sensations, experiences and feelings that could not be reduced to words, but which might, on the other hand, express themselves in art. Here we have a clue to the distinctiveness of Lyotard as a thinker which the appellations 'post-structuralist' or 'postmodernist' tend to obscure. Language, he wanted to say, is not all there is; and all there is could not be rendered in language. There were forms of experience and perception that eluded language and thus which underpinned the need for thinking of linguistic representation as somehow incomplete or limited. Such a view would of course bring him into conflict with the dominant intellectual fashion of the late 1950s and 1960s: the idea of language as coexistence with reality and thus of 'reality' as constructed via the 'play of signs'.

In the later *Discours, Figure* this problematising of what will become the basis of the post-structuralist approach to symbolisation is stated in more direct terms and indeed in terms that highlight the 'political' nature of the debate (Lyotard, 1971). Here, he argues that the world is constructed 'in language'; but – contra Derrida et al. – in some sense the world resists reduction *to* language. There is always an excess or a layer, the 'figural' that resists symbolisation or, rather, that is prior to symbolisation. Thus contra Lacan he could not posit the unconscious as 'structured like a language'. This would in turn imply that the figural had little place in the 'structuring' of the unconscious, and thus that it had to be regarded as a secondary influence. Instead the unconscious had to be seen as primarily mediated by phantasy and by the deep flows of desire that lay within, flows that were more likely to 'escape' in the process of artistic production which on this view was less susceptible to manipulation and containment than discourse. It is on this ground that Lyotard, like many of his generation, was encouraged to invest considerable hope in art as a mode of resistance. Discourse could never shrug off its origin in a symbolic order that is always already mediated by the forces of repression. Art, on the other hand, allows the subject to vent her frustrations on the world, to give 'voice' to that which would otherwise be sublimated or repressed. On this view resistance is not theorised as the posing of one social logic to another. Rather art becomes political in the sense of a resistance to capital, whose logic demands efficiency, orderliness, discipline.

Here in germ are what become constants in the Lyotardian 'political' refrain: the importance of that which escapes symbolisation for thinking outside of domination and oppression; the centrality of the figural and thus the importance of an aesthetic avant-garde in opposition to the utilitarianism of capitalism. What it also prefigured was the anti-intellectualism of the early Lyotard. The centrality of the figural, of the unconscious, of the pre-discursive in turn privileged the generic capacity to resist on the basis of subliminally held feelings and desires that could be released in artistic production. Like Deleuze and Guattari, Lyotard was to set his face against the privileged role of the intellectual, even whilst delivering ever more demanding syntheses of the philosophical, psychoanalytic and political canon. All this was to be considered less the prelude to the construction of some other world, than the basis upon which the thinking 'after' of capitalism could take place. It was such ideas that formed the basis of the programme and activity of the Lyotardian *22 Mars* group which made such an impact in the events of May 1968, and in turn accounts at least partly for the 'aesthetic' quality of those events. 'The Spectacle' of 1968 was not merely televisual in this sense, but also self-referential and intended as part of a strategy of '*détournement*', disrupting the pattern of consensus and acquiescence into which late capitalist citizens were held to be locked. Thus the graffiti and slogans ('Be Realistic: Demand the Impossible!') were implicated in the process of resistance, as opposed to merely paying witness to it.

In the wake of the failure of 1968 to produce any lasting monument to resistance, Lyotard's energies remain focused on the underlying structure of subjectivity in advanced capitalist society and the critical or emancipatory potential contained in the aesthetic. In *Libidinal Economy* we see this project come to full fruition albeit, so it seemed, at a price. Lyotard was later to describe *Libidinal Economy* as written in a 'scandalous' way, and it is easy to see why he might given the direction of his mature work (Lyotard, 1985: 4). Stylistically, it is free flowing, unencumbered and mesmerising. It obeys few rules and endorses even fewer principles being content to oscillate from (relatively) sober critique to energetic flights of fantasy. Ostensibly a fusion of currents from Marxism and Freudianism, *Libidinal Economy* is actually a highly original critique of both, departing radically from superficially similar works of 'synthesis' produced by earlier critical theorists such as Herbert Marcuse (*Eros and Civilisation*) and Erich Fromm (*The Fear of Freedom*). Underpinning the text is the same concern that one finds in Deleuze and Guattari's *Anti-Oedipus*, which appeared within months of Lyotard's work. The problematic common to both *Libidinal Economy* and *Anti-Oedipus* was, in general terms, the place of desire in animating action. Both texts were effectively post-mortems on the nature and origins of the 1968 events, the common consensus being that the sociologically driven class analysis of Marxism was wholly inadequate for explaining why it was middle-class students who led the rebellion rather than the 'alienated' workers, the majority of whom seemed only too pleased to see 'authority' restored after the heady utopian days of 1968. Here, however, their analyses diverged markedly.

Whilst Deleuze and Guattari attempt, as we have noted, to differentiate between the desire for freedom and the desire for enslavement, Lyotard insisted on the unity of desire as 'intensity'. The underpinning assumption of Lyotard's analysis was that under advanced industrial conditions desire had become an analogue of capital (and vice versa). Just as capital valorises exchange, so the libidinal could be seen as a valorisation of intensity. Capital and desire were thus held to mirror each other in promoting the exchange of equivalents in an anonymous process of 'circulation' and 'flow' with the object of circulation regarded as accumulation in and for itself (Lyotard, 1993a: 95ff.). In the case of capital this is an accumulation of money; in the libidinal economy it is an accumulation of intensity. All of which implied that there is no distinction to be made between desires or, more accurately, *within* desires. In Lyotard's view it was impossible to distinguish between, as Deleuze and Guattari put it, a 'fascistic' and an emancipated form of desire, but only between relative intensities of desire. Just as capital is neutral in regards to what is circulated (butter, money, guns), so desire can be read as neutral with regard to intensity. Intensities cannot be read outside of themselves; but only in terms of the overall quantum of effect produced. The more intensity we experience, the more complete our sense of life. The implication was that if we 'feel better' under a fascist regime than one based on council communism then little more could be said. Desire cannot in this sense be a false witness to itself. As Lyotard notes:

> [w]here there is intensity, there is a labyrinth, and to fix the meaning of the passage, of suffering or of joy, is the business of consciousness and their directors. It is enough for us that the bar turns in order that unpredictable spirals stream out, it is enough for us that it slows down and stops in order to engender representation and clear thought. Not good or bad intensities, then, but intensity or its decompression. (Lyotard, 1993a: 42)

There is no 'inauthentic' or 'alienated' desire, no way in which desire could be read from the 'outside' as Deleuze and Guattari contend.

If there was a politics to be found here then at best it was an individualistic one: seek that which enhances, which affirms one's own being in all its intensity. Seek not the transcendence of the given or some otherwise redeeming *aufhebung* as an end in itself, but only as the means to this sense of plenitude. *Libidinal Economy* thus endorsed the conclusion of the 'post-political' wing of the 1968 moment. May 1968 on this reading was less the beginning of something new, than a moment, a pure 'event' or spectacle whose intensity for its participants (including Lyotard) had to be treasured for itself and for the feelings it induced, and not because it pointed towards some possible 'space' beyond itself. This was May 1968 as the ultimate aesthetic experience, as the ultimate 'high'. *Libidinal Economy* was the consecration of the search for highs; but like most such quests it can be read as a markedly narcissistic and apolitical stance. Almost in spite of himself Lyotard had transcended what appeared at one level to be the aim of his critique, a reconciliation of Freud and Marx finding himself instead in the midst of a nihilistic vitalism reminiscent of Bergson and Nietzsche. *Libidinal Economy* thus marked the realisation of a particular conception of critique, of self, of the social. It was also, as he himself was to argue, a cul-de-sac on all these terms, necessitating some sort of turning back or recuperation of a critical perspective, even if this was not to be achieved by anything as grand as the elaboration of 'critique'. This, it quickly became apparent, was to be led by the concern for the very object that had so recently been surrendered in the baroque excess of *Libidinal Economy*, namely justice.

Libidinal Economy, as Lyotard came to argue, was at best an apolitical text and at worst a deeply individualistic one. It was evidently this sense of a 'betrayal' of the political that convinced Lyotard of the necessity to turn away from his preoccupation with a libidinally focused politics of subjectivity towards a pluralistically centred philosophy of subjects which was to become the basis of the texts in the late 1970s and early 1980s. On the other hand, what remains in the work that immediately follows *Libidinal Economy* is the sense of a final 'drift' from the problematic and form of critique associated with Marx and Freud towards Nietzsche who had loomed so dramatically in its unfolding (hence the title of one of his works of the period *Dérive a partir de Marx et Freud*, translated as *Driftworks*), Lyotard might have felt the need to temper the Nietzschean thrust of *Libidinal Economy*, but Nietzsche became an ever more important figure in Lyotard's theoretical project. What remained pertinent for Lyotard in Nietzsche is the suspicion of critique as grounded in the beyond or, worse, the 'above' of experience, of being, of life.

This in turn brought him back into the orbit of Foucault, Deleuze and Guattari, who, like Lyotard, were convinced of the undesirability and indeed impossibility of 'total' critique of the form associated with Hegelian and Marxian discourse and thus the necessity for 'localised' strategies of resistance (Foucault, 1977). What emerges in the essays marking the transition from *Libidinal Economy* to *The Postmodern Condition* (most notably *Dispositif Pulsionnel* and the 'pagan' writings), is that a total critique of the sort offered by Marx and his followers implied totalisation and the desire to dominate. Critique thus had to be informed by a sense of its own limitations and context, and the potential it contained for imperialism and the subjugation of the Other. It had to be local, delimited and contingent. Above all, one had to acknowledge the speculative, incomplete and thus 'imperfect' quality which Lyotard now attributed to the theoretical endeavour itself. Theory, Lyotard now held, could aspire to nothing more than *'theorie-fiction'*, a kind of writing that, in renouncing the claim to know, rests for its ability to convince on qualities other than writerly authority: on style, playfulness, affirmation. Gone, in other words, the drive to comprehend existence within some overarching narrative. Gone too the meta-politics of redemption, of reconciliation, of an end to the struggles hitherto epitomising the human condition. From here onwards, localised forms of critique would support localised, plural, diverse forms of struggle and resistance.

From 'pagan' to postmodern

Before the question of justice, however, Lyotard wanted to provide a more substantive basis for his account of the problems of grounding knowledge. The untranslated 'pagan' works (*Rudiment Paiens; Instructions Paiennes*) are suggestive in this respect, but the conclusions of Lyotard's rumination on the ground of knowledge were only fully clarified in *The Postmodern Condition* written in 1979. As should be clear, once the project of a meta-theory of the subject had been shelved (as it was shortly after *Libidinal Economy*), Lyotard's thought turns to the status of theory more generally: what could be believed, what was authoritative? Lyotard's Nietzschean conclusions to the question left him with the sense that what we believed we did so contingently, out of 'faith' in the necessity to believe in something, whether it be 'science', religion or Marxism. We were no longer believe*rs*, but at most *given to* believe, a fundamental distinction in the passage from traditional, feudal, theocratic societies to modern secular societies. In short we had become 'pagans': unconvinced of the necessity, let alone the desirability, for some bedrock of certainty beneath our contingently held opinions and beliefs.

In *The Postmodern Condition* the historical account of the decline in the basis of belief is underpinned by Wittgenstein's later philosophy and a 'pragmatist' account of language that stressed the rootedness of language in everyday life. Thus the issue concerning the origins of a decline in belief is supplemented with an account of why it is that the problematisation of the ground of knowledge should be regarded as a logical development out of the emergence of a pragmatist paradigm. The problem of 'foundations' should not be seen as a mere irrationalist response to a more general crisis of authority, but as a reasonable stance grounded in developments elsewhere in philosophy. It is this move that supplements the historical account that lies behind the double-meaning that 'postmodern' has in *The Postmodern Condition*. When Lyotard offers his now standard definition of 'postmodern' as 'incredulity towards meta-narratives' what he has in mind is not merely that we have – as a matter of historical fact – *become* incredulous towards meta-narratives, but also that we *ought* to be incredulous towards them, and hence that, for example, Marxists who could not match Lyotard in his 'incredulity' had better learn to do if they did not want to find themselves in the 'dustbin of history' (Lyotard, 1984: xxiv). 'Postmodern' is thus not only a descriptor for a kind of scepticism that emerges in the course of modernity, it is also a philosophical and political position to be defended against those who would maintain the legitimacy and credibility of meta-narratives in any particular domain of knowledge and discourse. Whether such a demand is, as Habermas famously describes it, a form of 'neo-conservatism' remains to be seen.

The historicised sense of the term 'postmodern' can be rendered in fairly straightforward terms. In Lyotard's view Enlightenment gave rise to an intense optimism about the degree to which increasing knowledge leads to increasing well-being to the point where we can imagine an end to all obstacles to human flourishing and self-realisation. Science would empower the species to rise above its current miserable condition. As Lyotard sees it, this thesis requires us to believe in the certainty of two propositions:

1   Science differs from other forms of discourse in that it is in some ultimate sense 'true'. 'Narrative' (i.e. non-scientific) forms of discourse such as religion or myths are only true by virtue of the fact that a given group of people holds a particular story to be valid.
2   Liberation can be equated to the realisation of some state of self-knowledge, to 'Absolute Spirit' in Hegelian terms. This implies that the achievement

of liberation as a 'scientific' undertaking as opposed to a narrative undertaking in which 'being liberated' is akin to accepting certain contingent premises about the nature of the good life.

Thus the fact that Marxism posited itself as 'scientific' is important, not merely in terms of the claim of certainty as doctrine, but also in terms of the nature of the 'liberation' that awaited humanity. This would be liberation as the culmination of a 'scientific' process, not one premised on the arbitrary choices emerging from collective action. The validity of 'Communism' as an ideal was one based on the status of communism as a 'true' or scientific doctrine and thus as a form of practice that would literally 'brook no argument'. A communist is someone with truth and rationality on his or her side – not mere ethical or moral 'right'.

The problem as Lyotard sees it is that the claim of science itself to extra-narrative validity was undermined as much from within the science camp as without, i.e. by the development of new 'narrative'-based scientific disciplines (cybernetics, informatics) and also by the efforts of philosophers of science to explain the difference between science and other kinds of undertaking (Popper, Kuhn, Gödel etc.). As Lyotard sees it, what seems clear is that a consensus has now formed around the view that science needs some extra-scientific argument concerning the nature of truth to demonstrate that it is capable of supplying 'truths'. In this sense science is no different to any other kind of discourse in that it requires us to be predisposed to the kind of truths it seeks to develop. Lacking this predisposition will result in a loss of faith in the certainty and rationality of the undertaking. The 'postmodern condition' is thus a description of the progressive sense of loss of certainty experienced over the course of the previous two centuries.

More controversially, Lyotard wanted to defend this sense of incredulity and to explain why it was a rational response to the all-pervasive crisis he documented. Here he drew directly on the work of Wittgenstein, a thinker who would loom over much of his subsequent work. In Lyotard's view, Wittgenstein had convincingly shown in his 'later' work (particularly *Philosophical Investigations*) that the function of language was not as earlier philosophers (including Wittgenstein himself) had held to 'describe reality'. As he attempts to show, language does not have a function or a purpose as such. What we call 'language' is rather an infinite set of overlapping and distinct 'games' that we deploy in different contexts for all manner of purposes and uses (Wittgenstein, 1958: 23). None of these games have, as it were, some ultimate grounding in 'reality' such that we could say that some games are more 'real' or meaningful than others. It is the players of the game who determine the 'meaningfulness' of any given practice, belief or discourse.

Lyotard was evidently deeply struck by these insights and more generally by the contextualisation of language associated with the pragmatist turn in philosophy led in the Anglo-American context by Charles Peirce and John Dewey. Given the absence of an extra-narrative basis for legitimating forms of knowledge Lyotard falls back upon this rich contextualisation to provide an account of how it is that some discourses come to be regarded as valid whereas others fall by the wayside. What seemed clear to Lyotard is that narrative validity is internally self-referential, which is to say that 'validity' is a description of a performative act of consent on behalf of those who are being asked to believe in the validity of a proposition. On this reading if we can point to a community of people who accept the proposition that the earth is flat, then for those people the earth is flat. It is irrelevant whether such a group can demonstrate to others' satisfaction that the earth is flat, which would be the 'traditional' modernist demand. If such a group believes the 'narrative' then the narrative is 'true'.

If we accept this account then it follows that truths are relative, contingent, 'local' and merely dependent on some sort of consensus for their 'validity' to be maintained. From this premise emerges an account of the 'postmodern' that is much more contentious than the mere description of a pervasive scepticism would otherwise allow, for what Lyotard is arguing is that in a sense postmodernism represents a transformation of our relationship to authority and truth generally. Scepticism is not, in other words, something to be combated. It is to be celebrated as a sign of our capacity to see the deeper meaning or significance in the production of knowledge as inscribed in different contextualised discourses. Of course for his critics Lyotard seemed to be revelling in the chaos of authority, in the lack of ultimate referents and in the 'unholy' mess he documented (some would say unleashed). But then in a sense he *was* celebrating it. Lyotard's thesis was merely an extension of the Nietzschean perspectivism he had been advocating over the previous decade. The difference now was that unlike *Libidinal Economy* and the pagan writings, *The Postmodern Condition* was a book that was widely read and debated. Indeed, it quickly became the reference point for anyone wishing to locate a distinctively postmodern 'position'.

Language games and the problem of justice

In view of his own equanimity concerning the question of the postmodern, the impression we get is that the examination of the condition of knowledge in modernity was intended merely to serve as a backdrop for two key issues. The first is the nature of the political under postmodern condition, a topic he addresses directly in *Just Gaming* and *The Differend*. The second is the nature of the sublime or incommunicable, which he addresses in his final major works *The Inhuman* and *Lessons on the Analytic of the Sublime* (Lyotard, 1991b and 1994, respectively). Although Lyotard went on to discuss further the nature of the 'postmodern', one senses that this is in response to 'market' demand rather than because he felt there was anything interesting to add to the account in *The Postmodern Condition*.

One of the paradoxes in considering the reception accorded to the idea of the postmodern was that the very quality others such as Habermas perceived to usher the death of the political was regarded by Lyotard as the very condition upon which politics could now take place. In his view the earlier dominance of meta-narratives as part of the self-understanding of the modern reduced the political to irrelevance. If science (or any other discourse claiming certainty for itself – such as Marxism) gave us 'insight' into the nature of the liberation to come, then what was the point of politics other than the realisation of some fore-ordained path towards the 'rational society'? Surely it was this approach that suffocated politics, that denuded the political of the 'agonistic' contingent character that otherwise marked modern life. On one reading therefore Lyotard was merely trying to rescue politics from the hands of those who would reduce it to a mere sub-domain of administration (such as systems theorists) and those who misguidedly saw consensus and the end of conflict as the goal of rational human endeavour (such as Habermas).

In arguably his most impressive work, *The Differend*, Lyotard draws again on Wittgenstein and also Kant to show how such moves must be resisted. The core of the argument rests on similar premises to those articulated in *The Postmodern Condition*. This is to say that the realm of human activity is characterised as a realm of language games, of diverse and plural forms of discourse, speech, action. Each 'game' has its own rules of conduct and norms of procedure, so that we can talk about different 'regimes' of activity governed by different systems of 'legislation'. Art criticism has one set of rules, international law has another, family disputes another, and so on. Within each regime there are, as Lyotard puts it, 'litigations' or disputes the resolution of which is determined by an application of the relevant rules in operation (Lyotard, 1988: 9). If I say that this artwork is 'rubbish' then this calls for a justification in accordance with the rules and 'phrases' of art criticism ('it is poorly executed'; 'badly conceived'; 'kitsch' etc.). Others may disagree or contest my judgement; but in order to do so effectively they too must remain within the domain of the litigation, which is to say the language and vocabulary of art criticism. The outcomes of litigations are 'damages', which is to say that some compensation, some recognition of a fault or a lack of judgement is offered. However, the litigants retain their dignity and self-respect, even where one has lost to the other.

As Lyotard argues, not all disputes have this litigious quality in which there is a certain agreement on the rules and phrases to be deployed. There are disputes that question the basis of the dispute itself and thus which challenge the 'totality'. An example he offers on a number of occasions is the relationship between capital and labour (Lyotard, 1988: 9–10, 178). Many labour disputes can, he observes, be resolved as a 'litigation' meaning that both parties tacitly endorse the legitimacy of the private ownership of the means of production. Labour presents its demands in a fashion that is consistent with the maintenance of the overall system, rather than in terms that challenge it, i.e. via the demand for more pay, better health and safety provision, fewer hours. Either the capitalist wins or labour wins, but either way the relationship between capital and labour remains intact. Labour is not destroyed if it fails to win more money for its members. Similarly, capital remains intact even where concessions are made in the form, say, of recognition of the right to form trade unions. Where, however, labour confronts the right of capitalists to dispose over the profit created by labour *as such* then this indicates a different kind of dispute, one that points towards the legitimacy of capitalism itself. It is this kind of conflict that Lyotard terms a *differend*. The presentation of a standard from outside the existing horizon of discourse causes a 'silence' or brute incommensurability of positions. As Lyotard puts it, 'the differend is not a matter for litigation; economic and social law can regulate the litigation between economic and social partners but not the differend between labour-power and capital' (Lyotard, 1988: 10). Here a new Idea, ideology or meta-narrative challenges the totality of that which exists. Such clashes cannot be resolved by mediation, compromise or an open-ended conversation, but only by the defeat of one particular 'totality' or view of the world by another. That which exists must therefore be reduced to 'silence' or even 'destroyed' for the other to 'win'.

Merely to describe the character of a differend is to get a sense of the political import of the analysis for Lyotard. For him a world of competing differends is a world of mortal combat, not a world of reciprocity or respect for the other. This is the politics of ideologies, of redemption and damnation and ultimately of the Gulag and the concentration camp. To be postmodern in this political sense is to turn one's back on the 'totality', on the idea that one can imagine a shift in the total character of life, economy, society. As he puts it, 'the totality is not presentable' (Lyotard, 1988: 10). This in turn implies returning to politics as 'micro-politics', namely a politics that is concerned with highly contingent and localised narratives of desert, merit, happiness and fulfilment. To ask for anything more is, we sense, to deny that we are bounded, 'local', contextual creatures, partaking of a multiplicity of 'games'. It is to imagine that there is some ultimate vision of the Good Life that we can conjure up in abstract contemplation. It is to think of ourselves as gods; which as 'pagans' we are now bound to resist.

Irrespective of one's sympathies to such a politics it is worth pausing to focus on the analytical claim being made here. This is that multiplicity, plurality and diversity are constitutive of social life as such. Language cannot be contained either in terms of the function it is alleged to perform ('picturing the world') or in terms of a totality of possible language games. As Wittgenstein implies, since it is forms of life that are constitutive of language games, to imply that there are a finite number of language games is to imply that there is a finite number of possible forms of life and activity. It is also to suggest that forms of life are in some strong sense commensurable, something he disputed in his later work. On this key point Lyotard agrees with Wittgenstein. This is to say, first, that it is impossible to reduce the complexity of social life to an Idea that could in turn account for the character of all possible language games. Thus something, someone, some 'form of life' always 'escapes'; or if it does not then its subsequent 'victimisation' as other or different serves as a reminder of the necessity for force to maintain the illusion of the whole and the true. Secondly, it is impossible to reduce language games to one 'genre of discourse' or meta-language (Lyotard, 1988: 128). As Wittgenstein insisted, language games are not ultimately reducible to each other such that we could say that witchcraft is the 'primitive equivalent' of science. We can only learn the 'meaning' or significance of witchcraft from within those forms of life in which witchcraft appears. Moreover, witchcraft may have a different symbolic meaning in one setting to another. It may have a different character or meaning dependent on the particular tribe or collectivity. Thus even the 'shared' practice of witchcraft conceals differences that are in some sense incommensurable and which defy translation from language into another.

To say that language games and forms of life are constitutive is thus to make a break from the strategies familiar in Western thought that insist on the availability of an ontologically grounded account of the world and reality. To be 'pagan' or 'postmodern' is to reject ontology in favour of the plurality of linguistic forms. It is to give up the search for ultimate answers or foundations. There is no being, only narratives concerning being. In turn, if there are only narratives then there is no authority *as such*, for there is no final answer to the question 'what is being?'. Authority dissipates and along with it the game to reinscribe authority from a privileged position *of* authority, that of the intellectual ('listen to *me*: I know what the answer is'). For postmoderns the 'game' is listening *and* speaking to the many, no matter how poorly 'qualified' to speak the 'many' may be. As Lyotard puts it in *Just Gaming*:

> For us, a language is first and foremost someone talking. But there are language games in which the important thing is to listen, in which the rule deals with audition. Such a game is the game of the just. And in this game, one speaks only inasmuch as one listens, that is, one speaks as a listener, and not as an author. It is a game without an author. (Lyotard, 1985: 71–2)

The game of justice, he wants to say, is a game not just of talking, of legislating, of founding through the performative utterance. It is a game of listening to others: an intersubjective continuous dialogue between those who have an interest in being together and living reciprocally. But it is of necessity a two-way game.

What should perhaps be highlighted at this point is that despite evident similarities to the project of Deleuze and Guattari, the plurality and diversity on offer here, is one constituted on quite different terms. Here the claim refers to the character of language rather than of 'desire' as in *Anti-Oedipus* or 'multiplicity' as in *A Thousand Plateaus*. Deleuze and Guattari offer what, from a Lyotardian point of view, are ontological claims, which is to say they are claims stemming from assertions concerning the nature of reality. In Lyotard the multiplicity and diversity are attributes of systems of representation, not of 'things'. The 'fact of plurality' in this case concerns the fact that the world can be represented in many different ways, which in turn makes the assertion of the validity of a single Idea, 'totality' or meta-narrative logically incoherent. Thus, whereas Deleuze and Guattari can maintain they are Marxists because of Marx's methodological and ontological materialism, in Lyotard's eyes that same insistence on ontological certainty becomes an imperialistic meta-narrative, in turn justifying the reduction of difference to the same. As for Wittgenstein so for Lyotard, King Lear's insistence on 'teaching differences' culminates in an anti-systematising philosophy of plurality and diversity as 'facts' that cannot be ignored without prompting violence, or 'terror' in Lyotard's lexicon. In this sense there is no world, there is no thing, no reality the totality of which can be described – only 'our' world, 'our' reality to be described in our language.

Language games and 'radical democracy'

As implied in the comments above, it is easier to get a grip on what Lyotard is against as opposed to what it is that he is for. What he is against is the totality, or rather the notion that the totality can be made known or 'present'. By extension he is against all forms of meta-narrative that tell the story of totality's 'coming to be', that tell us how the Absolute is to be 'realised'. Ideological thought – thought, that is, offering a 'closed' or 'fixed' point from which to view reality – is anathema to Lyotard. Where, however, does this leave politics? More particularly, where does it leave resistance to that which is in the name of some unrealised yet collectively held ideal, however defined or felt?

An aspect of Lyotard's thought that we have only hinted at is his critique of capitalism. His celebration of the 'postmodern' means that it is usually assumed that his work is complicit in the perpetuation of capitalism rather than providing resources for resisting it. It is all too easy to forget or overlook the fact that Lyotard thought of himself as a critic of capitalism, and thus as engaged in a politics of resistance, albeit one removed from the Marxian orbit. The problem for our purposes is that the critique of capitalism tends to sit alongside the critique of *anti*-capitalist politics – at least of the kind represented by Marxism. It should also be noted that he can be at his most acerbic when he talks about capitalism in the context of an examination of art and the artistic 'genre', as opposed to politics and the normative genre. In fact, as we have seen, the political and the aesthetic are closely tied in Lyotard's thought and remained so up to and including his last major works, *The Inhuman* and *Lessons on the Analytic of the Sublime*. Yet even these works serve as reminders of the critical thrust of his approach, particularly as regards the pernicious and dehumanising character of capitalism and thus the importance of an active avant-garde to combat the worst excesses of commodification. For Lyotard the logic of capital, or the 'genre of the economic' as he terms it in *The Differend*, is that of 'gaining time'.

Following Marx, Lyotard asserts that capital is constantly at war against the lag between idea and production, manufacture and commodity. Capitalists compete on the basis of time, the time it takes to make a commodity, to get it to the market-place. Capitalism is thus at war with the human itself, since as bounded, finite creatures capable of 'only so much' we are in our very being an obstacle to the boundless energy of capital itself. In a gesture reminiscent of an earlier generation of critical Marxists, particularly Lukacs and Benjamin, Lyotard asserts that art is a key weapon in the war against 'gaining time'. Modern art, in particular, is a game of questioning and thus of inducing the pause or lag. Art inserts conversation, play, reflection, where capital wishes to eliminate it. Art thus resists capital since, as an example of a primarily 'useless' kind of activity (particularly in its conceptual, 'high modernist' guise), it queries the logic of gaining time over thought, critique, decision (Lyotard, 1991b: 104–6). To be clear, Lyotard is not denying that art can itself become a commodity and thus implicated in the fetish character of modern life; he merely wishes to restore the sense of the importance of an avant-garde in art which in turn means non-realist forms of art that resist reproduction as commodity (as for example in installation art). The very irritation many feel today at much 'conceptual art', art that is which makes us ask 'what is art?', is thus on a Lyotardian view an entirely compelling reason for regarding it as avant-gardist: it resists, it queries, it annoys, and thus evades reduction to the machine. To those who stand irritated in its presence art promotes the very thing capital seeks to extinguish: thought, reflection, laughter, as well as irritation. Art thus provides a deinstrumentalised moment which evades the sheer utilitarian inhumanity of the market.

Lyotard's defence of the Kantian concept of the sublime is premised on similar terms (Lyotard, 1994). This is to say that the availability of the sublime, of the ineffable, of that which 'defeats' representation, is seen by Lyotard as a form of resistance to the monochrome world of capital where everything can be subsumed within everything else and thus where the differend is in danger of erasure. By contrast with those who regard the 'postmodern' as characterised by the celebration of kitsch, or playfulness induced by the juxtaposition of style over 'substance', Lyotard's stance could not be more different. For him the postmodern is characterised by invention rather than nostalgia, by turning away from the reductive realism of 'transavantgardism' and its desire to contain the excess of what is genuinely avant-gardist, i.e. that capacity to induce feelings of the sublime, the unspoken, the unrepresentable. Thus, far from being complicit in the reproduction of capital or merely the face of 'late capitalism', as Fredric Jameson for example argues, Lyotard's view is that contemporary art can and does have a critical function in these otherwise compromised times (Jameson, in Foster, 1985: 124). It must bear witness to that which cannot speak; it must induce thought, reflection on that which cannot be spoken; it must slow the passing of time. Above all, it must assert the primacy of the human over the machinic reproduction of life. Yet what is still to be established is how the critique of capitalism makes itself manifest in his *political* writings. What is the connection between critique and resistance?

Lyotard was, in his later writings, notoriously unforthcoming on such matters, perhaps in recognition as he might see it of the difficulty of 'mixing' genres. Nevertheless there are clues as to the overall thrust of his approach in his political writings. This is particularly so in the 1990 essay 'The Wall, the Gulf and the Sun: A Fable' (Lyotard, 1993b: 112–26). Here Lyotard describes the traditional progressive goal as 'emancipation', which in traditional leftist discourse was always theorised as a change from without, from outside the 'system'. This in turn necessitated a revolutionary strategy for capturing state power and radically transforming the system in order to bring about a 'genuinely' emancipated society. Yet for Lyotard the underlying narrative upon which such a strategy depends has been fatally undermined and, more generally, shown to be a 'myth' of limited validity. First, Lyotard is in agreement with those already covered: the working class does not and will not possess within itself the means for its own emancipation as that term would be interpreted in Marxist theory. Whatever identity it once possessed has been progressively eroded over time with the effect that the working class lacks the sense of common purpose with which to mount a serious collective effort of the sort required to alter the system.

Secondly, and more contentiously still, Lyotard argues that 'the system' (for which read 'liberal capitalism') has shown itself to be 'open' and 'flexible' enough not merely to withstand threats from within, for example from working-class struggle, but also to demonstrate its basic superiority over the other models of social organisation on offer (Lyotard, 1993b: 113). In an echo of Popper and Hayek, Lyotard goes on to explain that 'open' (market) systems are by nature flexible enough to adapt to innovation and novelty, permitting experimentation and profit maximisation, thereby in turn promoting social reproduction. In political terms this openness translates as a lack of extra-institutional 'authority', thereby facilitating the rotation of elites and the maintenance of a system that is itself open to reform. 'Emancipation' must therefore be theorised as change from within not without. It must be 'defensive' not 'offensive', that is seeking the overthrow of the system and its displacement by something radically different (Lyotard, 1993b: 113). The task of the political progressive is thus to argue for retaining and enhancing welfare benefits.

Translated into contemporary terms, what Lyotard appears to be arguing for is a defence of *already won* social democratic reforms and benefits against the neo-liberal juggernaut of market imperatives, private accumulation and 'gaining time'. Capital cannot, it seems, be challenged as such, or at least it cannot be challenged without a radical shift in the contemporary imaginary. All we can do is, as it were, tame capitalism in order to safeguard those rights and benefits that an earlier generation of radicals secured as the price for social peace.

What is striking here is the cold realism of Lyotard's approach, one which goes beyond a simple pessimism of the sort widespread among left radicals of all sympathies after the 'fall of the Wall', towards an at least partial endorsement of liberal-capitalism on its own terms. His comments on the 'openness' and 'effectivity' of capitalism do not imply that this is a 'second best' to some other type of system, but rather one that can be 'appreciated' on its own terms. This is tempered by the sense that it is not us who control capitalism, but capitalism that controls us. This is enough for Lyotard to write in melancholy terms, for example in *The Differend*, about the 'disillusionment' that attends our own impotence in the face of the market and the redundancy of traditional modernist radicalism. As he puts it himself, 'reformism cannot make anybody happy' (Lyotard, 1988: 180). We are doomed to act out a politics whose legitimacy and rationale is the possibility of change, whilst admitting in our private moments that 'nothing will change'. Politics has on this view become hijacked to the exigencies of the economic 'genre'; but given the 'choice' between the banality of consumer society and the primordial nihilism of Auschwitz, he implores us to take the former. This is a quite different view, as we shall see, to that espoused by 'radical democrats', one that equates to a faith in the supremacy of the political over the economic – or at least our potential to reassert the political over the economic. Lyotard is perhaps closer to Baudrillard in this respect than to, say, Heller or Laclau and Mouffe. He is closer to the notion that capitalism has become genuinely hegemonic, making alternatives unthinkable. Capitalism has become ubiquitous, unbounded and constitutive, so much so that whatever choice exists is one between forms of capitalism. Capitalism is an idea, a genre, and as such cannot be challenged without it seems evoking the totalitarian 'outside'.

'Post-Marxism' and the politics of a disillusion

One might expect the events of the 1980s and 1990s to have induced a certain pessimism or at least caution on the part of many on the left, but it is surely important to differentiate between those thinkers whose basic orientation is to accept the liberal-capitalist status quo as a feature of contemporary existence and those who assert the possibility (if not inevitability) of other 'forms of life', to mobilise Wittgenstein. As we think is clear, Castoriadis, and Deleuze and Guattari maintain a critical stance even in the face of the apparent omniscience of capitalism, always reverting back to an ontological or perhaps post-ontological position from whence critique can be launched. With Lyotard the availability of such a position from 'outside' is queried, not so much because of his realism, but because the conclusions of his enquiries into the nature of language prevent him looking too far beyond the world as it is. What is clear is his deep ambivalence to 'normative' gestures generally. We can see this essentially conservative (with a small 'c') nature of the analysis clearly in the account of the differend. Thinking back to this part of this discussion what Lyotard is objecting to is the notion that it is possible to step outside of where we are in order to judge the moral or ethical basis of the world of which we are parts. From this point of view he argues that it is wrong to posit (say) communism as a better system than liberal-capitalism. This would be to seek a point of critique from outside the totality, and, as we have heard Lyotard intone, the 'totality is not presentable'. Thus one can only take issue with *some part* of that which exists, some aspect, but not the whole. To judge the whole is to invoke an Idea, and invoking Ideas is to claim access to some *a priori* or transcendental truth. It is to claim the existence of an Archimedean Point when, as Lyotard asserts, no such point exists. We are all *of* the world we inhabit and thus have no recourse to anything beyond or outside it.

Plausible as such a reading of the obstacles created by 'plurality' may be, problems remain. Looking at Lyotard's own example of the capital/labour dispute is instructive. Lyotard says it is an illegitimate move to judge capitalism, the inference being that capitalism is 'all there is', and thus to do so would be to invoke the dreaded 'totality'. Yet capitalism was itself created out of something else, namely feudalism, and moreover co-exists with other kinds of system, including different variants of capitalism itself. 'Rhineland' capitalism is different to 'Latin' capitalism which is different to the frontier or 'Mafioso' capitalism of Russia, to take but three examples. There are also all manner of post-capitalist models challenging and competing with dominant neo-liberal-inspired capitalisms. To put the same matter differently, there are and always have been different 'regimes', whether considered as 'phrases' or socio-economic systems. This already implies the availability of choices *within* capitalism, and beyond that, *between* capitalism and non-capitalist or post-capitalist alternatives. More seriously, however, the notion intrinsic to Lyotard's stance that we are condemned to tolerate that which 'is' because the 'it' seems to be everywhere is a deeply problematical basis for critique generally. It is also morally and ethically objectionable as a basis for social analysis, effectively disarming critics of tyrannies and despotisms of whatever kind.

Without going any further it is difficult not to conclude that there is a mismatch between the position Lyotard wants to defend and the position that seems to follow from the claims he is making. What he *wants* to say is that we should regard ideologies and meta-narratives that use the cover of 'science' to present us with a normative schema of how the world should look as totalitarian because they do not permit 'justice' as the ongoing conversation on the nature of the just and true to take place. But what he *ends up* saying is that any normative schema that challenges liberal-capitalism and thus which requires radical change to the status quo in order to come into being should be rejected as totalitarian. These two positions are not the same, and the suggestion that in some sense they are should alert us to problems in the analysis. What in particular it highlights is the hiatus caused, in particular, by the distinction between differends and litigations which lies at the heart of the analysis in *The Differend*. This needs brief explanation.

Lyotard characterises radical schemas as differends that challenge the extant 'regime of phrases'. The problem, however, is in thinking that the source of differends is Ideas that rely upon some extra-discursive point of reference, some meta-narrative or philosophy of history whose claim to truth lies outside the discursive realm in which they originate. This is not always the case, although of course it *can* be the case (on Lyotard's terms). It is surely possible to arrive at a radical position without in a sense invoking the strong ontological or epistemological claims that Lyotard associates with radical politics. A radical political position can be arrived at on the basis of strong moral or ethical preferences – as opposed to some grandly narratological account of the nature of capitalism. We might, for example, hold that wage labour is a form of exploitation without signing up to Marx's account of how wage labour is implicated in the crisis character of advanced capitalism. In other words, we might find it morally obnoxious that one person is forced to work for another, in turn committing us to an economic vision of 'associated production' on moral or ethical grounds alone. Our position will thus *coincide* with that of a certain kind of ideologically committed socialist, but it is not the *same* as that position, deriving from ethical and moral objections to inequality as opposed to an account of why capitalism is economically unsustainable.

That Lyotard treats these positions as two species of the same reveals that what he is against is not so much Ideas that bring forth differends and thus the violence of the 'totality' so much as radical ideas *per se*. This in turn implies that, like Popper, he thinks that it is better for us to accept the current 'totality' and work within it to secure reforms to the system itself, rather than to offer up what the former termed 'aesthetic' schemes for social improvement for fear of unleashing forces that might inflict 'terror' on society (Popper, 1966: 157ff.). There are in these terms *no grounds* for rejecting a given political system outright, no matter how unjust or morally reprehensible it is. Political systems become immune to challenge as such because, whenever it is suggested that a fundamental change is required, existing elites can answer that this is invoking 'the totality' and thus necessitating violence.

It is not of course Popper, but the later Wittgenstein who is invoked to support the analysis from *The Postmodern Condition* onwards. Yet we should also note that Lyotard is arguably doing a disservice to his mentor and to the approach associated with the deployment of the later Wittgenstein in social critique – one that, as noted elsewhere, is highly significant in terms of the development of various Post-Marxist positions. Whilst the invocation of 'forms of life' and 'language games' does give us an image of complexity in relation to social life, it takes a leap of imaginative reconstruction to imply that the complexity of forms of life should be taken as a *constraint* on political action. This would be to argue that there was some underlying or hidden 'necessity' of an ontological kind that determines the nature of forms of life. As someone whose mature years were spent combating such a view, and thus opening the way to our 'imagining' radically different forms of life, such an account not only misrepresents his stance, but serves to inhibit the appropriation of his thought for the purposes of critique (Easton, 1983; Staten, 1984). What is arguably more in tune with a Wittgensteinian approach would be to insist that like any social practice political systems and practices are contingent and historically situated. No system exists out of necessity, or because it matches our 'deepest' needs or desires. Indeed as the 'earlier' Wittgenstein put it, '[t]here is no compulsion making one thing happen because another has happened. The only necessity is *logical* necessity' (Wittgenstein, 1961: 6.37; original emphasis). From this point of view political systems can be judged by the same moral and ethical criteria that we use to judge any other facet of human activity. It is not only individual actions than can be judged morally obnoxious, but political systems – particularly those that render the many subordinate to the few or which institute relations of oppression and domination.

Even in a brief presentation such as this what quickly becomes apparent in Lyotard's work is that, contra his critics, Lyotard's legacy for the development of a radical politics 'after' Marx is somewhat ambivalent. Nor is this merely a question of 'genres', as Lyotard seems to think it is. It is not merely a question of the difficulty of reading across his works in various fields to establish a 'core' orientation. There is, as we have sought to show, a core orientation, and it is one that is critical of capitalism both in abstraction and as an historical practice. Lyotard's critique clearly invokes Marx's in the sense of stemming from a rejection of the dehumanising – or possibly in-humanising – character of capitalist production as subjecting everything around it to the remorseless logic of 'gaining time' and surplus value. However, in his haste to abandon what he felt to be a redundant basis from which to develop a radical political practice, he throws out the ethical and moral basis of radical politics as such. This renders his own critique weaker as a resource for thinking through how the kind of resistances he documents could become the basis for a transformative politics. After all, there is resistance in Lyotard. As he reminds us in his last works, art gives witness to the unrepresentable, to our deepest feelings of alienation and anguish. It challenges, queries, questions and thus induces in others the facility to challenge, query and question.

On the other hand, the resistances unleashed are of a peculiarly attenuated kind, as if he thought it not merely unlikely but impossible that groups of individuals should feel sufficiently moved by the spectacle of their own alienation that they could bring themselves to act collectively in the name of some different logic or ethic. Here it is difficult not to speculate that the failure of 1968 to bring anything of any lasting significance or value prompted in Lyotard a deep pessimism concerning the prospects for any real challenge to capitalism. This, combined with the relative success of the incremental politics of social democratic reform in gaining something from the capitalists (if of a welfarist kind), conspired to induce in him a weariness as to the prospects of drumming up the necessary energies required to promote a more radical agenda.

Yet, there is a clear sense in which Lyotard's postmodern project was its own kind of cul-de-sac, producing a defence of liberal-democracy as a *de facto* bulwark against what was perceived to be less appetising alternatives. As is clear, Lyotard defended democracy less for what it is, than what it is not: totalising, oppressive, exclusionary (Lyotard, 1997: 133). What he thought he detected in contemporary liberal-democratic society was not merely a certain economic dynamism which could be of use in improving the condition of the least well off, but also a political dynamism of plural voices, albeit heavily mediated by all manner of interests. In this sense he thought he heard some sort of 'conversation', albeit one conducted in an atmosphere of power and inequality. However, any kind of dialogue was to him better than the monologue he associated with grand narratives generally, and Marxism in particular. That this dialogue was denuded of the power to challenge the status quo seemed ultimately to matter less than the fact that it was taking place at all.

What, however, is also clear is that in his unwillingness to radicalise the terms upon which the conversation might take place, his approach became complicit in the perpetuation of the very thing that remained the subject of a deep and far-reaching critique in another corner of his intellectual interests: capitalism. As his work in aesthetics testifies, contemporary capitalism is far from benign. On the contrary, it becomes increasingly intolerant as the impetus to 'gain time' requires the obliteration of all obstacles to accumulation. This included not merely artistic creation and innovation itself, but that very conversation at the heart of Lyotard's 'republican' politics. After all, neo-liberalism had as part of the object of its critique the 'overloaded' welfarist state to which latterly he was attached, with its 'public spaces' and autonomous institutions of learning. If there was any doubt as to what was primary between politics and economics, the neo-liberal revolution that swept the globe in the 1980s and 1990s surely settled the argument. The republican dream had been reduced to 'the administration of things', and the polite conversation of postmodern ironists confined to some corner of the academic Ivory Tower. Post-Marxism had in its Lyotardian rendition come to echo the fears of an earlier generation similarly immobilised by the fear of treading on the fragile catallaxy of 'forms of life'. What is recognised in the demands of contemporary activists, is precisely the point Lyotard was willing to countenance if only in relation to art: one of the principal threats to the plurality and diversity of forms of life is an unfettered market. Unlike the former, Lyotard was, however, unwilling to take that leap into a politics in defence of 'other worlds'.

Summary

- *Lyotard's aim*: primarily to investigate the potential of the 'unspoken' or 'unrepresentable' as the basis for developing a radical politics. He was consistently interested in the radical potential of the artistic avant-garde as a spark for resisting the imperatives of capitalism. This led him to explore the potentiality of phenomenology and psychoanalytic approaches, both of which stressed the limited horizon of the linguistic. In the wake of the failure of 1968, he was drawn to a critique of Marxism as a totalising 'meta-narrative', developing this critique into an analysis of the exhaustion of modernism generally, and science in particular. He turned latterly to pragmatism and the work of Wittgenstein to explore the nature of the postmodern condition and the 'republican politics' he thought such a stance entailed.
- *Background*: teacher and militant at the University of Paris. He had been involved with Castoriadis in *Socialisme ou Barbarie*, but left to create his own libertarian affinity group, the *Mouvement du 22 Mars*. After 1968 Lyotard combined teaching in Paris and the USA with the role of public intellectual.

- His most important early work is *Libidinal Economy*, which he later rejected as 'scandalous'. He sought in similar fashion to Deleuze and Guattari to find a creative synthesis of Marx and Freud. This was issued in a markedly individualistic stance valorising the circulation of intensities and desires.
- The failure of this project led him to develop a critique of 'meta-narratives' and an attempt to map out a postmodern account of knowledge that stressed the situatedness of all truth claims as 'narratives'. This appeared to abolish the distinction between science and 'fables', cementing his notoriety as the most 'relativist' of the post-1968 French thinkers.
- The failure of grand narratives implied a need to refine and develop 'justice' and democratic politics. This became the focus of much of Lyotard's later works, leading him to greater scepticism regarding the claims of radical politics and a respect – sometimes tacit, sometimes overt – for liberal-democratic institutions and practices.
- He retained, however, a critique of capitalism and its dehumanising tendency to instrumentalise creative thought and practice in the name of 'gaining time'.

Assessment

- *Strong points*: Lyotard was a highly creative thinker who drew on a huge range of sources of materials. He was instrumental in puncturing the illusion, widely shared, that the constant expansion of science and technology was a good in itself. His work also anticipates and enlarges upon the 'return of the political', which is a common theme in the work of Post-Marxists. He emphasised the possibility of disagreement both within and between 'genres', of the necessity for safeguards for political life, and the desirability of public spaces in which debate could take place.
- *Weak points*: Lyotard's eclecticism is witness to his often apolitical stance in relation to the phenomena he described. He was more absorbed by making theory 'work' than by searching for agents of change, causes to back or resistances to develop. His uncoupling of politics and economics makes the former the hostage of the latter, leaving his 'critique' resting on the qualities of avant-garde art as opposed to an avant-garde politics.

Sources and Further Reading

Browning, G. (2000) *Lyotard and the End of Grand Narratives*, Cardiff: University of Wales Press.

Castoriadis, C. (1997) *World in Fragments: Writings on Politics, Society, Psychoanalysis, and the Imagination*, trans. D.A. Curtis, Stanford, CA: Stanford University Press.

Dews, P. (1987) *Logics of Disintegration: Post-Structuralist Thought and the Claims of Critical Theory*, London: Verso.

Easton, S.M. (1983) *Humanist Marxism and Wittgenstein Social Philosophy*, Manchester: Manchester University Press.

Foster, H. (ed.) (1985) *Postmodern Culture*, London, Verso.

Foucault, M. (1977) *Language, Counter-Memory, Practice*, trans. D.F. Bouchard, Oxford: Blackwell.

Genosko, G. (ed.) (1996) *The Guattari Reader*, Oxford: Blackwell.

Lyotard, J.-F. (1971) *Discours, Figure*, Paris: Klincksiek.

Lyotard, J.-F. (1984) *The Postmodern Condition: A Report on Knowledge*, trans. G. Bennington and B. Massumi, Manchester: Manchester University Press.

Lyotard, J.-F. (1985) *Just Gaming*, trans. W. Godzich, Manchester: Manchester University Press.

Lyotard, J.-F. (1988) *The Differend: Phrases in Dispute*, trans. G. v. d. Abbeele, Manchester: Manchester University Press.

Lyotard, J.-F. (1991a) *Phenomenology*, trans. B. Beakley, Albany: State University of New York Press.

Lyotard, J.-F. (1991b) *The Inhuman: Reflections on Time*, trans. G. Bennington and R. Bawlby, Cambridge: Polity Press.

Lyotard, J.-F. (1993a) *Libidinal Economy*, trans. I.H. Grant, London: Athlone.

Lyotard, J.-F. (1993b) *Political Writings*, trans. B.R. w. K.P. Geiman, Minneapolis: University of Minnesota Press.

Lyotard, J.-F. (1993c) *The Postmodern Explained: Correspondence, 1982–1985*, Minneapolis: University of Minnesota Press.

Lyotard, J.-F. (1994) *Lessons on the Analytic of the Sublime: Kant's Critique of Judgment, [Sections] 23–29*, trans. E. Rottenberg, Stanford, CA: Stanford University Press.

Lyotard, J.-F. (1997) *Postmodern Fables*, trans. G. v. d. Abbeele, Minneapolis: University of Minnesota Press.

Popper, K.R. (1966) *The Open Society and Its Enemies*, London: Routledge.

Staten, H. (1984) *Wittgenstein and Derrida*, Lincoln, NE: University of Nebraska Press.

Williams, J. (2000) *Lyotard and the Political*, London: Routledge.

Wittgenstein, L. (1958) *Philosophical Investigations*, trans. G.E.M. Anscombe, Oxford: Blackwell.

Wittgenstein, L. (1961) *Tractatus Logico-Philosophicus*, trans. D.F. Pears and B.F. McGuinness, London: Routledge.

4

Laclau and Mouffe: Towards a Radical Democratic Imaginary

What is now in crisis is a whole conception of socialism which rests upon the ontological centrality of the working class, upon the role of Revolution with a capital 'r', as the founding moment in the transition from one type of society to another, and upon the illusory prospect of a perfectly unitary and homogenous collective will that will render pointless the moment of politics. (Laclau and Mouffe, 1985)

Laclau and Mouffe's highly original and ground-breaking work, *Hegemony and Socialist Strategy* (Laclau and Mouffe, 1985), was animated by the desire to expunge from Marxism all traces of the seemingly implacable Stalinist logic of its 'Jacobin imaginary'. They called for a 'radical and plural' democracy that would prevent the emancipatory dream becoming a totalitarian nightmare, as occurred in the Soviet Union and elsewhere. This nightmare, they proposed, could not be simply explained away by circumstance. There was something deep within the heart of Marxist theory that resisted an openness and tolerance necessary for democracy to work. The socialist agenda had to be augmented by liberal values and a respect for liberal-democratic institutions. Equally crucial, and more controversially, the core tenets of historical materialism had to be abandoned in favour of the post-structuralist theory of Derrida, Foucault and Lacan, as well as others, such as the later Wittgenstein. These political and theoretical moves were essential in order to resolve the 'crisis' of Marxism, whose authoritarianism made it incapable of connecting with the New Social Movements that had emerged from the 1960s.

Before *Hegemony and Socialist Strategy*

The easiest point of entry into *Hegemony and Socialist Strategy* (hereafter *HSS*) is through their preliminary works of the late 1970s, which were more 'neo-', than 'post-' Marxist. Laclau and Mouffe were still working *within* a Marxist framework, addressing the British Communist Party's Eurocommunist-inspired debates over the meaning and validity of the 'Broad Democratic Alliance'. Eurocommunism was an attempt to make European Communist Parties more voter-friendly through abandoning their old Marxist–Leninist vocabulary, such as 'dictatorship of the proletariat', distancing themselves from the Soviet Union and appealing to the New Social Movements. Laclau and Mouffe at this point still wanted to realise a socialist project through the overthrow of 'monopoly capitalism' in which the working class would play a decisive part, albeit in alliance with non-proletarian social forces. Theoretically, they were looking to resolve problems visible in Althusser's and Poulantzas's structuralist attempts to develop a 'Marxist' science of ideology and politics. In particular, they were dissatisfied with standard class reductionist Marxist explanations of ideology (of 'class belonging'), and Marxism's inability to become a hegemonic force in contemporary politics. It was unable to help the working class gain the support of the 'middle sectors', a weakness already evident in its strategy in countering fascism in the 1930s and in its approach to different kinds of Third World populism. Laclau argued that Marxists ignored the importance of the 'popular-democratic struggle', thereby vacating crucial political ground to the fascists and the bourgeoisie generally (Laclau, 1977: 110–11, 124). Marxists were also unwilling to see the significance of the petit-bourgeoisie's identification with 'the people', rather than defining itself as a distinct class, which had been crucial in the rise of fascism. Under contemporary conditions of 'monopoly capitalism', the petit-bourgeoisie given its social weight remained strategically important (Laclau, 1977: 135). The problem for Marxists was that the working class in keeping with its class identity could not speak 'hegemonically' in the name of 'the people'. Marxists did not acknowledge that the petit-bourgeoisie were not as deeply implicated in production relations as the proletariat, which meant that ideology itself played a decisive role in structuring political identity, rather than production relations (Laclau, 1977: 92, 114).

By the same token, Marxists had difficulty in analysing populism which played a large role in Latin American politics from the 1930s onwards. There existed a '"people"/power bloc contradiction' (Laclau, 1977: 108, 166), which was political and ideological, and autonomous from class contradictions stemming from production relations. This contradiction was ideologically far more enduring than those specific to particular social formations (Laclau,

1977: 167) and was 'dominant at the level of the social formation' (Laclau, 1977: 108). Yet, despite its autonomy, Laclau argued that this contradiction was 'overdetermined by class struggle' (Laclau, 1977: 108). In other words, different classes present their own objectives as the 'consummation of popular objectives' (Laclau, 1977: 109). Any residual loyalty to this 'class struggle' approach was abandoned in *HSS*, along with a bipolar, zero-sum conception of politics.

For Laclau the theoretical underpinning of his pre-*HSS* position derived principally from two elements of Althusser's account of ideology. The first was Althusser's theory of 'interpellation', which refers to the process by which individuals, as unknowing 'bearers' of social structures, are transformed through the 'interpellatory' process into 'subjects', who believe themselves to be autonomous choice-makers, as for example when an individual responds appropriately when hailed by a policeman. For Althusser this process occurs in all societies, and plays a vital part in the reproduction of all social and economic relations. The ideological process is therefore not seen primarily as the production of 'false consciousness' by the economically dominant class, disappearing in a classless society. This *potentially* non-class reductionist interpretation of ideology was emphasised in a second element in Althusser's thought, that of 'condensation' or 'over-determination', borrowed from the psychoanalytic interpretation of dreams. These concepts were used to explain the process of ideological *fusion* during periods of ideological/political crises. This process of fusion Laclau argued in contrast to Poulantzas, cannot be reduced to the 'class belongingness' of the composite ideological elements (Laclau, 1977: 93–4). Laclau's key point was that the evidence of different classes employing the same 'elements' of an ideology, such as militarism, nationalism, and even liberalism, demonstrated that they had no natural class home. Their class nature was only revealed when they were 'articulated' within a broader ideological discourse through a 'condensation' or 'overdetermination' of these elements with other elements (Laclau, 1977: 97–9). Given the crucial role of ideology in forming 'subjects', its autonomy from production relations and the fact that the 'middle sector' was particularly important under conditions of monopoly capitalism, a political imperative existed to combine popular with proletarian 'interpellations' (Laclau, 1977: 141).

Chantel Mouffe's work in this period strongly reflected their common concern to eliminate class reductionism and 'economism' from the Marxist conception of ideology and politics, especially in her treatment of Gramsci's theory of 'hegemony'. She suggested that Gramsci's definition consisted not merely of political/instrumental leadership within a class alliance of the exploited and oppressed, but also of 'intellectual and moral leadership', that is, of the ideological construction of a 'collective will' (Mouffe, 1979: 184).

This task of fusion entailed the production of 'interclass' subjects, irrespective of their economic class origins through the 'rearticulation of existing ideological elements' (especially the 'nation') rather than the imposing of a new ideology by a class vanguard (Mouffe, 1979: 188). Hegemonic practice (or the 'war of position') for the working class, in order to win over non-proletarian groups involved a process of 'disarticulation', of ideologically disconnecting the bourgeoisie from its non-bourgeois allies, and of 'rearticulation', so that they saw themselves as part of a new 'collective will' under working-class leadership. The working class in particular had to persuade these allies to accept its definition of the 'nation', of the 'national-popular' will. To achieve this the working class had to overcome its own narrow class identity and 'nationalise' itself, becoming a 'national' class, there being nothing intrinsically class-specific about the term 'nation' (Mouffe, 1979: 194). She concluded by suggesting that Gramsci's theory of hegemony provided the basis for a new, enlarged understanding of politics, which involved antagonisms based not just upon class. Indeed, 'politics is the very activity through which social relations are constituted (as a result of the relationship of forces existing between antagonistic subjects) [and] it becomes evident that everything in society is political' (Mouffe, 1981: 185). With this enlarged conception of the 'political', an alliance between the working class and 'new movements' could be effected.

What we shall see in *HSS* is the development of these anti-economistic arguments in such a way as to take Laclau and Mouffe 'beyond' Marxism, to become 'Post-Marxists' (although, as we shall see, they still wanted to claim *some* affinity to Marxism). Essentially, their critique of Marxism became more pronounced the less they were convinced by Althusser's (and Poulantzas's) project of establishing its scientific credentials and as they eradicated all forms of potential dualism, as between the 'economic' and the 'political', from their own thought. Here, they were following through the 'logic' of a non-economic reductionist, autonomous conception of ideology and its constitutive role, via politics, in the construction of social relations. Not only are the identities of the non-proletariat ideologically (or 'discursively') constructed, so too are the proletariat's. Theoretically, although the ideas of Gramsci (hegemony) and Althusser (over-determination and an anti-humanism which denied the idea of a fixed human essence) are still present, their intellectual trajectory led them into the interrelated areas of linguistics and psychoanalysis, into the worlds of Saussure, Lacan, Derrida, Foucault, the later Wittgenstein and others. The outcome of this intellectual journey was *HSS*.

What this new departure signified was that from now on Laclau and Mouffe held that meanings about the world and our place (identity) in it could never be fixed. Such meanings were inherently unstable as meanings in language itself were unstable. This was because, first, all meanings, being derived from language, were constructed in relation to other meanings which were themselves unstable since there existed no fixed meaning-giving 'centre' (e.g. God). Secondly, in psychological terms, individual striving for meaning and identity to make up for a fundamental 'lack' was potentially endless. And thirdly, language and meaning were 'hegemonically' constructed, privileging certain meanings over other meanings, thereby legitimating power relations throughout society, between individuals as well as between individuals and institutions. In other words, all social relations were at bottom political relations, and the secret of a successful hegemonic operation was to normalise or 'naturalise' these contingently constituted relations. Thus, in contrast to orthodox Marxism, which fixed meanings in an *a priori* way as 'essentialist' manifestations of the economic base, Laclau and Mouffe saw meanings and therefore identities as always open to change and negotiation. They drew the simple political conclusion that only liberal-democratic princi-ples and institutions fully recognised this unfixity of meaning, and attempts to fix meanings for all time would result in authoritarianism.

Hegemony and Socialist Strategy: the argument

The aim of *HSS* was to recast the political strategy of the Left in response to the 'crisis of socialism', to create a 'new politics' of 'radical and plural democracy'. This strategic reorientation entailed the theoretical reformula-tion of Marxist theory to the extent that their declared affinity to Marxism was simultaneously *'post-Marxist'* and 'post-*Marxist*', although in reality the first term of this paradox is a more accurate description (Laclau and Mouffe, 1985: 4). There are three interconnected themes in *HSS*. The first is a criti-cal account of Marxist attempts to get to grips with 'contingency', that is political, economic and social circumstances that are not readily explicable within the orthodox Marxist theoretical template, which gave rise to the concept of 'hegemony'. The second and most difficult theme develops a number of concepts and perspectives that inform their own theory of hege-mony. The third theme is an application of 'hegemony' to 'advanced indus-trial societies', demonstrating its relevance as a *general* theory of modern politics as well as advancing the Left's cause.

Critique of Marxist theory and the rise of hegemony

They urged the abandonment of basic Marxist categories, such as 'base', 'superstructure', 'false consciousness' and the teleology of 'historic necessity' that were grounded on mechanistic, 'essentialist' thinking, which had led to totalitarianism in the Soviet Union and elsewhere, to political ineffectuality in the West, with working classes generally embracing reformist identities, and to its inability to combat imperialism and fascism. This essentialism was most critically revealed in Marxism's portrayal of the ideological 'superstructure' as an *effect* of economic, production relations ('base'). Rather, ideology was all-pervasive, penetrating all human relations, whether they were economic, social or political, giving them a particular form. Because of this, all these relations were 'contingent', unpredictable and therefore 'opaque', since meanings about the world were potentially extremely ambiguous and open to contestation and new interpretation. Laclau and Mouffe held that for orthodox Marxists the meanings of all struggles were not understood in their specificity, but as fixed, *a priori*, essentialist expressions, class interests or stages of capitalist economic development. Put another way: for Laclau and Mouffe there existed no necessary, causal relation between 'social being' and consciousness, either because a given set of production relations did not generate a particular type of consciousness, or because ideas themselves were not class-specific. To repeat: ideologies had no 'class belonging'. A vital implication was that political identities were not preconstituted, to be *'discovered'* by a Marxist 'science' exposing 'false consciousness', but *constructed* through hegemonic discourses.

Laclau and Mouffe proceeded to demonstrate that Marxist attempts to cope with all the phenomena falling outside their theoretical model led to the emergence of two unreconciled 'logics', of 'necessity' and 'contingency', that is a 'dualism'. Marxists recognised the first 'logic', but until Gramsci had not sufficiently appreciated the significance of the second. To make their point they assessed various Marxist reactions to the lack of revolutionary working-class unity in Western Europe prior to the First World War. Rosa Luxemburg argued that unity could occur through a spontaneous mass strike, but she still clung to a notion of economically fixed proletarian identities. Karl Kautsky and George Plekhanov held that Marxist 'science' could guarantee the future unity as the underlying 'laws' of capitalist development meant a simplified class structure and deeper economic crisis. They thus underestimated the possibility that 'contingency' and class fragmentation was a permanent condition. Eduard Bernstein held that unity could be achieved through autonomous political intervention, but he was still in the grip of teleological thinking which attached *a priori* fixed meanings to different movements and struggles. And Georges Sorel, although still holding to the idea of Marxism as a science of capitalist development, stressed the indeterminacy of workers' identities, and therefore the need to construct a unity, a 'bloc', through the 'myth' of a general strike.

If Sorel was a forerunner to Gramsci in using the term 'bloc' as something that had to be constructed out of non-pre-given class identities, Russian Marxists provided Gramsci with the other key term 'hegemony'. It emerged in an under-theorized form in the unique conditions of Russia, where the bourgeoisie was too weak to lead a democratic revolution against Tsardom. This alien or 'external' task which naturally 'belonged' to the bourgeoisie, as orthodox Marxism argued, fell upon the proletariat. 'Hegemony' referred to the proletarian leadership within an alliance with other oppressed classes, especially the peasantry. Russian Marxists did not invest this term with much significance, because the need for 'hegemony' would evaporate, once proletarian revolutions had occurred in the West. Thus, Laclau and Mouffe noted that a democratic potential existed in Trotsky's conception of 'uneven and combined development' that necessitated a 'hegemonic' practice, because it acknowledged the co-existence of a 'plurality of antagonisms and points of rupture', but this narrative would disappear with the onset of proletarian revolution in the West (Laclau and Mouffe, 1985: 55).

More seriously, in the hands of Lenin and the Bolsheviks 'hegemony' had an undemocratic resonance. Not only was it merely part of a wider militaristic–instrumentalist conception of politics, within such an alliance 'the Party' was bound 'ontologically' to privilege the interests of the working class because it was a 'universal' class representing the interests of the whole of humanity (Laclau and Mouffe, 1985: 57). This was reinforced by an 'epistemological' privileging of Marxist 'science' which understood the laws of history. This led to a very dubious notion of 'representation', in which the working class's 'interests', represented by the Party, would take priority over those of the 'masses', although the former were in a minority (Laclau and Mouffe, 1985: 55–7). The lack of democratic potential also arose because within this alliance the division between the leading class (the proletariat) and the led (the peasantry) remained, as there was no 'hegemonic reconstitution' of working-class identity through an internalisation of a genuine commitment to democratic practice with all its potentially pluralistic implications. Rather, its identity remained static, since it had been pre-given by its position in the relations of production. After the Russian Revolution 'hegemony' became part of Communist political vocabulary in anti-fascist and anti-imperialist struggles, to the extent that it started using the term 'people', and recognised a multiplicity of antagonisms. But the economistically and statically conceived notion of class identity, and the privileging of the working class within 'the people' and the party 'representing' the historical interests of the working class, laid the basis for a manipulative and authoritarian political practice.

Gramsci's theoretical novelty lay in conceiving hegemony, in contrast to Lenin, not merely as political leadership with classes retaining their pre-given identities, but as 'moral and intellectual' leadership that possessed a genuinely democratic and pluralist potential. This was achieved through a 'hegemonic recomposition' of identities of the hegemonic agents, arising from the constitutive role of ideology. Gramsci's implicitly assumed that ideas and values had no intrinsic 'class belonging'. Ideology now played a key creative role in politics, no longer as an epiphenomenon of production relations. Rather, ideology is constructed through the practice of 'articulation', enabling 'subject positions' genuinely to 'traverse a number of class sectors' rather than through a process of representing abstractly conceived class interests (Laclau and Mouffe, 1985: 67). Because the elements forming this hegemonic ideology have no 'class belonging', they can be internalised by the hegemonising force, irrespective of 'objective' class categories. The meaning of the hegemonic tasks is no longer fixed externally according to class interests or historical laws. Instead they arise 'internally' through the articulatory process itself, consequent upon the hegemonic activity of binding disparate social fragments into a 'collective will'. The resultant 'collective will' provided the ideological cement required to form a new 'historic bloc', independent of the class origins of the hegemonic agents. This 'hegemonic recomposition' was underlined by Gramsci's interpretation of ideology as a 'totalising' force which possesses a 'materiality', embodied in the totality of society's institutions, rather than being confined to the 'superstructure'. As a result of all this, the actual practice of hegemony means that the hegemonic subject changes, so that it does not take state power, but through a 'war of position' *becomes* the 'state', conceived as a social totality, as an 'integral state' (Laclau and Mouffe, 1985: 69). However, Gramsci ultimately displayed a vestigial economism in which there is a single unifying principle in every hegemonic formation, grounded upon a 'fundamental class'. The 'economy' is perceived as 'homogenous space unified by necessary laws', rather than as hegemonically constructed solely through the contingent activity of class struggle itself (Laclau and Mouffe, 1985: 69). Thus, Gramsci's Marxism remained ultimately dualist with the process of identity-formation occurring on the economic plane, separate from where hegemonic articulation arises.

Laclau and Mouffe's theory of hegemony

After demonstrating that for Marxists 'hegemony' was essentially an ad hoc add-on, a flawed, theoretically dualist and politically authoritarian response to the problem of contingency, Laclau and Mouffe then proceeded in Chapter 3 (theoretically the most important, as well as complex, in the book) to construct their own, democratic theory of hegemony. This, they regarded as central to understanding the politics of 'advanced industrial societies' and to furthering the Left's egalitarian project. As suggested earlier, they built on the insights, concepts and critical methods of Continental post-structural linguistics, philosophy and psychoanalysis, in order to prove that ultimately the meanings of language and identities could never be finally fixed, and that therefore the ideological cement sustaining social practices was always open to subversion. Crucially, this lack of stability of identities constituted the conditions in which the battle for hegemony between different social groupings was played out.

We should first note that their analysis had an historical dimension. The precariousness of identities only fully revealed itself in advanced industrial societies, which experienced a growing proliferation of differences (Laclau and Mouffe, 1985: 96). Sites of antagonism which have the potential for multiplying political spaces had expanded as a result of changes in modern society associated with the bureaucratisation of the welfare state, the expansion of mass communications, the rise of a 'democratic consumer culture', increased commodification of all aspects of society, decline of the traditional family, and capitalism's effect on the natural environment. So unlike earlier societies, an asymmetry arose between the growing proliferation of differences and the difficulties of a discourse in attempting to fix these differences as 'moments' within an articulatory structure. These numerous spaces were, or had been, open to hegemonic contestation in the modern era between the Left (egalitarian), the Right (inegalitarian and hierarchic) and the totalitarian (Right or Left, but equally centralising and repressive).

Moving on to their theoretical framework, Laclau and Mouffe base hegemony on the idea of 'articulation', which is a form of discursive practice turning different 'elements' (or 'floating signifiers') into 'moments' within a discursive totality whose identities thereby become 'modified' (Laclau and Mouffe, 1985: 105). Thus, 'signifiers' (verbal or written terms referring to a 'signified' concept) can have no clear, fixed meaning unless relationally embedded within a discourse, and then remain only 'partially fixed' as 'nodal points'. Language, and therefore human subjectivity and identity, is a vital component of discursive practice in which the meaning of one term is derived 'internally' and relationally in comparison with others (e.g. father/son). So, following Saussure, meaning is a result of a 'system of differences', rather than produced 'externally' with reference to an external object. As a consequence the changes of meaning of certain terms – 'signifiers' – within such a system impact upon other terms within the system. By analogy, if the differences in social and political identities of an individual or group changes, this impacts upon the identities of other individuals and groups.

This discursive approach also meant that all meanings about the 'external' world were discursively constructed, so that physical events, such as earthquakes, have no meaning outside language. Equally significant, discourse is more than language. It also includes a 'material' element, so for example, following Wittgenstein, the co-operative activity house building is 'discursive' in the sense that this activity involves the interaction of both linguistic communication and physical co-operation, and thus constitutes a 'language game' (Laclau and Mouffe, 1985: 108). Thus ideology, Laclau and Mouffe argue, has a material character and is not a mental, epiphenomenal reflection of the material world. It was essential in the construction of all social practices.

Here we come to a key stage in their argument: following Foucault and Gramsci, discourses were hegemonically (that is, power-politically) constructed and form stable, apparently 'necessary' and 'objective' social practices as well as linguistically created identities or 'subject positions'. In reality, the meanings contained within such discourses were prone to subversion, with the possibility of the meaning of 'signifiers' becoming dislodged within a discursive structure, not merely for historically contingent reasons in the modern era, associated with changes in social relations. There were linguistic and psychological reasons too. To explain this precariousness of meanings and identities Laclau and Mouffe introduce a number of terms and concepts. The embeddedness of ideology in social practices manifests itself in the sense that the latter are in some way symbolically constituted. Here they radically develop Althusser's use of the term 'over-determination', which was derived from Freud's analysis of dreams, and entailed a 'condensation' of the symbolic with a plurality of meanings and identities, or a 'displacement' of the meaning of a term within a given discourse by another. From this Laclau and Mouffe drew the conclusion that social relations were 'over-determined' in the sense that they lacked an 'ultimate literality' (Laclau and Mouffe, 1985: 98). The other concept underlining the symbolic dimension of the social is 'suturing' derived from Lacanian psychoanalysis (Laclau and Mouffe, 1985: 88, note 1). All individuals, beginning with the traumatic separation from their mother in early childhood, desire 'fullness', experience a primordial 'lack' of a satisfyingly stable identity based upon a sense of oneness with the 'Other'. According to Lacan's hypothesis, the full recognition by the 'Other' of the self is always open to doubt. Hence the 'Other' in all its symbolic forms can be blamed for the blocked identity and hence the continuing possibility of antagonism (Laclau and Mouffe, 1985: 125). The suturing process involves a 'filling in' or a fixing of meanings through symbolisation to make up for this 'lack'. However, such symbolisation can never be stable, presupposing a closed, fixed, 'objective', 'positive' and transparent order of meanings.

This is so, Laclau and Mouffe hold, owing to the existence of 'antagonism', or 'negativity', in which the 'presence of the "Other" prevents me being totally myself' (Laclau and Mouffe, 1985: 125). For example, the peasant cannot be a peasant if the landowner has expelled him from his land. But this antagonism is not a direct, objective relation between landlord and peasant, but occurs at the imagined, symbolic level, as a 'symbol of my non-being', overflowing with a 'plurality of meanings' preventing my 'being fixed as full positivity' (Laclau and Mouffe, 1985: 125). Antagonism limits 'positivity' or objectivity, which consists of seemingly unambiguous linguistic meanings, and sits at the interface between 'experience' (including imagination) and language, and serves to disrupt any stable system of linguistically created 'subject positions'. It prevents the final 'suturing' of society which language attempts to achieve. They infer from this that 'society' itself is an 'impossibility' in the sense that 'society' as a signifier can have no ultimately fixed, agreed meaning, and neither can the consequential 'subject positions'. Given the existence of antagonism and the fact that all identities are relational, meanings are likely to be even more precarious.

In the modern world the instability of meanings and the subversion of the 'social' (that is, the attempt to fix the meaning of 'society') arises through the interplay of two competing 'logics' of 'equivalence' and of 'difference'. Their point is that different identities can only be made equivalent (and therefore becoming a different identity at the symbolic level) through antagonism, in opposition (for example) to a real or potential oppressor. But these equivalents are always precarious because they also prevent differences from fully constituting themselves. From this Laclau and Mouffe deduce that this interplay meant that society was 'not totally possible, neither ... totally impossible', that is, as an 'objective' and universally agreed concept – or 'signified' (Laclau and Mouffe, 1985: 129). Hegemonic, articulatory practice, they posit, involves attempting to fix the meaning of the floating signifiers, or 'elements' by making them into 'moments', creating 'chains of equivalence', hoping to expel successfully any 'surplus of meaning', creating 'nodal points', and preventing opposing forces from articulating these terms. A thoroughgoing contingency, or 'openness of the social' is presupposed, along with the idea that conflict does not occur in a 'single political space' (Laclau and Mouffe, 1985: 137). The conditions for hegemonic activity occurred therefore when, owing to a proliferation of antagonisms, the relational system defining political and social identities weakened (Gramsci's 'organic crisis') led to a 'generalized crisis of social identities' and a multiplicity of 'floating elements' (Laclau and Mouffe, 1985: 136).

The new strategy for the Left: applying hegemony to advanced industrial societies

Left-wing hegemony could only be established if the 'floating signifiers' of 'liberty' and 'equality' were fixed within a democratic discourse, in contrast to the right's meanings, which in effect detached liberty from democracy and therefore licensed inequality and preserved social hierarchies (Laclau and Mouffe, 1985: 174–5). Thus Laclau and Mouffe did not 'renounce' liberal-democratic ideology, but wanted its deepening and expansion in the 'direction of a radical and plural democracy' through the multiplication of political spaces (Laclau and Mouffe, 1985: 176). They called for 'a new extension of egalitarian equivalences, and thereby the expansion of the demo-cratic relation in new directions', especially through anti-racist, anti-sexism and anti-capitalist struggles (Laclau and Mouffe, 1985: 158). They saw advancing radical and plural democracy in terms of changing conscious-ness, where necessary relations of 'subordination' (that is, where an indi-vidual is subjected to the decisions of another) are transformed into relations of 'oppression' (that is, where the former relations become ones of 'antagonism'), and thereby becoming perceived as illegitimate relations of 'domination'. This occurs when those subject to relations of subordination (of 'difference'), such as women, slaves or serfs, have been exposed to a dis-cursive 'exterior', for example to the 'logic of equivalence' of individual rights discourse (Laclau and Mouffe, 1985: 153–4). What happens here is a process of 'equivalential displacement', when these subordinated groups start to internalise egalitarian discourses (Laclau and Mouffe, 1985: 158).

In advanced industrial societies this discursive 'exterior' consisted of the ideology emerging from the French Revolution of 1789, which initiated the 'democratic revolution' (a term coined by de Tocqueville), beginning a nar-rative of growing individual equality and liberty in all spheres of human relations. It started with formal political relations and then throughout the nineteenth century extended into the economic realm (socialism is now seen as a 'moment' in the democratic revolution). By the late twentieth century it had moved into sexual, gender and ethnic relations, as well as into underlying issues to do with peace and ecology, as espoused by the New Social Movements. Laclau and Mouffe expanded the notion of the 'political', as these movements increasingly indicated the extent to which all social relations are in a sense 'politically' constructed, resting on power rela-tions. This expansion of the 'political' reinforces their thesis that the demo-cratic revolution is an open road, since we are unable to predict where new sites of antagonism are likely to occur. Indeed, they drew on Claude Lefort's idea of democracy, as the site of power, is an 'empty place' in which law, power and knowledge no longer stem from a unitary centre as prevailed under feudalism, as embodied in the king. Thus, the 'democratic revolution' meant that all laws, resting on no assured or agreed foundations, are open to question, as are social divisions previously suppressed by an unchal-lengeable central authority (Laclau and Mouffe, 1985: 187).

A left-wing form of hegemony had to unite all the disparate struggles of both the New Social Movements and workers, creating a 'nodal point' of 'radical and plural democracy' what this entailed was the 'struggle for a max-imization of spheres on the basis of the generalization of the equivalential-egalitarian logic' (Laclau and Mouffe, 1985: 167). Here workers had no *a priori*, externally generated privileged position according to the 'laws of history', because all groupings within such a 'historical bloc' were based on their own 'principle of validity' (Laclau and Mouffe, 1985: 167). But presumably these groupings could be united by the 'overdetermining' 'symbolization' of the 'democratic revolution', which would become a 'new common sense' (Laclau and Mouffe, 1985: 183). Laclau and Mouffe wanted a 'new utopianism' mixed with pragmatism, which institutionalises the moment of tension and openness, enabling society to manage 'its own impossibility' (of becoming a harmonious, fully transparent or 'sutured' society) (Laclau and Mouffe, 1985: 191). Interestingly, they call upon the elements of this 'historic bloc' to internalise Marx's notion of reciprocal freedom: the free development of each should be a 'condition for the freedom of all' (Laclau and Mouffe, 1985: 183). This would lead to the 'production of *another* individual', unsullied by 'possessive individualism', where natural rights were held as prior to society rather than as socially constructed. Equivalence and individual autonomy had to be combined, which meant that there had to be a space for 'logics' of complete identity and pure difference to be renegotiated (Laclau and Mouffe, 1985: 188).

In short, they were insisting that a 'hegemonic' view of politics was the only desirable and possible one in the modern era, in which social institutions are unravelling in a way that revealed their precarious, political/ antagonistic construction. The essentialist certainties of 'history', 'the economy', 'ontology' and 'epistemology' must be abandoned in favour of the discourse of 'hegemony'.

Summary of their basic arguments in *HSS*

1 Orthodox Marxism must be rejected because *theoretically* its essentialism in all its manifestations meant that it could not grasp the contingently/ symbolically/ideologically, in short, the discursively, constructed nature of *all* social relations (including the economic sphere) in the modern era, that is, when the meaning of the 'political' could not be established *a priori*. And it had to be rejected *politically* because its theory was inherently totalitarian (the 'Jacobin imaginary') since it ontologically privileged the 'interests' of the proletariat, which it claimed to 'represent', and its epistemology, its 'science' of history, privileged the Party. Marxism's only serviceable residue was Gramsci's theory of hegemony and Althusser's concept of over-determination, both suitably radicalised through purging them of any vestigial essentialism.

2 Thus there was a need for a new general theory to grasp the 'political' as different types of social antagonism proliferated. Their theory of hegemony, 'articulation' and associated concepts, they thought, provided

the most adequate understanding of this process in advanced industrial societies.

3 The Left can only become effective if it abandons the imagery associated with the class struggle, and embraces a much more inclusive, democratic and pluralistic form of discourse, that counters the Right's attempts to promote inequality and hierarchy through 'disarticulating' the freedom/democracy couplet.

After *Hegemony and Socialist Strategy*

A clear intellectual division of labour emerged after *HSS*. Laclau's energies were devoted to consolidating and developing their theoretical and political positions outlined in this text: of 'fine-tuning', tying their theory in more closely with Derrida and Lacan, resisting critical refutations by Mouzelis (1988) and Geras (1990). Mouffe, on the other hand, extended their thesis into political philosophy. They also acted jointly in 'hegemonic' activity, the search for intellectual allies (Rorty, Derrida and Zizek, to name a few) and the cultivation of support from younger academics.

Laclau

His refinement of their thesis first of all embraced further explorations of the contingent, 'political' construction of the 'sedimented' 'social'. Secondly, it involved a clear formulation of the particular/universal relations, as there was a danger of misinterpreting them as advocating only particularity, thereby making any kind of negotiated democratic hegemony impossible. In underlining their anti-essentialist, contingency perspective Laclau embraced more fully Derridian terms associated with his theory of deconstruction, especially 'undecidability', and Husserl's 'forgetting of origins'. He also utilised his own category of 'dislocation' closely associated with that of antagonism, possibly in order to resist charges of voluntarism (see Rustin, 1988), as well as integrate the categories of free will and determinism. All this was designed to reinforce the idea of how the 'real' or 'objective' and 'subjective' or 'imagined' worlds and therefore meaning were contingently constructed. Equally significant, there was a 'Lacanian turn' (Smith, 1998: 81) in Laclau's work, prompted by Zizek's criticism that if Lacan's ideas were more fully embraced, identity would be seen not merely as a result of external antagonism, but also of internal self-blocking (Laclau, 1990: 251).

In consolidating their contingency perspective, Laclau, following Derrida's deconstructive register, argued that decisions that constitute the social were not 'algorithmically' formulated (as in mathematics), but arbitrary, based upon an 'undecidability' between incommensurable choices in which power (and therefore hegemony), involving the repression of other possibilities, was ultimately decisive. But the fact that choices involve the *need* to repress meant that power had its limits, making all 'objectivity' the result of a decision potentially unstable (Laclau, 1990: 60–1). This was so because individuals, following Lacan, ceaselessly searched for identifications in order to achieve an impossible 'fullness', which stemmed from the trauma of the 'real' that occurred at the pre-linguistic stage in early childhood. The 'mirror-image' process attempts to make up for the 'lack' of coherence and wholeness by providing a frame and self-image for the child. The 'signifier' of the socio-political order, the product of 'decision', however, always ultimately failed to fully represent the subject: 'not everything is reflected in the image-mirror, and what remains on the other side is the impossible, the primarily repressed' (Laclau, 1994: 32). Thus, there existed an unstable relation, a 'split', between individual identification and representation at the ideological-symbolic and formal political levels, between the ordering ('the Law', that is, 'framing') function of identification, which all subjects desire, and the precise contents of that order. Under conditions of modern democracy different parties and movements will compete within this 'empty place' of order to achieve an impossible 'fullness' of representation, to speak in the name of the 'universal', in effect, however, to signify the 'lack' (Laclau, 1994: 36–7; 1996: 35). However, Laclau was keen to stress that although the origins of the problem of representation were psychological, they were also associated with the intensification of fragmentation, complexity and proliferation of antagonisms in contemporary capitalism, creating the 'dislocation' of identities, and therefore the need for a 'centre' and identification. Nevertheless, the satisfaction of this need was ultimately impossible (Laclau, 1990: 39–41). Thus, particularly in times of 'organic crisis' (Gramsci) conflict reactivated the awareness of the political and contingent construction of the 'social', thereby 'de-sedimenting' it and opening up possibilities for hegemonic contestation in attempting to represent the absent 'fullness'.

Laclau's second refinement concerned the 'universal/particular' couplet. He opposed the Marxist idea of the working class as the 'universal class', owing to the dangers of substitutionism arising from its ontological privileging of the party or leader claiming to represent the interests of this class, when it was in reality merely making its own particular – as opposed to universal – demands (Laclau, 1990: 25). He also recognised the politically regressive dangers of celebrating the 'particular' (e.g. Apartheid) (Laclau, 1990: 29), as well as making democratic hegemonic construction highly problematic. Laclau argued that the universal/particular couplet made democracy – indeed, contemporary politics – possible. Because the universal had no particular content (it was an 'empty place') different groups competed to give their 'particularisms a function of universal representation. Society generates a whole vocabulary of empty signifiers whose temporary signifieds [that is, providing "empty signifiers" with a content] are the result of a political competition' (Laclau, 1990: 35). In a democracy, particular groups representing a 'universal' chain of equivalents will always eventually expose their own particularity, because they are unable to 'fill in' the 'absent fullness' of a community, especially given the 'unevenness', heterogeneity and antagonism in society (Laclau, 1990: 57). In other words, the universal and particular constitute the political fulcrum around which the undecidable logics of difference and equivalence operate. Thus, he rejected the idea that 'universality' had any substantive content, although he admitted that democracy was impossible without the notion of universal human rights (Laclau, 1990: 122). But this discourse was a *contingent* historical product' (Laclau, 1990: 122; original emphasis). He also endorsed the universalism of Enlightenment values, as long as they were presented as 'pragmatic social constructions', rather than as grounded in 'reason' (Laclau, 1990: 103–4).

Mouffe

Mouffe's post-*HSS* trajectory was in many respects different from Laclau's and perhaps more adventurous, although the ultimate message of 'radical and plural democracy' remained the same. She attempted what could be interpreted as a 'hegemonic' manoeuvre within contemporary and not so contemporary Anglophone political philosophy. This entailed a series of 'disarticulations' and 'rearticulations', of critically appropriating the insights and perspectives of contemporary thinkers (often whose politics were incongruous with their own position) in order both to buttress and show the validity of their political–theoretical framework. In *the Return of the Political* her most important book, she sought to demonstrate that contemporary political philosophy, especially in its liberal form, was not really *political* philosophy at all, but moral philosophy (Mouffe, 1993b: 113, 147). It failed to understand 'the political', which pointed to the need to adopt a position of 'agonistic pluralism', whose meaning was consonant with their 'radical and plural democracy' platform, and involved challenging all forms of subordination by extending liberal and egalitarian values into new areas of social existence. She derived her notion of 'the political' from the German conservative political philosopher Carl Schmitt, who understood it in terms of the ineradicability of passion-driven, human conflict and the attendant propensity of individuals and groups to define themselves as 'friends' and 'enemies', as a 'we' and as a 'them' in constructing their identities (Mouffe, 1993b: 2–3). Yet Schmitt's weakness was that he had no understanding of how liberal-democracy could transform 'enemies' into friendly 'adversaries' (Mouffe, 1993b: 4), of how it could domesticate the passions created by anta-gonism, so that 'the political' could become 'politics' (Mouffe, 2000: 101–2). Schmitt's negative view of liberal-democracy, its inability to resolve the tension between (individual) freedom and (democratic) equality (Mouffe, 1993b: 119–20) meant that he was blind to its primary virtue in legitimising and transforming human conflict into something less destructive. Indeed, the 'paradox of democracy' lay precisely in its inability to eliminate conflict, especially between the 'logics' of equality and liberty (Mouffe, 2000: 4–5). It contained the 'promise' of being able to do so, yet such a promise was impossible to realise (Mouffe, 1993b: 8). The stance of 'agonistic pluralism' recognised this paradox, the inevitability of difference and antagonism and the belief that liberal-democratic ideology and its institutions could create a climate of toleration thereby preventing the socially and physically destruc-tive implications of such conflict. Thus, in the contemporary debates on citizenship she argued that citizenship should be based upon the 'common political identity of persons who might be engaged in many different enter-prises and with differing conceptions of the good, but who are bound by their common identification with a given interpretation of a set of ethico-political values' (Mouffe, 1993b: 83–4).

We can now look briefly at Mouffe's critical appropriation of various frame-works of contemporary political philosophy. In passing we should note that this process of appropriation by and large excluded Marxism. She had 'given up the idea of a radical alternative to the capitalist system' (Mouffe, 2000: 15) and Marxism was 'unlikely' to recover because of its discredited totalitarian association and its inability to respond to the aspirations of the new social movements owing to its class reductionism (Mouffe, 1993b: 9). As for social-ism, if defined as the democratisation of the economy, this was a 'necessary component of the project of radical and plural democracy', and could only be attained through a liberal-democratic regime (Mouffe, 1993b: 90).

As a background to her critique of liberalism and Habermasian-inspired deliberative democracy, she put herself in a critical relation to the Kantian aspi-rations to, and assumptions of, universalism, rationalism and individualism that were characteristic of the Enlightenment and modernity. She was not opposed to these notions *per se*, but only to a failure to recognise that they were discur-sively constructed through language games involving power, antagonism and exclusion, and consequently they could assume different meanings. As for con-temporary liberalism, she had much sympathy with Rorty's tradition-based, non-foundational liberalism (Mouffe, 1993b: 15), but was critical of his confla-tion of political (good) and economic (bad) liberalism (Mouffe, 1993b: 10).

Again she had sympathy with Rawls's position, especially with his argu-ment that modern democracy, in prioritising the 'right' over the 'good', con-tained no 'single substantive common good' (Mouffe, 1993b: 55) and with his 'progressive' idea of 'justice as fairness' in opposition to neo-liberalism (Mouffe, 1993b: 52). However, his 'perfect liberal utopia' (Mouffe, 1993b: 51) failed to recognise 'the political', in at least three senses. First, in assuming that all differences could be relegated to the private sphere through the construction of a procedurally based rational consensus (Mouffe, 1993b: 49), he ignored the possibility that conflicts over political values were irresolvable. Indeed, conflict in the public sphere over the meanings of liberty and equality was the defining mark of the liberal-democratic regime. He left no space for indeterminacy required for the modern democratic process to operate successfully. Secondly, this rationalistic process of relegating dissent to the private sphere was in itself in effect a covert political manoeuvre, entailing the construction of a 'We' in opposition to the 'Them' of a 'constitutive outside' that excluded non-liberals (Mouffe, 1993b: 140–1; cf. Mouffe, 2000: 24–30). Thirdly, in assuming that a rational public consensus was possible Rawls conflated political and moral philosophy which focused upon individual morality. He was thus unable to construct an 'ethics of the political'. This dealt with the ethical consequences of being a member of a political association, which meant that in a liberal-democracy political principles involved irresolvable conflicts over the meaning of liberty and equality for all (Mouffe, 1993b: 56, 113). She later mobilised similar arguments against Habermasian-inspired theorists of deliberative democracy, who in seeking to create procedures that would generate a rational consensus ignored the endemic nature of human conflict, and the fact that 'social objectivity' and social identities are constituted by power/hegemony relations, that made the quest for harmony and transparency illusory (Mouffe, 2000: 95–100).

She had critical sympathy with the communitarian critique of Rawls's initially abstract individualist position of the 'disembodied subject', but rejected the Aristotelian-derived 'ancient' conception of the common good that excluded a plurality of views, that gave up on liberalism, of Sandel and MacIntyre (Mouffe, 1993b: 30, 32). Nevertheless, she endorsed Walzer's 'modern' notion of 'complex equality', based not upon a universal abstract principle, but on Western liberal-democratic culture and institutions, as well as Taylor's 'modern' liberal-friendly communitarianism (Mouffe, 1993b: 33–6). Yet she most strongly applauded the civic republican tradition advanced by Quentin Skinner in his interpretation of Machiavelli. This espoused the value of political participation of all citizens in order to protect the liberty of the individual to pursue their own ends, thereby combining the liberty of the 'ancients' with the 'moderns' (Mouffe, 1993b: 38).

She had least sympathy with Habermas's 'rationalist longing' for an undistorted communication and social unity based upon a rational consensus. His position was 'antipolitical', ignoring the 'crucial place of passions and affects in politics' (Mouffe, 1993b: 115). Politics could not be reduced to rationality. Rather, it indicated the 'limits of rationality' (Mouffe, 1993b: 115; original emphasis). Political philosophy's role, she concluded, was not in deciding which notion of justice, equality, liberty were true, but in 'proposing different' interpretations (Mouffe, 1993b: 115). This brings us to her crucial point: she strongly resisted the implication that her overall argument was relativistic, or nihilistic. She maintained distinctions between justice and injustice, and so on, could always be made, but only from the standards provided by a particular tradition. An 'external', universal standpoint was impossible (Mouffe, 1993b: 15). And modern democracy was not based upon a relative conception of the world, but upon a 'certain set of "values"' (Mouffe, 1993a: 12). Indeed, a Wittgensteinian defence of liberal-democratic principles as 'constitutive of our form of life' was appropriate (Mouffe, 2000: 66). Although, following Foucault, the distinction validity and power (as well as logic and rhetoric) had to be collapsed, this had no nihilistic inference, because within a given 'regime' of truth, there were still rules of argument, which could be respected in contrast to those who wanted merely to impose their power (Mouffe, 1993b: 15).

Assessment

This assessment will take two forms. First, we show – as a concluding summary of their ideas – to what extent Laclau and Mouffe, true to their purposes, were both *Post*-Marxists and Post-*Marxists*. Then we shall look at the various strengths and weaknesses of their position.

Their *Post*-Marxism manifested itself in a number of ways. Most importantly they abandoned 'class' as an explanatory category. For them ideology had no 'class belonging'. It did not arise from 'material' production relations, but was a hegemonic construction, the outcome of political struggle. As a result of its essentially 'non-belonging', contingent nature, a ruling ideology was always vulnerable to subversion. Class also disappeared in a normative sense: the 'logic of equivalence' required to establish the 'nodal point' of 'radical and plural' democracy meant that the needs of the working class were not privileged above the needs of any other oppressed or exploited group. They rejected the Marxist idea of proletarian revolution and its supposed 'Jacobin imaginary', either as a possibility or a desirability: multiplying political spaces within liberal-democracy was practically and ideally the best option. They also rejected Marxism's historical teleology which united the 'fact' of proletarian revolution with the 'value' of communism. For them 'history' was, broadly speaking, an open book, full of possibilities with no predictable outcomes. This historical openness derived from their psychoanalytical/ linguistic account of the formation of human identity. The relational character of identity formation and the 'impossible' desire for 'fullness', prevented by the 'Other' in times of 'organic' crises, made identities and ideological allegiance precarious, and open to hegemonic reconstruction. Finally, in keeping with their former Althusserian 'anti-humanist', affinity, they departed from the young Marx's essentialist theory of human nature from which human beings were, under capitalism, alienated.

Evidence of their Post-*Marxism* lay first of all in their theory of hegemony, which they derived from Gramsci, suitably shorn of 'classist' connotations. Gramsci's anti-economism is taken on board, allowing for ideology and politics, rather than an effect of the economic base, to play a constitutive role in forming social relations. Moreover, they embraced Gramsci's notion of identities as subject to change through the hegemonic process itself in creating a 'collective will'. In addition, their anti-essentialist theory of human nature, as an ideological and social construction, had much in common with the later Marx. And linked to this, although as we shall see Mouffe was at pains to deny it, they shared with a certain type of Marxism, a relativist position arising from their notion of the 'political'.

Turning to the strengths of their argument, their critique of a certain *kind* of (Stalinist) Marxism and elements to be found in Marx that contributed to it can be sustained. The crude, 'scientific', technological determinist, base/superstructure Marxism of Marx's *Preface to a Contribution to Political Economy*, which fixes 'subject positions' in a predetermined way and privileges those with a 'scientific' understanding of history, can certainly be construed, if taken in isolation from many other of Marx's pronouncements, as laying the seeds of a repressive Marxism that privileges the 'Party' in guiding and representing the proletariat in its 'true' 'historic mission'. They convincingly demonstrate how 'essentialism' and its kindred 'isms' can provide the slippery slope to the most undesirable 'ism' of all – totalitarianism. Further, their registering of identity formation as a complex process and of the socially fragmentary nature of modern capitalism underlines how problematic an October 1917-style revolution would be in the twenty-first century.

Indeed, their focus on human consciousness and the multiplicity and ambiguity of meanings associated with human inter-communication and their complex effects on human behaviour and motivation that required linguistic and psychoanalytic forms of explanation suggests that Marxist analysis of ideology as 'false consciousness' falls short. Put another way, they underline what many Marxists have realised: that Marxism is not a self-sufficient doctrine that has no need to go beyond Marx's unique amalgam of German philosophy, French socialism and 'English' political economy. Marxists have often attempted, for a variety of reasons, to incorporate other bodies of knowledge, whether, for example, from Darwin (Kautsky), Kant (the Austro-Marxists and Habermas), Hobson (Lenin), Freud (Fromm and Marcuse), Croce (Gramsci) or Lacan (Althusser). What Laclau and Mouffe have sought to explain is why the Marxist aspiration of a unified, revolutionary class-conscious proletariat has not materialised under conditions of advanced, liberal-democratic capitalism, and why the radical passions of the New

Social Movements have focused on questions of identity rather than class. This explanatory quest required the deployment of linguistic and psychoanalytical paradigms. And in using these paradigms they did so in an original way, and although they upset 'classical' Marxists, they were attempting to address problems for which 'classical' Marxism did not offer convincing answers, especially in relation to questions of nationalism and reformism, and the multitude of individual and group identities that provided enormous obstacles to working-class solidarity.

A second positive quality is their argument for toleration and democracy, if some kind of authoritarian regime is to be avoided. They dignify human experience in not dividing it, 'a priori' fashion, into either 'true' revolutionary, or 'false' consciousness. And their stress on contingency, the multiplicity of meanings and identities, the complex nature of human desire and the depth of human antagonism reinforces an experientially based notion of human emancipation that requires a democratic framework. Not only does this perspective unequivocally value non-proletarian struggles against oppression, but it also ensures that an openness to new forms of struggle can be maintained and allows human conflict to assume a less aggressive, more 'agonistic' form. What they say is a useful reminder that 'politics' is unlikely to 'end' even in the most egalitarian, tolerant and co-operative of societies, which orthodox Marxists do not clearly spell out. The dignifying of human experience is also visible in Mouffe's post-*HSS* works, where she attempts to recruit in a critical fashion communitarian and conservative thinkers to her cause as a corrective to the rationalists' understanding of politics and their failure to confront 'the political'. Again there is here an important lesson for those with an egalitarian impulse who hope to avoid the totalitarian trap of wanting to master the seemingly transparent foundations of society.

As for the vulnerabilities in their argument, without rehearsing criticisms made elsewhere (e.g., Wood, 1986; Mouzelis, 1988; Geras, 1990), these can be suggested by raising a number of questions. First, we have already noted that they effectively criticise a certain *kind* of Marxism, but we can still ask whether their critique of Marxism in general was as incisive as they hoped. There is a general question of whether they adequately noted that various economic, political, social and cultural circumstances were important in creating a certain *kind* of Marxism that they want to criticise. Thus, totalitarian Soviet Marxism was different from the democratic Marxism of the West, which from Marx and Engels to Kautsky and the Eurocommunists saw parliament as pivotal to socialist transition, having little to do with the foundational, 'Jacobin imaginary' of the Russian Revolution. Neither should we ignore the Council Communist tradition of Gramsci, Bordiga, Pannekoek and Gorter who took seriously Lenin's radically charged democratic, anti-parliamentary position, as outlined in *The State and Revolution*, which could be 'articulated' with liberal, non-property-owning individual rights. Thus, more proof is needed to show that, historically, democratic Marxism was an oxymoron. This, of course, is not to ignore the fact that Marx and European Marxists based their strategy on the assumption of a proletarian majority in society. The Russian Marxist strategy was, however, far more speculative, and the idea of hegemony in these circumstances clearly had authoritarian dangers, especially if disconnected from a democratic political practice. In addition, they tend to gloss over the many tensions within Marx's writings, especially between his determinist/teleological stance on the one hand, and his commitment to genuine, non-tendentious empirical research on the other. And whatever the elitist implications of 'science', historical teleology and fixed 'subject positions', his commitment to the idea of proletarian *self*-emancipation and 'winning the battle of democracy' with its explicit anti-elitist, anti-Jacobinism (or anti-'Blanquism') cannot be ignored. Neither can the 'essentialist' theory of human nature explicit in the early Marx and implicit in the later, which, in proposing to realise human potentials under conditions of co-operative, reciprocal freedom, has a democratic logic to it, as is perhaps suggested by their own affiliation to his idea of freedom (Laclau and Mouffe, 1985: 183).

A second question is whether their own theory of discourse (in contrast to Marxism's base/superstructure epiphenomenalism), which attempts to transcend linguistic and extra-linguistic differences in order to deflect charges of idealism actually succeeds. Whilst their example of house building, derived from Wittgenstein, involves material (that is, non-linguistic) elements, manifest in physical co-operation, this does not rule out the possibility that the *explanation* of the general activity of house building may well involve 'materialist' and indeed biological, essentialist categories associated with universal human needs. Of course, there may be a multiplicity of meanings attached to specific house-building activities, but the answer to the fundamental question of why human beings build houses *in general* has to contain the fact that the human body is not well equipped to resist all climates in all places at all times of the day. This raises the issue of whether *all* forms of signification are relational and whether all forms of human society have words to denote, *refer to*, common physical objects and human activities, whatever the additional meanings that might be given to them. Indeed, whilst all sorts of human activities and signifiers may be associated with a multiplicity of meanings, does this exclude the possibility that some *explanations* are truer than others, verified by commonly held notions of logic and evidence? Whilst a Kuhnian-paradigmatic explanation, to which they subscribe, may have an important insight into the *process* of scientific progress, the process itself still involves evaluating the power of a hypothesis according to forms of logic and empirical verification that all human beings could potentially recognise, and on which their own arguments for historicity and contingency are based. Also lurking behind this issue is whether universalism cannot only be a discursive 'empty place', but can also denote something substantive about objective properties that are characteristic of all human beings. The notion of a discursive 'empty place' only makes sense if we are trying to understand the 'political' rather than the 'objective', natural world, which includes human 'nature'.

Moving to their own normative framework, the third question is whether they have said enough, consistent with their anti-foundationalism (anti-humanism and anti-substantive universalism), to establish firmly their own 'progressive' values of 'radical and plural democracy' in the sense of being able to persuade anybody who does not already share their values. True, they denied the charge of relativism, which makes persuasion difficult except as a plea for toleration, on the grounds that appeals to justice and legitimacy can only be given from 'within a given tradition, with the help of standards that this tradition provides' (Mouffe, 1993b: 15). This, however, does not avoid the awkward problem that traditions are *relative* to each other and the fact that 'radical and plural democracy' could be rightfully regarded as illegitimate from within a totalitarian tradition ('it's-not-the-way-we-do-things-here'), just as totalitarianism could be from within a 'radical and plural tradition'.

Other questions are raised as to whether they generate convincing arguments in favour of a 'radical and plural democracy'. Can a 'progressive' politics be derived from their concept of the 'political', if all values and discourses are 'undecidable'? They could appeal to the 'logic of equivalence', but then equally they appeal to the 'logic of difference'. They can also appeal to the unfolding principles of the 'democratic revolution' that began in France in 1789. This would not cut much ice with certain kinds of Burkean conservative or neo-Platonist. There appears to be a gap between their description and explanation of the 'political' and their own political–ethical preferences in the sense that the former is no sure guide to the latter. At best the 'ethical' is viewed as a by-product of the 'political' fact that human relations are inherently conflictual (Mouffe, 1993b: 112). Perhaps Laclau's admission that the ethical side undeveloped in their theorising is of little surprise (Butler et al., 2000: 295). Indeed, in denying foundational arguments which appeal to a common human essence (albeit subject to difference, like leaves of a tree), or universal moral principles, it becomes difficult to see whether they offer the intellectual resources to enable 'the political' to become domesticated as an agonistic, 'politics'. Another tension in their value position is that they do not want an alternative society (Mouffe, 1993a: 2), but seek to end all forms of social subordination, which entails the democratisation of the economy. This involved the need to 'disarticulate' political from economic liberalism (Mouffe, 1993a: 2). Yet this egalitarian logic could easily lead to an alternative society, if property relations were significantly transformed.

A fourth question that may be raised is whether they too become guilty of the things for which they criticise Marxism, involving them in some kind of performative contradiction. For example, their Tocquevillian conception of the unfolding 'democratic revolution' that characterises liberal-democratic societies seems to have teleological connotations. Further, they attack Marxism's notion of 'false consciousness', yet the whole thrust of their position is to expose the way in which the 'sedimented' 'social' is a contingent, politically constructed discourse. Their own theory of ideology, based upon Lacan's notion of misrecognition (Smith, 1998: 77), seeks to expose the 'false consciousness' of a bogus essentialism of 'suture', and 'transparency' and the other 'isms' of closure. Indeed, we seem to be confronted by a form of 'totalising' discourse. Further, in relying on Lacan's psychoanalytic paradigm, derived from a subject's fundamental 'lack' they seem to be returning to some diluted – if rather unhappy – form of essentialist humanism. Additionally, although they want to indicate how the meaning of 'floating signifiers' becomes hegemonically fixed, they too wish to fix meanings, for example, of 'universality' and 'democracy' as 'empty places' and the 'classical notion of emancipation' (that is, Marxism) as 'eschatological messianism' (Laclau, 1990: 75). This 'fixing' may be for the best of motives, but have they not used arguments that rely on what they would hope to be persuasive notions of objectivity and rationality? In sum, does their anti-foundationalism depend upon *some* kind of foundationalism, of shared ideas about the fundamental nature of the world, fixed meanings of certain words and concepts, so that they will be understood, and a form of reasoning of which all humans are potentially capable?

These comments are not intended to undermine Laclau and Mouffe's efforts, merely to emphasise the extent of unresolved issues, whose resolution may take them into unwelcome territory. Whatever the difficulties of their position, there is much of value, not merely in their plea for toleration and anti-dogmatism, worthy of J.S. Mill, as against those (especially mechanical) Marxists who claim to know 'the truth'. Their intellectual framework, drawing on the insights of post-structuralism, helps to erode stultifying disciplinary boundaries within academia, and remind us not only of the importance of the role of ideology in politics, but also of just how complicated is the process of understanding 'the political'. Yet, although their position is an important counterpoint to more structuralist and 'objective' understandings of the 'political', it is by no means clear whether their vision could actually replace such frameworks, as Laclau, Mouffe and their followers perhaps hope.

Summary

- *Their aim*: to ensure that radical egalitarian imaginary does not become totalitarian, need to combat Marxist essentialism and develop an anti-essentialist, democratic theory of politics.

- *Background*: 1970s crisis in official Communist theory created by totalitarian model of communism and the rise of New Social Movements. Problem of Marxist, class-based theory of ideology in accounting for strength of fascism and populism. Problem of ideology/petit-bourgeoisie relation. Ideology's non-class 'belonging'. Ideology's autonomy in relation to the economic 'base' and its role in forging political identities. Althusser and the production of a non-class theory of ideology. Gramsci and the potential autonomy. The 'articulation' of class with ideology and psychoanalysis. The avoidance of dualism through the linguistic and psychoanalytical 'turn'. The unfixity of identities and their need to be politically and hegemonically constructed through democratic hegemony.
- Critique of Marxist notion of the 'political' – emergence of concept of hegemony to cope with historical contingency, especially the role of the proletariat in creating a 'bourgeois' revolution in Russia before 1917.
- Laclau and Mouffe's theory of hegemony – precariousness of identities in 'advanced industrial societies' and proliferation of antagonisms and meanings. Problem of unfixity of identities for linguistic ('symbolic') and psychological ('lack') reasons.
- Left's hegemonic strategy – articulating freedom with democracy in contrast to those who detach them, preferring freedom and hierarchy. Need to multiply democratic spaces for New Social Movements, and need to transform 'subordination' into discourse of 'oppression' – internalisation of 'egalitarian discourse' and transcendence of 'possessive individualism' – as part of the ongoing 'democratic revolution'.
- After *Hegemony and Socialist Strategy* – division of labour between Laclau and Mouffe.
- *Laclau*: consolidation of theory – aim of avoiding logic of particularism of identities undermining the 'universal', and problem of representing the 'universal'.
- *Mouffe*: intervention in political philosophy, concept of the 'political' ('We'/'Them') critique of Schmitt. 'Agonistic pluralism'. Contemporary political philosophy insufficiently 'political' in not acknowledging the centrality of human 'passions' and conflict, and the historical contingency of values.

Assessment

- *Strengths*: as critique of orthodox Marxism (economic determinism, base/superstructure, ideology). Identify some of democracy's prerequisites: importance of 'experience', complexity of identities and meanings, and continuation of the 'political' in a classless society.
- *Weaknesses*: critique of a certain *kind* of non-democratic Marxism, and still room for 'objective' and materialist explanations. Problem of relativism,

and relation between the 'political' and their own politico-ethical preferences. Difficulties in creating an 'agonistic politics'. Their limited radical aspirations. Performative contradictions: the teleology of the 'democratic revolution' and the foundational anti-foundationalism.

Sources and Further Reading

Butler, J., Laclau, E. and Zizek, S. (2000) *Contingency, Hegemony and Universality*, London: Verso.

Critchley, S. and Marchart, O. (eds) (2004) *Laclau: A Critical Reader*, London: Routledge.

Geras, N. (1990) *Discourse of Extremity, Radical Ethics and Post-Marxist Extravagances*, London: Verso.

Howarth, D. (2000) *Discourse*, Buckingham: Open University Press.

Laclau, E. (1977) *Politics and Ideology in Marxist Theory*, London: Verso.

Laclau, E. (1990) *New Reflections on the Revolution of Our Time*, London: Verso.

Laclau, E. (1994) 'Minding the Gap', in E. Laclau (ed.), *The Making of Political Identities*, London: Verso.

Laclau, E. (1996) *Emancipations*, London: Verso.

Laclau, E. and Mouffe, C. (1985) *Hegemony and Socialist Strategy, Towards a Radical Democratic Politics*, London: Verso.

Mouffe, C. (1979) 'Hegemony and Ideology in Gramsci', in C. Mouffe (ed.), *Gramsci and Marxist Theory*, London: Routledge & Kegan Paul.

Mouffe, C. (1981) 'Hegemony and the Integral State in Gramsci: Towards a New Concept of Politics', in G. Bridges and R. Brunt (eds), *Silver Linings*, London: Lawrence & Wishart.

Mouffe, C. (ed.) (1993a) *Dimensions of Radical Democracy*, London: Verso.

Mouffe, C. (1993b) *The Return of the Political*, London: Verso.

Mouffe, C. (2000) *The Democratic Paradox*, London: Verso.

Mouzelis, N. (1988) 'Marxism or Post-Marxism?', *New Left Review*, 167: 107–23.

Rustin, M. (1988) 'Absolute Voluntarism: Critique of a Post-Marxist Concept of Hegemony', *New German Critique*, 43: 146–73.

Smith, A.M. (1998) *Laclau and Mouffe: The Radical Democratic Imaginary*, London: Routledge.

Torfing, J. (1999) *New Theories of Discourse*, Oxford: Blackwell.

Wood, E.M. (1986) *The Retreat from Class: A New 'True' Socialism*, London: Verso.

5

Post-Marxist Feminism: Within and Against Marxism

[My aim is] to build an ironic political myth faithful to feminism, socialism, and materialism. (Donna Haraway, 1985)

These issues, in which I would tend now to locate feminism even more firmly within a liberal humanist tradition, make the alliance with Marxism as traditionally understood very problematic. (Michèle Barrett, 1988)

The 'second-wave' feminist movement in Europe and North America was the first significant post-1960s 'new social movement' to challenge the orthodox Marxist self-understanding that Marxism was *the* theory of human liberation. Indeed, this movement has produced probably the most interesting and insightful radical social theory in the latter part of the twentieth century. It raised deeply troubling issues for Marxist theory and practice. Marxists hitherto thought they had few problems in explaining and condemning other movements and ideologies that divided the working class politically and intellectually, whether it was nationalism or reformism, as forms of 'bourgeois'- induced 'false-consciousness'. Although some Marxists maintained that feminism was a middle-class phenomenon, and that the 'women question' would be sorted out *after* a communist revolution (made in part by women who were predicted to have joined the wage-labouring workforce in increasing numbers), when private property and classes were abolished, it soon became clear that some kind of social 'revolution' was taking place without a rupture in the capitalist order and that a new, gender 'frontier' was forming, even within the working class. Moreover, many women within male-dominated Marxist organisations were not prepared to put this issue in abeyance (Rowbotham et al., 1979).

This impelled female Marxists such as Juliet Mitchell to state: 'We should ask the feminist questions, but try to come up with some Marxist answers' (Mitchell, 1971: 99). The attempt to develop Marxist answers rapidly moved Marxist-influenced feminist thinkers on to a Post-Marxist terrain. This chapter, after sketching the background, maps and evaluates this political and intellectual development.

In order to understand the contours of this new topography an important paradox must be signalled. Although very few Anglo-US feminist thinkers were prepared to label themselves as 'Post-Marxist', a significant amount of post-1960s feminist literature can indeed be described as such. Many key feminist thinkers started off their intellectual/political lives committed to some form of Marxism, only to move in a 'post' direction for various political, intellectual and 'professional' reasons. Although some feminist thinkers were anti-Marxist, with their post-structuralist and radical feminist sensibilities telling them that Marxism, with its 'production paradigm', was inherently 'phallogocentric', many theorists adopted (either wittingly or unwittingly) what might be called either a 'strong' or a 'weak' Post-Marxist position. A 'strong' Post-Marxism (or 'socialism', see e.g. Weedon, 1987: 26; Tong, 1998: 105) can be defined as a commitment to feminism that involved a critical *preservation* and *transcendence* of Marxism. Such a position, however, is not meant to imply that such categories can be neatly integrated into some Hegelian 'Absolute'. This 'Post-Marxist' stance was most graphically expressed in Heidi Hartmann's famous 'dual systems' thesis, which held that *both* capitalism and patriarchy were responsible for women's oppression, allowing for some form of 'cultural' patriarchal autonomy from the economic 'base' (Hartmann, 1981). She was adding to, rather than rejecting, Marxism. This 'adding' could of course consist of methodologies as well as ontologies (such as patriarchy). In contrast, the 'weak' Post-Marxism of Barrett and Haraway, involved a more ambiguous attitude. They oscillated between an abandonment of Marxism (Barrett's later 'encounter' between Marxism and feminism), especially its strong materialism, use of structural explanation and 'realist' epistemology on the one hand. Yet they also embraced Marxist historical sensibilities by grounding their feminism on the 'new times', and did not seek to abandon materialist explanations altogether, or objective notions of truth. Simply put, if 'strong' Post-Marxists veered in a Post-*Marxist* direction, 'weak' Post-Marxists were more *Post*-Marxist. Yet in undertaking such a taxonomic and mapping activity one has to hastily add the qualification that in keeping with the 'linguistic turn' within feminism this naming is deeply problematical. As Haraway suggests: 'It has become difficult to name one's feminism by a single adjective – or even to insist in every circumstance upon the noun. Consciousness of exclusion through naming is acute' (Haraway, 1991: 155).

Background

Initially, in response to the rise of feminism of the 1960s, some Marxists (to demonstrate Marxism's relevance) looked at the relation of women to paid work (especially as a 'reserve army'), the family and the state. However, the two most significant Marxist 'answers' to women's oppression lay, first, in the realm of ideology – especially familial ideology as functional to the reproduction of capitalism (Barrett, 1988). Secondly, and relatedly, the material realm of domestic labour, in which was embedded the sexual division of labour, consisted of male 'breadwinners' and female 'home-makers'. This analysis, which underwent a number of mutations in the 1970s, held that women were exploited: their unpaid domestic labour was crucial to capitalist reproduction. Whatever the strengths of this position, leaving aside the fact that many women performed wage labour too, it could not satisfactorily answer the question why women performed most domestic labour. Just as significantly, it could not explain the possibility that working-class men received non-reciprocated benefits from women's domestic labour. Additionally, this 'production' paradigm either devalued or misunderstood activities in the process of human reproduction (Benhabib and Cornell, 1987: 2). Furthermore, there were many other forms of male oppression whose roots were not obviously capitalist, such as rape, sexual harassment, 'heteronormivity', male cultural domination in language and knowledge, male domination in the workplace and in politics. All this seemed to lend force to the radical feminist argument that for women the real problem was men, not capitalism. In other words, even on a most sympathetic reading, Marxism could not account for the totality of women's 'experience' of oppression, and of course an unsympathetic reading suggested that Marxism was inherently hostile to feminism, because it viewed 'experience' itself as a manifestation of 'false consciousness' (see e.g. Campioni and Grosz, 1991: 386). As Michèle Barrett remarked, 'the personal voice of experience has recently acquired a new authority' (Barrett, 1991: 17).

Indeed, not only did what we might term 'plain' Marxism have theoretical problems by the late 1970s and early 1980s, but the liberal and radical feminist schools of thought also ran into trouble. Although liberal feminists found it difficult to rebut successfully the radical feminist charge that calling for equality with men meant accepting patriarchy's values, radical feminism also became theoretically and politically vulnerable. It essentialised the differences between men and women thereby obscuring differences *between* women, particularly between women of colour and white women, and between 'straights' and 'gays'. All this meant that no one could claim to speak on behalf of *all* women. This difficulty became compounded by the post-structuralist-inspired 'linguistic turn', which suggested that even the term 'women' contained an unstable 'excess' of meaning.

In the 1980s, Marxist influence on feminist thought declined for another reason: Marxism itself was undergoing a deep theoretical and political crisis, indeed partly as a result of its limitations in understanding women's oppression (Aronson,1995: 133–6). *Politically*, the Left, both Marxist and social democratic, was on the defensive in this period in the United States and Britain as a result of the ascendancy of the New Right, and by the end of the decade the Soviet Empire collapsed, soon followed by the demise of the Soviet Union itself. Whatever Western Marxists might have thought about the Soviet Union, that it was a 'deformed' version of socialism or 'bureaucratic state capitalism', in the popular imagination its demise suggested that Marxism (or socialism) could not work, and that Fukuyama was correct in his judgement that liberal-democratic capitalism was the only show in town. All this prompted Zillah Eisenstein, formerly a committed socialist, to assert, 'socialism seems to hold out little new theoretical or political promise for feminism' (Segal, 1991: 90). This led some socialist feminists to embrace various forms of liberalism or 'radical democracy' (Ferguson, 1998: 522–3). Or, the 'exit' from Marxism could take a post-structuralist form in the case of Nancy Fraser and Linda Nicholson (1990). The stark fact was that although the socialist idea was becoming less popular, feminism as part of a 'new social movement' remained politically vibrant, and had a political agenda that did not seem to require a linkage to Marxism.

The undermining of Marxism's claims to *theoretical* superiority came from the French post-structuralists, especially Foucault, Derrida, Lyotard and Lacan (who, however, refused the appellation 'post-structuralist') and their French feminist followers, who initiated the so-called 'linguistic' or 'cultural turn' in Western humanities scholarship in the 1980s. Their style of theorising, apart from challenging different forms of what was (perhaps mistakenly) construed as radical feminist essentialism of, say, Chodorow and Gilligan (see e.g. Fraser and Nicholson, 1990: 31; Scott, 1990: 134; Weedon, 1999: 31) and feminist 'grand narratives' and notions of female 'difference' (Weedon, 1999: 3, 23), resonated with many feminists because they focused on questions of subjectivity, the body, sexuality and identity, which led them into areas of language, psychoanalysis and power. This move away from Marxism arose in part because the agenda-setting question changed from 'why oppression and how to end it?' to 'what does it *mean* to be a woman?', developing De Beauvoir's famous thought that one is not born a woman, one 'becomes' a woman. So the question changed to that of female representation that focuses on all the issues surrounding female subjectivity, a move away from material to symbolic structures of meaning, whose oppressive forms do not require material/structural change – the concern of Marxism. In a way this was a logical development for those Marxists, such as Barrett, who had rooted their own analysis in Althusser's theory of ideology that limited the causal role of the economic structure, and yet helped explain its 'naturalising' effects on women. The net effect of this 'turn' was a move away from structural and materialist analysis that involved an 'objective' 'scientific' approach and a concern with the origins or explanations of women's oppression, whether of Marxism or the social sciences in general (Barrett, 1988; Benhabib, 1996: 31; Brooks, 1997: 7). This 'turn' at its most extreme saw Marxism as intrinsically hostile to women's emancipation, because it was 'phallogocentric' (Campioni and Grosz, 1991: 367, 375).

The development of different approaches as well as fluidity of positions adopted by feminist thinkers was perhaps a reflection of the growth of academic feminism – women's and cultural studies, or within English and philosophy (Jackson and Jones, 1998: 5). Indeed, perhaps the so-called 'cultural' or 'linguistic' 'turn' might equally be described as the 'academic turn', with feminists from many backgrounds emerging within academia, producing theory that was usually not far away from 'the political' and their own experiences. Interestingly this meant that feminist thought had no pretensions in aspiring to 'Archimedian' objectivity (the view from 'nowhere'), unlike much academic culture, even in the humanities. Furthermore, unlike male radical academics who were 'political' they were not necessarily speaking on 'behalf' of exploited or oppressed groups, classes or nations, because they too were oppressed (and exploited). Additionally, given that feminists were reflecting on the totality of women's experiences their thinking criss-crossed the academic disciplines. Finally, given that there was no pre-existing feminist 'canon' there has been an intriguingly exploratory and fluid dimension to the whole enterprise.

Nevertheless, the academicisation of feminism has had various effects. These disciplines in which feminism most significantly developed were less concerned with material structures and explanations – the focus of political economy – and more concerned with meaning, and academic feminism's emergence helped to weaken the political imperative to engage actively in overthrowing patriarchy. In other words, it served to weaken the theory/practice nexus: theory and other kinds of research could become ends in themselves (Epstein,1985: 103; Brenner, 2000: 239–40). Nevertheless, given the male domination of academia for these feminists the theory/practice link could never be completely broken, although it became harder to discern, as a result of the post-structural notion that the category 'woman' was a discursive construction, whose meaning was fundamentally unstable (e.g. Riley, 1988; Butler, 1990; Brooks, 1997: 97–101; Jackson, 1998: 138). By the same token post-structuralist insight meant that 'man' too was an unstable category, and that therefore the female/male antagonistic frontier was indeterminate. Indeed, the deconstruction of white, Western upper-middle-class heterosexual 'women' did not require a sophisticated theoretical post-structuralist apparatus, as different types of women, reflecting their own particular backgrounds, experiences and interests, began to assert themselves within US academia in the 1980s, so-called 'post-colonial', 'Third World Women', lesbians, women of 'colour' and so on (see e.g. Brenner, 2000: 255–6). The agenda-question changed once more: 'What does it mean to be *which* woman?' These developments would appear to have made Marxism irrelevant to women's concerns.

'Weak' Post-Marxism

'Weak' Post-Marxism is best exemplified in the work of Michèle Barrett and Donna Haraway. They sought to move 'beyond' Marxism in keeping with the 'new times'. They distanced themselves from any kind of orthodox Marxism, although neither wanted to cut the umbilical cord. And neither came to favour a 'strong' Post-Marxism of Marxism-'plus'.

Michèle Barrett

All of Barrett's feminist thinking, whether early or later, can be viewed as an attempt to balance between competing material and ideological/cultural forms of explanation. In her early, widely read *Women's Oppression Today* (*WOT*), first published in 1980, she embraced Althusser's anti-economism and the notion of the 'relative autonomy' of the ideological superstructure from the economic base, allowing for the ideological, non-class-based construction of gender ideology (p. 30). Yet as 'relative autonomy' also suggests, she rejected the notion that women's oppression was completely ideological in origin. Rather she insisted that notions of femininity and masculinity were deeply embedded in the division of labour and capitalist production relations (pp. 60–79), but avoided charges of capitalist 'essentialism' by holding that pre-existing forms of oppressive gendered divisions of labour became the material basis of capitalist production relations. Thus historical, contingency-based explanations had to be combined with capitalist-oriented ones.

However, in the late 1980s and early 1990s, within a political/cultural climate of 'New Times' debates within the British Communist Party, her balancing assumed other forms as she (hesitantly) moved from a 'strong' Post-Marxism to an explicit (weak) 'Post-Marxism'. In *The Politics of Truth, From Marx to Foucault* (Barrett, 1991: 11), she critically aligned herself with Laclau, who detached ideology from class, and more importantly with Foucault. In her 1988 introduction to *WOT*, whose sub-title changed from 'Problems in Marxist Feminist Analysis' to 'The Marxist/Feminist Encounter', she signalled her desire to revise her views (although not the original text) in the light of black feminist criticism (her concept of the family did not allow for racial/ethnic variation) and the development of post-structuralist thinking which she believed could more adequately answer questions concerning women's subjectivity and experience (and the 'body') (cf. Barrett, 1991: 4). Here Foucault's concept of discourse seemed more relevant. The question of whether ideology was class-based and whether it should be seen primarily as epistemological ('false-consciousness') or as descriptive, historical class consciousness, could with Foucault's help be circumvented. Instead we could talk about discursive 'regimes of truth', which were produced by 'power', rather than class, and understood in 'processual and micro-social' rather than in terms of social structure (Barrett, 1988: xviii). Yet she still wanted to retain the concept of 'familial ideology' because it spoke to and beyond the experience of the individual subject, helping to investigate the relation between the psychic and the social (Barrett, 1988: xix). Moreover, it helped to understand the construction of gender identity in the workplace and the specific sexual division of labour in the workplace, since this ideology saw men's responsibilities as primarily financial and women's in the form of domestic labour and childcare (Barrett, 1988: xxii). She did not want to abandon materialist explanations, but she now believed that it was impossible to write in such a 'confidently materialist vein' (Barrett, 1988: xxxiii). Later, in her essay 'Words and Things' (Barrett, 1992: 202) she seemed to go further down the 'weak' Post-Marxist road in holding that post-structuralism had 'decimated' the Marxist assumption that consciousness was 'dependent on matter' and that economic relations were 'dominant'.

Politically and theoretically Marxism seemed to be less relevant to feminist concerns: theoretically, black women were more effective in addressing the questions of class, inequality, poverty and exploitation to a wider public than white socialist-feminists (Barrett, 1988: xxiv). Indeed, questions of men and class had been displaced by women's social and psychic differences with men (Barrett, 1988: xxiv). She also held that traditionally feminism was politically closer to liberal humanism than revolutionary Marxism (Barrett, 1988: xxiii). Thus, an alliance between Marxism, as 'traditionally understood' and feminism was 'very problematical' and now less 'desirable' (Barrett, 1988: xxiii). She had 'abandoned' her earlier project to reconcile Marxism and feminism through challenging Marxist reductionism in understanding the social (Barrett, 1988: xxii). Perhaps this abandonment was partly because she acknowledged that she had not offered a satisfactory theory of the material basis of gender ideology and had resorted to historical argument, although no one else had resolved this issue (Barrett, 1988: xvii). All the more reason to embrace Foucault. Overall for her 'times' had moved on: we now lived intellectually and culturally in 'post-modern' times, which meant abandoning grand political projects such as socialism and feminism (Barrett, 1988: xxxiv).

Her attempt to retain a balanced position within a 'weak' Post-Marxism was also evident in two other texts produced in this period. In her work on Foucault, *The Politics of Truth*, which discussed the implications of his discourse theory for the study of ideology in the light of what she regarded as the failure of the Marxist theory to deal adequately with questions of culture and subjectivity (Barrett, 1991: 4, 139), she stressed that he was not a cognitive relativist and that his statements on epistemology contained truth claims. In 'Words and Things' she noted that Foucault was attempting to provide a 'truer' account of mental illness (Barrett, 1992: 210). She still wanted to retain the notion of ideology as mystification, provided it was not tied to social class (Barrett, 1991: 157, 167). She did not want to reject the claims to objective, scientific knowledge or universal scientific truths. Nevertheless, she thought that we had to take on board Foucauldian sensibilities that linked discourse/truth/knowledge to power (Barrett, 1991: 163, 143).

In 'Words and Things' again she sought a balance, for example, between a rejection of 'classical materialist presuppositions' which were 'harder to apply usefully' to the feminist issues of sexuality, subjectivity and textuality, and a recognition that losses were attached to the 'wholesale abandonment of the disciplines of political economy, sociology, politics and economics (Barrett, 1992: 215). By the same token she stood between modernist and postmodernist positions asserting that feminism 'straddles and thus destabilises the modern–post-modern binary divide' (Barrett, 1992: 216). She acknowledged that 'modernist', Habermasian theory committed to rationalism, egalitarianism and autonomy helped rescue feminism from the 'irrationalism and political limitations of the post-modern perspective', and yet she rejected its assumption that political values and principles could be derived from scientific analysis. They sprang from 'aspiration rather than proof' (Barrett, 1992: 216–17).

Overall we can see that her move from 'strong' to 'weak' Post-Marxism involved a twin-track strategy. She relied, first, on what might be called a 'reportage' strategy, reporting in effect that 'new (post-modern) times' were reflected by new feminist agenda-setting questions around female subjectivity, sexuality and the like that required new post-structuralist paradigms that emphasise issues concerned with meaning (textuality) rather than explanation and material structures. Thus the relevance of Marxism for women's emancipation is diminished by an appeal to contemporary cultural/intellectual 'facts'. Her second strategy to negotiate this move entailed attempts to maintain some kind of equilibrium to avoid any post-structuralist excesses, whose logic dispensed with any notion of epistemic truth and undermined the feminist political agenda.

How convincing are these strategies? The problem with the 'reportage' strategy, which ironically parallels the Marxist historical teleological in appealing to a new contemporary 'reality' (epoch?) is that we are invited to shelve the 'old' Marxist materialist methodologies rather than ask how Marxist explanations might still be relevant even in 'new times'. Although she does not completely reject materialism, we get few hints as to what its explanatory strengths and limits are. This brings us to perhaps the more important question concerning her 'equilibrium' strategy in the transition from 'things' to 'words' (the linguistic 'turn'). She endorsed Laclau's Heideggerian distinction between the existence ('thinglikeness') of objects and their 'being' (language or social-rule-giving meaning) as well as Saussure's structuralist notion of language where the meaning of words is internal to language itself. Yet she also wanted to retain a notion of ideology as mystification that relies on a correspondence theory of truth; that is, a notion of meaning that is external to language. Although one might wish to retain both concepts of language with words whose meaning is both relational and referential we would want to know more about how both are related to the feminist project, and where both notions conflict which side she would be on and why. Her commitment to ideology as mystification led to another tension: she is opposed to any notion that science and presumably rationality are important in establishing political principles and values, and yet is not one of science's functions to penetrate the appearance of things such as ideologically constructed or naturalised social relations (e.g. capitalism and patriarchy) to understand their reality in order to show their exploitativeness and oppressiveness? Although she noted that talk of 'proletarianization' and 'exploitation' by global capitalism appeared to be an 'anomaly' in contemporary feminist discussions (Barrett, 1992: 216), the ideological demystification of the language used to justify these processes would seem to be eminently 'scientific' and political tasks.

Indeed, this issue raises the question of whether from a feminist angle the total severing of ideology from class is a good idea. The 'Third Way' ideology of 'rights' and 'responsibilities', seeking to reduce 'dependency' on the welfare state, which aims to avoid an anti-capitalist redistributive agenda, hits single-parent, working-class women particularly hard. We might also want to know which class in certain situations benefits the most from certain forms of patriarchal ideology, for example women as home-makers in times of high unemployment. This criticism can be put in another way: because she thinks of class only in terms of its failure to construct identities, she seems unwilling to think through the way her epistemological notion of ideology is linked to the 'materialism' of capitalist socio-economic relations, justifying unequal benefits and burdens. While she can reject with good reason the notion that ideology is a set of ideas that serves class interests if conceived as part of a capitalist conspiracy even if we are uncertain about the 'causes' of ideology, we still want to assess its effects in terms of its costs and benefits to different sections of society, especially if it makes class itself invisible. In addition, we ought to think further about how capitalist 'materialism' in a not obviously 'class' sense might shape ideology so as to control women. The most obvious candidate here is the capitalist-organised division of labour, which of course assumes some salience in *WOT*. This has clearly changed in 'post-modern times' and so has the popular, media-created conception of women, who are expected to undertake the double shift as breadwinners and home-makers. We might also note the link between the circulation of commodities and the sexualised imagery of women. The upshot of this discussion is not to suggest that Barrett's position(s) ought to be rejected: rather that her earlier 'strong' Post-Marxist position could have been strengthened rather than abandoned. Whilst it is true that between the 1970s and the 1990s the agenda-setting questions changed for women, this does not mean that either the 'old' materialist insights and issues are irrelevant to women, or that in (macro)contextualising questions about sexuality, reproduction and subjectivity the fact that both men's and women's lives are so powerfully shaped by living in a capitalist society is no longer an important consideration. Maybe there is a need for a friendly 'encounter' between Marxism and feminism.

Donna Haraway

Haraway's 'A Cyborg Manifesto: Science, Technology, and Socialist-Feminism in the Late Twentieth Century' (Haraway, 1991), first published in 1985, is one of the most famous Post-Marxist feminist texts, and among other things exhibits a Derridean, deconstructive imprint. In common with Barrett she bases her argument and perspective on the explicit assumption that we live in 'new times', which she characterised as the 'informatics of domination' (hereafter *IOD*). Similarly, a 'weak' Post-Marxism is in evidence: although she deliberately avoided technological determinism, central to her explanation of the 'informatics of domination' is the 'superstructural' development in the sciences of biotechnology and information technology, leaving the role of capital and relations of class in this process unclear. This concern with the 'superstructural' is also evident in her (Derridean) focus on language, culture and meaning, encapsulated in the cyborg, a composite, hybrid, image of machine and human which inhabited social reality and fiction and in between. This image was inspired by Piercy's *Women on the Edge of Time* (Haraway, 1995a: xvi) as well as the post-colonial fiction by 'women of colour' struggling for survival, living on the boundaries, and feminist, 'cyborg' science fiction, exploring potential forms of embodiment in a high-tech world. Indeed, the boundary between social reality and science fiction was an 'optical illusion' (Haraway, 1991: 149). She wanted to overcome women's technophobia by exploring 'all kinds of linguistic possibilities for politics'. More specifically, her purpose was to 'build an ironic political myth faithful to feminism, socialism and materialism' (p. 149). Her 'ironic' pose, contrasting with the stereotypical socialist feminist left, expressed itself in her playful use of the cyborg figure and equally in her unwillingness to let contradictions be resolved into larger wholes. Rather the 'tension of holding incompatible things together' had to remain 'because both or all are necessary and true' (p. 149). She wanted to reconstruct socialist-feminist politics by addressing the social relations of science and technology, including 'crucially the systems of myth and meanings structuring our imagination' (p. 163). This myth was about the pleasures to be derived from 'transgressed boundaries, potent fusions, and dangerous possibilities which progressive people might explore as *one part* of needed political work' (p. 154; emphasis added) Or this myth helped overcome what we might term 'dichotomic' thinking that led to oppressive dualisms, such as mind/body, nature/culture, animal/human, organism/machine, primitive/civilised (p. 163). The cyborg was a creature of a post-gendered world without 'genesis', without 'innocent' mythic, pre-oedipal or unalienated origins, that eschewed notions of organic wholeness (p. 150). It embraced a postmodern 'otherness, difference and specificity' (p. 155). Indeed, in opposition to Marxism's and feminism's espousal of 'imperializing and totalizing' revolutionary subjects, grounded upon an implicitly Western, white, phallogocentric humanism (p. 160), the cyborg's identity could not represent a pre-given, 'essential' unity, given the existence of postmodern partial identities and contradictory standpoints. Rather there was a need for coalitions, based on affinity, and inspired by women of colour's oppositional consciousness, grounded upon their skills of re-signification or 'coding'. Haraway called for a re-signifying strategy to overcome boundaries between women and nature and women and machines.

A cyborg politics' transgressive, pleasure-giving potential arose because we lived culturally, intellectually and materially in a 'new times' epoch, rendering the overcoming of fundamental dualisms both desirable and possible. Developments in evolutionary biology increasingly blurred the distinction between human beings and animals, facilitating animal rights movements as well as giving 'bestiality' a new status in the 'cycle of marriage exchange' (p. 152). Perhaps more crucially the boundaries between human and machine as well as between the physical and non-physical were becoming less clear as a result of biotechnologies and modern electronics, which were 'crucial tools recrafting our bodies' (p. 164).

> Communications sciences and biology are constructions of natural–technical objects of knowledge in which the differences between machine and organism is thoroughly blurred: mind, body, and tool are on very intimate terms ... The boundary-maintaining images of base and superstructure, public and private, or material and ideal never seemed more feeble [p. 165].

Haraway characterised these 'new times' as a 'new industrial revolution', as a transition from an 'organic, industrial society to a polymorphous, information system – from all work to all play, a deadly game' and from 'old hierarchical dominations to the scary new networks' of the 'informatics of domination' (p. 161) and from things that could be coded as 'natural' to something microelectrically or biotechnically derived. The 'dichotomies' she suggested included: 'organism/biotic component', 'organic division of labour/ergonomics/cybernetics of labour', 'family/market/factory/women in the integrated circuit', 'labour/robotics', 'mind/artificial intelligence', 'white capitalist patriarchy/informatics of domination' (pp. 161–2). The *IOD* integrated/exploited a world system of production/reproduction and communication (p. 163). All this brought about the feminisation of both work and poverty in a 'homework economy', of which the Silicon Valley was 'prototypical', undertaken by women of colour, within huge changes in the spheres of home, market, paid workplace, the state, clinic-hospital and church (pp. 170–2). The result was fragmented, denaturalised and often degendered identities, and reinscribed female bodies.

Although there were signs of opposition to the effects of high-tech culture, for example, by unionising, female office workers in the United States, she focused on 'disrupted unities' caused by the *IOD*, which created possibilities for a 'subtle understanding of emerging pleasures, experiences, and powers with serious potential for changing the rules of the game' (p. 173). She noted that 'real life' cyborgs, South-East Asian village women workers in Japanese and US electronics firms were 'actively rewriting texts of their bodies and societies' (p. 177). Nevertheless, she was inspired by the cultural resistance of the marginalised, 'sister outsider' women of colour in their novels and poetry who demonstrated their power to survive through subverting the language by which they are marked as 'other', subverting 'origin' stories of original, 'organic' wholeness, and opposing the perfect language of phallogocentrism. All this opened up the possibility of rejoicing in 'illegitimate fusions of animal and machine' celebrated in feminist science fiction (pp. 176, 178–80). Cyborg language challenged the dualisms of domination of women, people of colour, nature, workers and animals that arose from the distinctions of self/other, mind/body, culture/nature and so on. Such a language resonated because high-tech culture had made it unclear 'who makes and who is made in the relation between human and machine ... what is mind and what body in machines that resolve into coding practices' (p. 177).

Written over twenty years ago the *Manifesto* has proved prophetic: the cybernetic and biotech revolutions increasingly impact upon the daily lives of the global population. Moreover, the wit, eloquence, conceptual breadth and command, and ludic iconoclasm of this manifesto continue to dazzle, but the question of the success of this 'ironic' stance remains unresolved: does this high-wire act manage satisfactorily to hold on to the competing strands of socialist-feminism and postmodernism as she intended? Overall, her socialist-feminism takes a back-seat as a result of her excessive stress on the 'superstructure' of high-technology and emphasis on the role of myth and meaning in bringing about political change. Her 'new times' approach, which suggests that the 'informatics of domination' is now the main 'enemy' rather than 'white capitalist patriarchy' (p. 162) leaves the role of a social-ist feminist politics unclear. Indeed, she later stated, 'I have almost lost the imagination of what a world that isn't capitalist could look like. And that scares me. I really don't ...' (Haraway, 1995b: 519). Leaving aside the vexing question of imagining a post-capitalist society, there is a more mundane issue. That 'white capitalist patriarchy', along with the 'old hierarchies of domination', has disappeared is far from self-evident. And if this is so, then the road to a post-gendered society, however desirable, is going to be a long one, and it may even be longer if the strengths of socialist feminism are not clearly incorporated into her vision. She focuses much of the time on the effects of high-technology, making its embeddedness in capitalist relations of production invisible, thereby weakening her materialism. The weakening of the capitalism/high-tech link is manifest in her tacit assumption that the Left's and women's distrust of technology is attributable to an innate con-servatism. Her enthusiasm for science means that she is unable to contem-plate that this distrust could as easily spring from technology's capitalist embeddedness, because there is no genuine commitment to *responsible* research that fully takes into account its social, economic, ecological and political effects.

If the capitalist-driven nature of this new technology was fully acknowl-edged then the limitations of 'tropic', cyborg resistance could be more easily appreciated too. The 'recoding' and re-significations needed that Haraway sees as analogous to the resistances seen in writings of 'women of colour', who sub-vert the oppressors' language and symbols for their own ends (p. 175), does not quite work as a strategy for storming the citadels of white capitalist patri-archy. Although she later claimed (Pedley and Ross, 1991: 14) that the *Manifesto* is not an attempt to be strategic, some indication of how her postmodern 'recoding' would fit into some kind of strategy would have been useful from a socialist-feminist viewpoint. Although the internet is clearly a potent tool in anti-capitalist struggles, it is not clear that 'progressives' have the resources to undertake any major 'recoding' within capitalism, except at the occasional symbolic level, because they do not control the means of high-tech production. Thus, although she mentions that technicians might want to convert arms technology for less militaristic purposes, the question is whether they would have the time and resources to do this successfully, even apart from the ques-tion of whether they could keep their jobs. Similarly with genetic technology. And whilst she refers to women of colour 'surviving' the identity-fragmenting 'homework economy' through cultural resistance, within capitalism there is perhaps not just the issue of surviving, but of surviving well, which would appear to make the socialist, anti-capitalist agenda relevant.

This indeed brings us to the question of the efficacy of her suggested form of cultural resistance embodied in the form of the cyborg. She stresses the joys of boundary transgression arising from a host of oppressive dualisms, including that of gender. Although there may be many good reasons to blur and transgress boundaries that are oppressive, certain distinctions/dualisms may be important from a 'progressive' viewpoint. For example, making the distinction between 'external reality' and 'internal' fantasy, because the latter is externally untranslatable, may be pleasure-creating for being precisely what it is: a fantasy. Or alternatively, where modern technology may allow body reshaping fantasies to be literally translatable we may want to consider such translations within the context of patriarchal capitalism, where women's bodies are always found 'wanting' (Hawthorne, 1999: 208). In other words, *a priori* there is nothing necessarily beneficial about boundary blurring.

By the same token there is nothing inherently oppressive about dualistic thinking if what is involved is merely the activity of making distinctions. Thus, Haraway wants to blur the distinction between human beings and animals. Yet even if we argue that human beings and animals are deemed to be of equal moral worth, this does not mean that differences are not significant in terms of species-specific needs. Put another way: the issue should be not whether we create dualisms and distinctions; rather it is how accurate they are and to what use they are put. Pressing this line of thought further, dichotomy and distinction-making are unavoidable in knowledge construction, and Haraway unsurprisingly rests some of her case upon her 'epochal' distinction between 'white patriarchal capitalism' and the 'informatics of domination' in order to underline the need for a cyborg myth.

Similarly, although she opposes the idea of taxonomic exclusions she found it hard to resist them on her own account. She objects to what she sees as the oppressive potential of 'perfect communication' (p. 176), yet we have to ask whether perfect communication has to be necessarily oppressive, and indeed whether the epistemological 'realism' associated with this desire has an emancipatory potential in uncovering mistaken beliefs. Indeed, elsewhere she acknowledges the progressive potential of 'no-nonsense ... faithful accounts of a "real" world' (Haraway, 1991: 187; cf. Harding, 1986: 194). Similarly, Marxist humanism is excluded because it is identified with its 'pre-eminently Western self' (p. 158). Although obviously its origins are Western, does this mean that it is impossible for it to be a 'floating' signifier that can be refashioned 'progressively' in non-Western contexts? Again, although she clearly aims to overcome the nature/culture dichotomy, her explicit anti-'organic' naturalism, from which such a humanism stems, seems to forbid a genuine interaction between 'nature' and 'culture', with invariant (natural) human needs assuming diverse cultural forms. Rather, 'nature' is viewed in semiotic terms, however much she wishes to cleave to epistemic realism as well as social constructionism. Although in keeping with her anti-naturalism she would prefer to be a cyborg rather than a goddess; why not choose to be a cyborg *and* a goddess?

In sum, her 'ironic' stance could have been more 'faithful' by holding more firmly to the socialist-feminist strand and a 'strong' materialism that fully recognised that the embeddedness of high-tech in capitalist production relations means that 'progressive' politics requires more than the cultural resistance of re-signification or 'recoding'. Holding together socialist-feminist and postmodern strands also requires a greater acceptance of epistemic 'realism' (as opposed to social constructionism), naturalism and humanism, even if they do not provide an absolutist and essentialist grounding. Equally important, her 'epochal' juxtaposition of 'white capitalist patriarchy' and the 'informatics of domination' is not wholly convincing, if only because white capitalist patriarchy in the public realm still seems as dominant as ever, and although the impact of high-tech has been great, it has been globally uneven.

'Strong' Post-Marxism

What defines 'strong' Post-Marxist feminists is their clear belief that Marxist notions of epistemology (objectivity) and ontology (materialism and social constructedness of 'human nature') are still relevant to the feminist agenda, whatever their doubts about Marxism's substantive propositions privileging male wage labour, and naturalising, or 'invisiblising', many women's roles. This section examines two types of 'strong' Post-Marxist feminism, namely, 'feminist standpoint theory' and 'materialist feminism', although 'multi-systems' (e.g. hooks, 2000: 161) explanations and 'postcolonial' feminism (e.g. Mohanty, 1992) could equally be used as further examples of this category.

Feminist standpoint theory

By the late 1970s and early 1980s as different types of feminism were emerging based upon many experiences of what it meant to be a 'woman', feminists with Marxist affinities became uncomfortable with the notion that women's experience could be simply reinterpreted through a Marxist prism, yet they were equally uncomfortable with the notion that unmediated 'experience', however authentic, should be deemed authoritative in the struggle for women's emancipation. In other words, neither 'theory' nor 'experience' could claim, *a priori*, to be the 'truth'. A number of theorists, including Dorothy Smith, Sandra Harding, Donna Haraway, Jane Flax, Alison Jaggar, Hilary Rose and Nancy Hartsock, either working independently or in conjunction with each other, fashioned 'feminist standpoint theory' (see Harding, 1986: 142–62). Although they all came up with slightly different renditions of the theory depending partly upon disciplinary background, they were not fundamentally incompatible with each other, and these theorists did not devote any energy to show how their version was different from, or superior to, another version. And certainly they had much in common: an unwillingness to isolate political, epistemological and ontological issues, as well as a firm belief that women's experience could not be faithfully represented by phallogocentric Enlightenment binaries of mind/body, reason/emotion, abstract/concrete, subject/object and culture/nature. Crucially, knowledge had to be 'situated', to use Haraway's term, and 'embodied'. It could not be transcendental, from 'nowhere' and potentially irresponsible. Rather, it had to come from 'somewhere', and be accountable and power-sensitive. Finally, many standpoint theorists acknowledged the importance of the gendered or sexual division of labour in shaping women's experiences. They all hoped these insights would contribute to the creation of a post-Enlightenment 'successor' science.

Nancy Hartsock's feminist standpoint theory, although not superior to other versions, will be considered here because she is the thinker most obviously associated with the theory (see Heckman, 2000: 9). Her landmark essay, 'The Feminist Standpoint: Developing the Ground for a Specifically Feminist Historical Materialism', was in response to Iris Young's call for a 'specifically feminist historical materialism' (Hartsock, 1998: 127). Her own distinctive, standpoint, version owed something to Marx and to a lesser extent Lukacs, as well as psychoanalytic object relations theory.

The inspiration for the 'standpoint' idea came from Lukacs's essay in *History and Class Consciousness*, entitled 'Reification and the Standpoint of the Proletariat'. Lukacs argued that the exploited could have, at least potentially, a more accurate, 'de-reified', non-ideological account of production relations than the exploiters (capitalists). She also derived from Lukacs the idea that the theory was a 'method' of analysis. Her larger debts were firstly to Marx, especially his 'meta-theory' of epistemology and ontology as suggested in his *Theses on Feuerbach*, rather than his political economy. Thus, more 'certain' (rather than 'true') knowledge could be 'achieved' through understanding the practical (productive and reproductive) activities of women and their struggles against oppression. These activities were primarily shaped by the institutionalised sexual division of labour and were common to most women. Women's labours included housework, childrearing with its gender role-creating activities as well as the 'double-day' involved in producing goods and human beings. There were also the common natural, bodily experiences unique to women, of menstruation, coitus, pregnancy, child-birth and lactation. From a progressive viewpoint, however, the institution of motherhood was crucial because childrearing involved the experiences of change and growth, of helping another to develop and learning about the limits of control (p. 115).

The other major source for her theory was psychoanalytical object relations theory that accounted for the contrasting male and female genders. The net result of contrasting of post-oedipal breaks was the construction of rigid ego boundaries for men, with boys having to sharply distinguish themselves from, and in opposition to, their mothers, modelling themselves on absent fathers. This kind of 'othering' gave rise to an 'abstract masculinity' in contrast to the fluid, empathetic egos of women who were not compelled to separate sharply from their mothers and whose sense of self is based upon concrete experience. 'Abstract masculinity' led to potentially dominating and destructive dualisms of abstract/concrete, mind/body, culture/nature and the like, in contrast to women's experiences of positive relations of continuity with others and the natural world. In sum, women's activities in effect transcended the binaries normally experienced by men, and the potential or 'achieved' knowledge gained from them could be generalised to the social system as a whole, encouraging the creation of a fully human community structured on connection rather than separation and opposition. In response to a number of criticisms she later modified her position, fully recognising the need to pluralise standpoints rather than subsume the marked categories of 'color' and lesbian under the single unmarked category of white/straight (p. 239; Hartsock, 2000: 36). Nevertheless, she recognised that there was still the need to provide some theoretical basis for female solidarity.

In assessing her theory, if we leave aside the difficulties of admitting, as Hartsock does, that there are a multiplicity of standpoints all of which have claims to 'objectivity', we can start with the small but perhaps significant point that she prefers the term 'sexual division of labour' to the 'gendered' division of labour in order to emphasise the invariant biological properties of women. Yet she also relies on the psychoanalytical object relations account of the development of male and female psyches. Although this theory possesses naturalistic inferences, it also seems to involve 'gender' analysis in contrasting male and female consciousnesses, for she admits that childrearing is something that is culturally variable (p. 112). The problem of combining some kind of materialism with object relations theory becomes compounded once we also ask the question of whether her dropping of Marx's political economy in favour of his 'meta-theory' and the notion of the sexual division of labour is an unproblematic move. This ignores the central fact that men and women live in a world structured by the *capitalist* division of labour. This not merely interacts with pre-existing sexual or gendered divisions of labour, but it also shapes them, and in doing so can easily impact upon the 'institution' of motherhood, with greater flexibility of parental roles. In the contemporary world, especially in the West, notions of masculinity and femininity and motherhood have been destabilised. Although this tendency should not be exaggerated, it does suggest the *possibility* of a reduction in 'abstract masculinity'. This may be crucial in realising any kind of socialist agenda, to which Hartsock still adheres, involving an alliance with men, and which is grounded upon some kind of material 'conditions of possibility'. Class could also be important here, in promoting such an alliance as well as promoting solidarity between women of different standpoints. A final consideration is that although standpoint theory is premised upon women's experiences derived from their various practices that require some kind of theoretical 'mediation', it is not clear who does this mediating and in what circumstances of accountability. Clearly there is a need for some kind of democratic practice, of arriving at the 'truth' together. What is the role of academic feminists in this unity of theory and practice?

Even if the above criticisms have some validity, this should not be construed as seeing standpoint theory as a dead end in the sense that it still holds fast to a number of Marxism's strengths in the face of postmodern criticism, especially to some notion of 'truth' or 'certitude', or 'epistemic grounding' (McLennan, 1995: 393) that implies the existence of a power-insensitive 'false consciousness', a commitment to some kind of materialism and liberatory practice, all of which can get lost in the infinite regress of deconstructing the category of 'women', or in the endless play of signification.

Materialist feminism

The association of the term 'materialism' with feminism began in the 1970s. Christine Delphy (1984), as well as Annette Kuhn and AnnMarie Wolpe (1978) working within the Marxist tradition used the term to register the specificity of women's oppression (Kuhn and Wolpe, 1978: 8; Delphy, 1984: 215) that had not as yet been explained satisfactorily by Marxists. Their position can still be defined as 'strong' Post-Marxist in the sense that patriarchy, whether as a descriptive or an explanatory category, has to be added to Marxism. By the 1990s, however, some feminists in the wake of poststructuralism had diluted their Marxism, so that their 'feminist materialism' referred mainly to either the 'materialism' of the 'body', or to the material effects of discourse or language (Ebert, 1996: 26–30; Gimenez, 2000: 25). Yet others chose to fly under the flag of 'feminist materialism' for various reasons, although they were clearly 'strong' Post-Marxists, with the 'material' productive and reproductive activities given great significance, especially within the sexual division of labour. Although there were 'weak' Post-Marxist renditions of 'feminist materialism', the better developed versions were in a 'strong' vein.

Ann Ferguson's 'strong' 'feminist-materialism' (Ferguson, 1991: 1) was based upon a concept of 'modes of sex/affective production', involving sexuality, social bonding and parenting, grounded primarily in the sexual division of labour. Ferguson then suggests that this form of production also takes place within racist and class 'systems' of domination, all of which helped to create a 'multi-systems' theory of oppression. She explicitly agreed with the postmodernist rejection of universalist humanist assumptions. She did not presuppose a common, yet alienated, human nature or a unified concept of self. Although she called for anti-racist, anti-patriarchal and anti-capitalist coalitions, ultimately she saw the need for socialism and the abolition of capitalism, which would help degenderise all aspects of social life (Ferguson, 1991: 107). And although she recognised differences between women she noted the cross-cultural persistence of women as biological mothers and the fact that most women were mothered rather than 'fathered', laying the basis of male domination through a 'sex/affective' division of labour (Ferguson, 1991: 67). Finally, she held that women were a 'revolutionary class' as a result of their position within the sexual division of labour and the growing contradictions between the social relations of capitalist production and the social relations of patriarchal, sex/affective production in the family, with single mothers often working for a subsistence wage or dependent on meagre welfare payments (Ferguson, 1991: 44). Women's oppression was increasing through the intensifying work of reproducing both the capitalist and patriarchal relations of production.

Ferguson is advocating what we have termed a 'strong' Post-Marxist case, in response to developments in feminist thought in the 1980s, and is basically a dual-systems analysis, plus some 'sexual' and 'racial' layering. How adequate was her response? Although she makes some kind of concession to the postmodern critique of an 'essentialising', unified concept of self and an alienated 'universal' human nature, in practice she does not depart from the universalist assumption that democratic socialism and the degenderisation in all forms of social life would constitute a universal good for women (Ferguson, 1991: 107). Thus, there is a difficulty in understanding precisely the extent to which she has abandoned the 'early' Marx concept of human nature. Another problem is that although in departing from orthodox Marxism she sees women as a potentially revolutionary class, she does not consider fully the impact of changing divisions of labour, which may in a limited fashion alter the power relations between the sexes. Finally, she does not consider the possibility that class might be a considerable source of unity and disunity amongst women, creating both differences based on differences of wealth and working conditions, yet also potentially overcoming racial, ethnic and gender differences based upon similarities of wealth/income and working conditions.

Rosemary Hennessy, in espousing a 'materialist feminism', echoed many of Ferguson's ideas and insights, concerning dual (or effectively, 'multi-') systems, sex/affective production or the division of labour. Her 'post-modern Marxist feminism' (Hennessy, 1993: xiv) also reflected postmodern sensibilities, not so much as anti-humanism and fragmented subjectivities, but in her concern to analyse contemporary subjectivities as discursively constructed and in her rejection of a foundational grounding for feminist knowledges. Nevertheless, her materialist commitment led her explicitly to distance herself not only from Laclau and Mouffe (Hennessy, 1993: 22–5, 62), but also from Haraway, Landry and others who saw differences in terms of the interplay of signifiers rather than ultimately deriving from the (late) cap-italist forms of production and circulation of commodities, thereby down-playing the importance of extra-discursive conditions. In particular she was interested in the production of new subjects of sexual desire through the disruption of gender distinctions as a result of changes in the division of labour, property and consent law (Hennessy, 2000: 101), which unhinged sexuality from its procreative function (Hennessy, 2000: 103). Furthermore, the erosion of hetero-normative sexuality corresponded to the more 'fluid' forms of the commodity (Hennessy, 2000: 109).

Although her 'political economy' emphasis is a refreshing contrast to the 'cultural materialism' (i.e. concerned with the 'material' effects of culture, especially on the 'body'), does this require, as Hennessy suggests, the post-modern rejection of epistemology (Hennessy, 1993: 26)? Although she opposed foundationalist 'God, Reason, Science' or any 'master discourse' claims, she still maintained that the relationship between what counts as knowledge and the 'truth' was important. Truth claims should be established in rela-tion to other discourses that also make claims about the 'real' (Hennessy, 1993: 28). Yet truths were 'political', not 'metaphysical', and were derived from their explanatory power, i.e. 'their effect on the "ideological construc-tion of reality"' (Hennessy, 1993: 28). This explanatory power was based upon success in solving problems that the theory has set itself, although it could be contested by other discourses. She held that every theoretical framework was partisan. Thus, for Marxism, its effectivity had to be measured in relation to its quest for an equal distribution of resources and the end of exploitation.

Does her commitment to a Marxist-informed materialism and a 'political', postmodern epistemology gel? Although much feminist thinking, along with Foucault and Derrida, has certainly made us sensitive to the extent to which knowledge (and language) can be contaminated (mediated) by power and domination, conventional notions of truth and falsehood based upon 'objec-tivity' derived from correspondence theories, consistency and epistemic 'real-ism' should not be abandoned for either 'political' or 'metaphysical' reasons. Whilst descriptive/explanatory postulates may be necessarily linked to political projects either wittingly or unwittingly, they still need to be analytically separated. If explanatory power is based upon the 'effect on and intervention in the ideological construction of reality', it is not clear where this effectiveness comes from. What if it is the result of rhetoric? One of the virtues of standpoint theory is that it presumes a sharp dichotomy between the dominant ideology and the (material) lives of the marginalised. As a result of the standpoint of the latter, there is a greater potential for an 'objective' understanding of society, whatever the political project. All ideologies contain a mixture of descriptive, explanatory and value postulates, and in order to undermine the value aspect of an ideology that benefits a dominant minority, its descriptions and explanations of the world have to be challenged. This is achieved through forms of reasoning and experience that do not presume unbridgeable perspectives, which is the 'localising' tendency of postmodernism to which Hennessy tacitly veers. Although Hennessy claims that she has not abandoned standpoint theory, her worries with Harding, Haraway and others' formulations concerning their quest for authoritative, epistemic foundations grounded in marginalised women's lives (given their diversity), prompt her to revise it. Instead, the focus, she argues, should be on the 'effects of knowledges as always invested ways of making sense of the world' (Hennessy, 1993: 97; original emphasis). Harding (1993: 54), however, did admit that a marginal life in itself does not provide a guarantee of knowledge, and may only prompt a 'maximising objectivity' question by a non-marginal (white, middle-class) feminist. Nevertheless, she held that her materialist understanding of much of women's labours in caring for bodies provides an 'objective' critical standpoint from which to explore how patriarchal and capitalist ideologies, making these labours invisible or undervalued. Thus with patriarchal ideology women internalise male expectations (caring for male and children's bodies?), and as a result of capitalist ideology women's labour has use value but little exchange value, and if it has exchange value it will be relatively small, given the ubiquity of caring skills. Such lives provide the basis for demonstrating how such ideologies of domination are *mistaken*. To maximise the 'effects' of feminist knowledges without the epistemic/material as grounding, suggested by Harding, can only serve to weaken feminism politically, potentially leading to an unbridgable, postmodern perspectivism.

Perhaps the most challenging 'strong' Post-Marxist feminist thinker is Teresa Ebert. Her only concession to postmodern 'times' is to describe herself on occasion as a 'resistance post-modernist' (Ebert, 1996:132), although she also names herself as a 'red feminis[t]' (pp. xiii, 24). Her *Ludic Feminism and After: Postmodernism, Desire, and Labor in Late Capitalism*, an enormously rich and instructive work, matches the incisiveness and passion of Rosa Luxemburg and, more contemporaneously, of Ellen Wood. The comprehensiveness of her attack on 'ludic' feminism, which ultimately reduces 'reality' to 'excessive' semiotic and representational play can only be noted.

Her critique of 'ludic' feminism, which included thinkers as wide ranging as Butler, Haraway, Barrett, Cornell, Grosz and the French post-structural feminists (especially Irigaray and Cixous) boiled down to its lack of emancipatory potential for women as a whole, owing to its limited transformative objectives, which were concerned only with 'superstructural' matters of signification, rather than relations of production that involved an unequal gendered division of labour and exploitation. Gender, sexuality, pleasure, desire and needs – all matters of subjectivity – could not be separated from the material, praxis/labour conditions that produced individuals (Ebert, 1996: 30, 81). Ludic feminism's emancipatory endeavours were also stymied by its focus on meaning or 'experience' (as the 'limit text of the real') rather than explanation (or Foucauldian 'origin'), required if a critique of the social (exploitative) totality was to be developed. In particular ludic feminism offered little explanation of the relation between the discursive and non-discursive (p. 42) and was often guilty of discursive reductionism (p. 40) with 'value' interpreted not as a material relation, as in Marxism, but as a linguistic pun. The focus on meaning rather than explanation was also manifested in the form of their commitment to materialism, which either viewed language itself as 'material' (presumably in its effects, or as 'practical consciousness' [Marx]), or the (ahistorical) body as 'material in potential resistance' (à la Foucault) to discourse, or saw the discursive/non-discursive (i.e. material) relation as 'indeterminate'. For Ebert, on the other hand, materially grounded social relations were 'prior' to significations and were 'objective' (p. 38).

Not surprisingly this lack of emancipatory ambition sprang from the fact that 'ludic' feminism's exponents were 'upper-middle-class Euroamerican women', and their lack of theoretical self-reflectivity meant that they were unable to understand how their own concerns with desire and difference were in effect the product of capitalism's underlying contradictions (Ebert, 1996: 33). Indeed, their theorising served *in effect* to 'occlude' or reconcile these contradictions (p. 150). Notions of difference (signs, identity/textuality) were used to discredit calls for collectivity and universality, thereby justifying the 'interests of the ruling class' (p. 152). In so far as ludic feminism was radical it was individualistic and anti-authoritarian (p. 220; cf. Segal, 1999: 33) and substituted 'verbal empowerment for economic and social enablement' (Ebert, 1996: 292).

Whilst Ebert's aim to refocus feminism in an anti-capitalist direction is laudable and her exposure of just how far ludic feminism has departed from the material and 'global' factors that are so pressingly problematic for the overwhelming majority of women of the world, her materialist 'stick-bending' (to use a phrase of Lenin's) does not wholly convince. Although polarising positions can often be useful in exposing their competing logics and consequences, her enthusiasm for stressing the importance of the economic 'base' perhaps provides too much justification for potential ludic critics to ignore her. We have already noted that for her social relations are 'prior' to signification. Moreover, she views patriarchy (Ebert, 1996: 90, 92, 136) solely in terms of its economic benefits for, or the product of, capitalism, as is teenage pregnancy, homosexuality (p. 96), rape (pp. 19, 20), desire (p. 49) heterosexuality (p. 65) and breast-feeding (p. 238). Or she proposes that struggles over meanings should be 'grounded in the priority of economic struggles' (p. 123). Occasionally, something more qualified creeps in so that the base/superstructure relation is portrayed as 'dialectical' (pp. 172, 178), and she urges interventions in *both* capitalist production relations and its superstructural forms (p. 182; original emphasis). And she can equivocate: within one passage (pp. 95–6) sexuality and desire can be 'related' to the organic composition of capital, and teenage pregnancy is not only the product of desire and patriarchy but 'also part of the law of motion of capital', or (more strongly) sexuality is 'determined by the mode of production'. She also admits that feminist deconstructive strategies have been 'quite effective' at the superstructural level in denaturalising patriarchal ideology (p. 168).

From all this we are left with a number of problems. The first is that her reductionist gloss that explains ludic feminism as serving the interests of upper-middle-class women veers strongly towards the 'ad hominem', and does little to explain why this post-structuralist, 'ludic' turn has felt little need to refer to Marxism in a theoretical sense. We get little indication of how this 'turn' might reflect some of Marxism's aporias as far as women are concerned, or why Marxists such as Gramsci and Althusser and many others have wrestled with the base/superstructure problem. Moreover, in proposing that social relations are 'prior' to signification she ignores the post-structuralist (and Gramscian) insight that these relations are themselves constituted by significations. Admittedly, as we have just seen, she qualifies her position with reference to base/superstructure relations so that mono ('base') causality is substituted by a 'dialectical' causality. The problem here is that this concession is purely gestural and carries little weight in her overall critique, so that we get little sense of how 'ludic' insights might be *combined* with Marxist frameworks, and indeed how 'ludic' concerns, suitably decoded, might in fact be useful to the struggles of working-class women of all races and nationalities, just as the issues raised by the upper-middle-class suffragettes did in the last century. However, raising these objections should not detract from her overall point that 'ludic' feminists, if they are seriously committed to the emancipation of (sexed) women, are unlikely to impact on a majority of women's lives without the rich, praxis-based materialism of Marxism that seeks to explain and change them for the better.

Assessment

This chapter has attempted to map out and evaluate both the 'weak' and 'strong' Post-Marxist feminist responses to the post-structuralist challenge, which itself was a response to the growth of differences within the feminist movement (especially over race, sexuality, ethnicity and post-coloniality). The method of evaluation has largely been in the form of an internal critique, exploring the tensions within the various responses. The upshot of this approach has been to demonstrate that a 'strong' Post-Marxism from the point of view of women's emancipation is preferable to a 'weak' Post-Marxism, in that it aims to keep feminism, Marxism and the insights of post-structuralism in some kind of dynamic tension.

Nevertheless, the underlying theme of this chapter is that both forms of feminist Post-Marxism in their different ways have made too many concessions to post-structuralist sensibilities (although perhaps too few in Ebert's case). Thus, Barrett was unwilling to spell out how her continuing commitment to the notion of ideology as mystification works within the context of patriarchal capitalism, except in terms of 'familial ideology'. We get little sense of how capitalism is a formidable obstacle to women's emancipation (especially through controlling the division of labour, and having an enormous impact on women's self-understanding in relation to their labouring roles, sexuality and so forth), and how Marxism, whatever its shortcomings, more profoundly than any other theory, understands the totality of its workings. Haraway, although she too is committed to some notion of objectivity, also tends to detach ideology from capitalism, with the new target becoming the 'informatics of domination', and her chosen mode of struggle relies excessively on a strategy of re-signification in the form of a cyborg. Further, this strategy seems only loosely connected to her continuing commitment to socialist-feminism. Strong Post-Marxists such as Hartsock and Ferguson, although much more materialist than the 'weak' Post-Marxists, also concede too much in tacitly assuming that class has little relevance to women's struggles, not in the sense of understanding the construction of identity, but in understanding the distribution of the benefits and burdens of labour and how they are justified. Hennessy's concession is to reject conventional forms of epistemology in favour of a 'political' version. In doing so we are not clear whether she is committed to a robust form of objectivity irrespective of political belief that can provide the basis of ideological critique.

Yet, even if this overall judgement of Post-Marxist feminism is endorsed it is not intended to invite the corollary that we ought to return to the debates within feminism prior to the advent of post-structuralism and the emergence of feminisms that could not be neatly labelled 'liberal', 'Marxist', 'radical' and 'socialist'. Rather, what has been shown is that successfully maintaining a dynamic tension between feminism, Marxism and post-structuralism is a difficult enterprise, yet is preferable to abandoning, from an emancipatory viewpoint, such a threesome, especially if we include other areas of women's oppression not discussed here, involving race and post-coloniality. In particular, a 'strong' Post-Marxist feminism which fully acknowledges the importance of labour – its benefits and burdens – in *all* its forms to women's lives, offers the greatest possibility of holding the 'local' of discursively constructed 'experience' and the 'global' of explanation and epistemology together. Yet there can be no return to 'plain' Marxism whose discussion of the construction of female subjectivity – the 'meaning' question – was confined to the (not unimportant) labouring body. Neither can we think of a 'strong' Post-Marxist feminism as some kind of totalising 'core' that explains everything. Rather, it should be seen more as part of what Walter Benjamin described as part of a 'constellation', by which he meant a 'juxtaposed rather than an integrated cluster of changing elements that resist reduction to a common denominator, essential core, or generative first principle' (Bernstein, 1993: 206).

Such a position might be dubbed a 'tool-kit' approach, and criticised because it ignores the deep incompatibilities between different versions of Marxism, post-structuralism and feminism. This is of course true of certain versions, but letting the argument stop there is to encourage non-dialogue between these positions in the face of ongoing women's struggles, which do indeed – often given their multi-layeredness – invite a synthetic approach. In sum, women's freedom requires as many theoretical instruments for self-reflexivity as possible, whether post-structuralist or Marxist, given that 'experience' and meaning can never be innocent and non-revisable.

Summary

- The inadequacy of orthodox Marxism's response to the rise of feminism.
- 'Strong' and 'weak' Post-Marxism.
- *Background*: differences within the women's movement, the move from explanation and solution to women's oppression to the 'meaning'/experience question. The political and theoretical decline of Marxism in the 1980s.
- The move away from the 'material' to the symbolic, from explanation to meaning.
- Growth of academic feminism.
- *'Weak' Post-Marxist feminism, 'New Times'*: *Michèle Barrett* – influence of Laclau and Foucault, delinking of class and identity, abandons socialist/feminism project.

- Her balancing strategy. Its tensions. Problems in totally eliminating the question of class and ignoring the effects of capitalism on women's needs and identities.
- *Donna Haraway*: concern with effect of biotechnology and information technology on women's consciousness and implications of post-colonial and cyborg science fiction. Wants to overcome narrow 'boundary' thinking of oppressive dualisms in order to 'build an ironic political myth faithful to feminism, socialism and materialism'.
- Wants a resignifying strategy to overcome boundaries between women and nature, and women and machines. 'New Times' of 'informatics of domination'. Difficulties: non-embeddedness of science, problems of 'resignification' strategy and boundary transgression, her own dichotomies.
- *'Strong' Post-Marxism: standpoint theory* – attempt to combine 'experience' and 'truth'.
- *Nancy Hartsock*: women's common experience: the sexual division of labour, not only in production of goods, but in the production of human beings, physically and psychologically. Production of 'abstract masculinity', male binaries, in contrast with the women's connectedness. Problems with concept of sexual division of labour, relation of academic feminists to women's struggles.
- *Materialist feminism: Ann Ferguson*: concept of 'sex/affective division of labour': internal tension, effects of division of labour and class.
- *Rosemary Hennessy*: capitalism and changing sexual identities, postmodern rejection of conventional epistemology, problems with her 'political' epistemology of 'effects'.
- *Teresa Ebert*: critique of postmodern feminism, as 'ludic': reality reduced to excessive semiotic play, overly focused on superstructures and individualistic.
- *Assessment*: problems of both renditions of 'weak' and 'strong' Post-Marxist feminism, but need to maintain a dynamic tension between feminism, Marxism and post-structuralism.

Sources and Further Reading

Alcoff, L. and Potter, E. (eds) (1993) *Feminist Epistemologies*, London: Routledge.

Aronson, R. (1995) *After Marxism*, New York: Guilford Press.

Barrett, M. (1988 [1980]) *Women's Oppression Today*, London: Verso.

Barrett, M. (1991) *The Politics of Truth, From Marx to Foucault*, Stanford, CA: Stanford University Press.

Barrett, M. (1992) 'Words and Things', in M. Barrett and A. Phillips (eds), *Destabilizing Theory, Contemporary Feminist Debates*, Stanford, CA: Stanford University Press.

Benhabib, S. (1996) 'From Identity Politics to Social Feminism: A Plea for the Nineties', in D. Trend (ed.), *Radical Democracy*, New York: Routledge.

Benhabib, S. and Cornell, D. (1987) *Feminism as Critique*, Cambridge: Polity Press.

Bernstein, R.J. (1993) 'An Allegory of Modernity/Postmodernity: Habermas and Derrida', in G.B. Madison (ed.), *Working Through Derrida*, Evanston, IL: Northwestern University Press, pp. 204–29.

Brenner, J. (2000) *Women and the Politics of Class*, New York: Monthly Review Press.

Brooks, A. (1997) *Postfeminisms*, London: Routledge.

Butler, J. (1990) *Gender Trouble: Feminism and the Subversion of Identity*, New York: Routledge.

Campioni, M. and Grosz, E. (1991) 'Love's Labours Lost: Marxism and Feminism', in S. Gunow (ed.), *A Reader in Feminist Knowledge*, London: Routledge, pp. 366–97.

Delphy, C. (1984) *Close to Home: A Materialist Analysis of Women's Oppression*, London: Hutchinson.

Ebert, T. (1996) *Ludic Feminism and After: Postmodernism, Desire, and Labor in Late Capitalism*, Ann Arbor, MI: University of Michigan Press.

Epstein, B. (1985) 'The Impasse of Socialist-Feminism', *Socialist Review*, 15: 93–110.

Ferguson, A. (1991) *Sexual Democracy: Women, Oppression and Revolution*, Boulder, CO: Westview Press.

Ferguson, A. (1998) 'Socialism', in A.M. Jaggar and I.M. Young (eds), *A Companion to Feminist Philosophy*, Oxford: Blackwell, pp. 522–3.

Fraser, N. and Nicholson, L.J. (1990) 'Social Criticism without Philosophy: An Encounter between Feminism and Postmodernism', in L.J. Nicholson (ed.), *Feminism/Postmodernism*, London: Routledge.

Gimenez, M. (2000) 'What's Material about Materialist Feminism?', *Radical Philosophy*, 101 (May/June): 18–28.

Haraway, D. (1991 [1985]) *Simians, Cyborgs, and Women, The Reinvention of Nature*, London: Free Association Books.

Haraway, D. (1995a) 'Cyborgs and Symionts', in C.H. Gray (ed.), *The Cyborg Handbook*, London: Routledge.

Haraway, D. (1995b) 'Nature, Politics, and Possibilities: A Debate and Discussion with David Harvey and Donna Haraway', *Society and Space*, 13: 507–27.

Harding, S. (1986) *The Science Question in Feminism*, Milton Keynes: Open University Press.

Harding, S. (1993) 'Rethinking Standpoint Epistemology. What is "Strong Objectivity"?', in L. Alcoff and E. Potter (eds), *Feminist Epistemologies*, London: Routledge.

Hartmann, H. (1981) 'The Unhappy Marriage of Marxism and Feminism: Towards a More Progressive Union', in L. Sargent (ed.), *Women and Revolution*, Montreal: Black Rose Books.

Hartsock, N.C.M. (1998) *The Feminist Standpoint Revisited*, Boulder, CO: Westview Press.

Hartsock, N.C.M. (2000) 'Comment on Heckman's "Truth and Method: Feminist Standpoint Theory Revisited": Truth or Justice?', in C. Allen and J.A. Howard (eds), *Provoking Feminism*, Chicago and London: University of Chicago Press.

Hawthorne, S. (1999) 'Cyborgs, Virtual Bodies and Organic Bodies: Theoretical Feminist Responses', in S. Hawthorne and R. Klein (eds), *Cyberfeminism*, Melbourne: Spinifax Press.

Heckman, S. (2000) 'Truth and Method: Feminist Standpoint Revisited', in C. Allen and J.A. Howard (eds), *Provoking Feminisms*, Chicago and London: University of Chicago Press.

Hennessy, R. (1993) *Materialist Feminism and the Politics of Discourse*, London: Routledge.

Hennessy, R. (2000) *Profit and Pleasure: Sexual Identities in Late Capitalism*, London: Routledge.

hooks, b. (2000) *Where We Stand: Class Matters*, London: Routledge.

Jackson, S. (1998) 'Theorising Gender and Sexuality', in S. Jackson and J. Jones (eds), *Contemporary Feminist Theories*, Edinburgh: Edinburgh University Press.

Jackson, S. and Jones, J. (eds) (1998) *Contemporary Feminist Theories*, Edinburgh: Edinburgh University Press.

Kuhn, A. and Wolpe, A. (eds) (1978) *Feminism and Materialism*, London: Routledge.

Landry, D. and MacLean, G. (1993) *Materialist Feminisms*, Oxford: Blackwell.

McLennan, G. (1995) 'Feminism, Epistemology and Postmodernism: Reflections on Current Ambivalence', *Sociology*, 29: 391–409.

McLennan, G. (1996) 'Post-Marxism and the Four "Sins" of Modernist Theorizing', *New Left Review*, 218: 53–74.

Mitchell, J. (1971) *A Women's Estate*, Harmondsworth: Penguin.

Mohanty, C.T. (1992) 'Feminist Encounters: Locating the Politics of Experience', in M. Barrett and A. Phillips (eds), *Destabilizing Theory, Contemporary Feminist Debates*, Stanford, CA: Stanford University Press.

Pedley, C. and Ross, A. (1991) 'Cyborgs at Large: Interview with Donna Haraway', in C. Pedley and A. Ross (eds), *Technoculture*, Minneapolis: Minnesota Press.

Prokovnik, R. (2002 [1999]) *Rational Woman: A Feminist Critique of Dichotomy*, Manchester: Manchester University Press.

Riley, D. (1988) *'Am I That Name?' Feminism and the Category of 'Woman'*, Minneapolis: University of Minnesota Press.

Rowbotham, S., Segal, L. and Wainwright, H. (1979) *Beyond the Fragments*, London: Merlin.

Sargent, L. (ed.) (1981) *Women and Revolution*, Montreal: Black Rose Books.

Scott, J. (1990) 'Deconstructing Equality-versus-Difference', in M. Hirsch and E.F. Keller (eds), *Conflicts in Feminism*, New York: Routledge.

Segal, L. (1991) 'Whose Left? Socialism, Feminism and the Future', *New Left Review*, 185: 81–91.

Segal, L. (1999) *Why Feminism?*, Cambridge: Polity Press.

Tong, R.P. (1998) *Feminist Thought*, Boulder, CO: Westview Press.

Weedon, C. (1987) *Feminist Practice and Post-Structuralist Theory*, Oxford: Blackwell.

Weedon, C. (1999) *Feminism and the Politics of Difference*, Oxford: Blackwell.

Zavarzadeh, M. and Morton, D. (1991) *Theory (Post)Modernity Opposition*, Washington, DC: Maisonneuvre Press.

6

Agnes Heller: Radical Humanism and the Postmodern

Progress is not characteristic of history as a whole. It was born in the modern age and it may disappear with it. While creating progress and maintaining it by this very act, one can only believe (not know) that it will continue. Future progress is not a necessity, but a value to which we are committed and it is through this act of commitment that it becomes a possibility. (Heller, 1987: 307)

As with numerous others covered in this book, one has to exercise considerable care in describing Agnes Heller as a Post-Marxist. Her reputation as an audacious and original thinker was made as a 'Marxist', albeit of a humanist kind. Indeed the Budapest School, of which Heller was, with Gyorgy Lukacs, the leading member, is usually described as a school of 'humanist Marxism' (Tormey, 2001: Ch. 1). Nevertheless, with the folding of the School in 1976 Heller developed a radical critique of Marxism that echoes many of the concerns of others looked at here. Whilst breaking with Marxism she never gave up on the broader ambition to redevelop radical critique for 'new times'. Far from it, a number of works, including *Radical Philosophy* (1984b) and *Beyond Justice* (1987), retain much of the radicalism of her earlier work, drawing as they do on the radical republican tradition, various utopian socialisms, as well as work by Habermas and other neo-Marxists. From the 1980s onwards, however, her work is marked by the conviction that the distinctively modern concern with understanding the trends and tendencies of social life has given way to a postmodern scepticism about the grand narratives, as she – following Lyotard – was to describe 'totalising' doctrines such as Marxism. This necessitated a turn towards the subject of the political, namely the citizen, and more particularly towards the moral and ethical sphere in the search for maxims and norms of conduct that might inform a radical politics of 'everyday life'. 'Post-Marxism' on these terms is indeed postmodern in the sense that it starts from an acceptance of the limited field of the political, and the bounded and contingent nature of life generally. This is not to say that it had to be a politics necessarily resigned to the 'present', however defined. It might reinvestigate ways in which the individual as opposed to the class or the Party could 'make a difference'. It meant being self-consciously circumspect in the demands and expectations we have of others. Above all else, it meant taking seriously the Kantian admonition to treat others as ends in themselves. As Heller vehemently argued, a politics that strayed from that edict would only repeat the disasters witnessed at close hand by Heller in her life under 'actually existing socialism'.

Heller was born in 1925 to Jewish parents. With the onset of the Second World War, the Jews of Hungary were harassed and hounded by Horthy's pro-Nazi regime. Heller's father, Pal, was captured and sent to Auschwitz, where he was to perish. After the war, Heller studied chemistry, but quickly switched to philosophy. This brought her into the orbit of Lukacs with whom she was to study and work over the course of the next three decades. Initially sympathetic to communism, if not 'actually existing socialism', Heller was swept up in the events of 1956 when the regime was overthrown by a popular uprising. As for Castoriadis so for Heller the directly democratic councils that sprang up were a source of inspiration and wonder for many years to come. In the wake of the reimposition of communist control, however, Heller was cast into the wilderness, despite the brilliance of her earlier writings and their only oblique criticisms of the communist regime. As the harshness of the regime thawed, so Heller and her colleagues in the Budapest School – Ferenc Feher, Gyorgy Markus, Andras Hegedus and others – gained in prominence through their criticisms of the limited extent of the reforms. However, with the Prague Spring, all forms of heresy ('Marxist' or otherwise) were outlawed. Heller was called for a show trial and placed in internal exile. Heller managed finally to leave for Australia in 1976 where she was to remain for a decade working at La Trobe University, Melbourne. Much of her most political work was written there and secured her reputation in the West as a leading critic of communist regimes from a left humanist perspective. These works included *A Theory of History* (1982), *Radical Philosophy* (1984b) and the collaborative work *Dictatorship over Needs* (Feher et al., 1983), which stands today as one of the most penetrating analyses of the origins and nature of communist systems. In 1986 Heller moved to the New School for Social Research in New York, since when her work has taken a more obviously philosophical turn. She has at all times remained the model of the engaged intellectual, speaking around the world on a variety of subjects as well as intervening regularly in political debates in Hungary.

The break: Marxism after the grand narrative

Heller's Marxism was forged directly in opposition to the official Marxism of the USSR to which she was subject after the war had ended. This meant a Marxism of a reductionist, if not Stalinist kind. It was one that insisted that all social phenomena could be understood from the point of view of the development of the forces of production. It was a Marxism that disdained the notion of the individual as anything other than a 'social product' with discrete needs or wants of her own. History was the history of class struggles, and the individual's only place in the story was as part of the class. This was a Marxism that appeared to ignore the very subject of Marx's critique of capitalism: the estranged creature alienated from the products of her work, from those around her, from herself. Heller's work shows clearly her disdain for such notions, helping in turn to explain why much of it was unpublished under the Communist regime.

Her first widely read work, *Everyday Life* ([1967] 1984a), defended a Lukacsian reading of the potential of individuals to escape from the suffocating weight of inherited roles, including that of class itself – the Marxian master 'role'. It explored the potential of a variety of what she termed 'for itself objectivations', claiming that exposure to art, science and philosophy could promote a critical intellect and thus a way around the suffocating trap of bourgeois ideology. It also described the possibilities available to exemplary individuals to lead the search for a way out of the alienated present towards a society of 'rich individuality'. On the face of it such a manoeuvre mimicked the 'vanguardist' intellectual strategies of those she was otherwise critical of. Yet her point was that there was a role for intellectuals in unpacking the contingent nature of social relations so as to make clearer the options that confronted us for the radical transformation of those relations. This did not necessitate the construction of a Party or a privileged position for a new class of 'educators'. It meant encouraging those with insight into the nature of the present to engage with a public hungry for solutions to the far-reaching problems of advanced industrial society.

This distinctly individualistic politics of rebellion against the 'given' nature of alienated life received an at least partial 'correction' in two works written shortly after *Everyday Life*: 'Towards a Marxist Theory of Value' (1972) and *The Theory of Need in Marx* (1976). Here, Heller outlined what was to become the familiar humanist refrain of Budapest School writings in insisting that Marx placed the individual and his or her needs at the core of his critique of capitalism and thus at the core of his idea of an emancipated society. Heller drew heavily on the reservoir of materials unearthed by Lukacs and in particular the *Economic and Philosophical Manuscripts of 1844* and the *Grundrisse*. These were the works in which Marx developed the category of alienation and thus where the recuperation of 'species essentiality' lies at the heart of the analysis. Concepts such as 'social need' and 'social interests' which sustained the 'anti-humanist' Marx were carefully dissected and shown to be categories that pertained to *alienated* society, not a society of associated production with its emphasis on the development of the many-sided individual, on human wealth and the satisfaction of human needs. Heller argued that Marx's thought is explicitly as well as implicitly ethical, resting as it does on the critique of bourgeois value from the point of view of superior 'communist' values such as abundance, human wealth and qualitative needs. This is not to say that she read Marx as a 'liberal' or that she invoked the contest of needs and values as being at the heart of social life. Rather she insisted that Marx was attached to an ethical conception of the world that posited the satisfaction of human needs as the expression of the good life. In this sense Heller attempted to maintain the by now deeply unfashionable view that Marxism was not an 'anti-essentialist' or indeed structuralist doctrine (as had been insisted upon not only by the Communists, but also by Althusser and other leading thinkers of the time). Her view was that without the humanism Marx's work was a mere approximation of bourgeois social science and hardly capable of inspiring political action or of connecting to the 'post-materialist' radical movements springing up across the world after 1968. Without appealing to the individual as the bearer of radical needs and as the subject of 'emancipation', Marxism would remain a stultifying doctrine fully implicated in the plight of millions suffering under bureaucratic rule.

Yet even whilst defending one particular reading of Marx, she at the same time argued that there were certain tensions in his account that served to undermine the libertarian message she thought lay within his thought. This is particularly so in relation to the teleological nature of his philosophy of history that posited an ideal endpoint or goal as the rational outcome of the historical 'process'. This came into conflict with what she terms Marx's 'ontology of Praxis' as articulated in the *Eighteenth Brumaire* where he famously asserted that 'men make their own history'. The necessity Heller thought was appropriate to the Marxist project was what might be regarded as *ethical* necessity: the injunction to fully develop our species potential. Communism was necessary because it held that the free development of each was the condition for the free development of all. Those who held that the task of a progressive politics was to develop the conditions whereby humanity as a whole could take advantage of 'wealth' should thus be 'communists'.

As with Castoriadis, Heller's rejection of Marxism stems initially from her disappointment that the kind of *radical* Marxism she had in mind, which was to say a *humanist* Marxism, failed to establish itself as the dominant interpretation. It is as if having staked everything on a widespread acceptance of her humanist reading of Marx, the indifference towards the radical promise contained within it forced a reconsideration of the desirability of maintaining a Marxist 'front'. The world had moved on. Marxism had become the stultifying doctrine of bureaucratic regimes and parties, whilst the proliferating New Social Movements had largely rejected Marxism as an irrelevance. Heller thus felt she too needed 'to move on' to reflect as well as fully embrace the concerns of this new constituency for radical ideas. In *A Theory of History* Heller fully announces her break via what will become a familiar theme in the Post-Marxist critique: the rejection of historical materialism as an overall account of the development of rationality and as a philosophy of history.

If, Heller argued, Marxism meant the ability to comprehend the totality of the historical process from inception to goal then this implied the death of human action, of contingency and the possibility of morality. If history is a foreordained process then how could we be considered the authors of our own actions? How could we ascribe blame or guilt to actors? Historical materialism destroyed any basis for understanding the human in action and thus destroyed the project of emancipation as the *self*-emancipation of ordinary men and women. In Kantian mood she now asserted that the philosophy of history 'annihilates freedom' for 'it transforms us into mere effects and thus leaves no scope for human action, for exercise of the will' (Heller, 1982: 263, 173). The philosophy of history is a philosophy 'beyond good and evil'. It takes responsibility from the human subject and posits it in the flow of the historical, in process. Philosophies of history thus posit a form of meta-utilitarianism in which actions are judged, not in accordance with moral criteria, but in terms of whether they serve to advance or delay the realisation of the historical *telos*, namely the construction of communism. From here it is, she argues, but a short step to the kind of moral reductionism of the kind displayed by the Bolsheviks. 'Eggs' are to be 'smashed' to make 'omelettes' and 'generations sacrificed in order to build socialism'. Interestingly, Heller thinks these expressions of 'Bolshevik' ethics to be entirely inconsistent with Marx's ethics which posited *all* class morality as deeply alienated. This again demonstrates the degree to which Heller separates 'her' Marx from that of Lenin and his followers, thereby preserving the hope that Marx would one day be read as the radical humanist thinker she evidently still took him to be. It was not a case of valorising the morality or values of one class over all others, but on the contrary valorising the morality of the species, of humanity as a whole. In this sense Marx's intention was to celebrate in Enlightenment fashion the possibility of a truly *human* society and ethics, not a partial or self-interested class vision of the kind associated with Bolshevism and, indeed, most later Marxisms.

Nonetheless (as Heller was to insist) if this is what Marxism had 'become' then it had not merely to be rejected, but opposed as a pernicious and debilitating doctrine. Her view, articulated initially in *A Theory of History*, is that genuinely progressive individuals needed to recast themselves as socialist not communist. Socialism is a partial position. It offers its doctrine in terms of a 'theory' of human development among other theories, not a 'philosophy' that admits of no competition, let alone refutation (Heller, 1982: Pt IV). Socialists fully accept the contingency and historicity of human action and thus the availability of choices to situated actors. To this end she urged left radicals to embrace Kantian thought, just as an earlier generation of 'Austro-Marxists' such as Otto Bauer had done before her. Left radical practice certainly could not be a holistic and 'totalising' doctrine without destroying the very possibility of freedom read as self-directed activity. Socialism had to be recast as a utopia of the present, not a science or doctrine for some far off Tomorrow. It had to be an explicitly normative schema that individuals could reject or embrace – but whether they embraced or rejected it was less a question of class position or class interests than of whether the normative vision on offer was felt to articulate the values we possess as concerned individuals.

In light of such a view it comes as little surprise to find the Heller of the late 1970s and 1980s tinker with various schemas in 'utopian' manner. Some of these reflected her own experiences in the Hungarian Uprising of 1956 and come close to the descriptions of self-management offered by Castoriadis, among others. A common feature of these schemes was, first, the embrace of plurality and diversity of values, norms and visions of how the world should look. Critique could not proceed from the standpoint of an anticipated or actual coalescence around one ideal. Differences of opinion, of outlook and needs necessitated recognition of the inevitably *political* character of social life. This necessitated rights to protect the freedom of speech and minorities. It thus also necessitated a judiciary to enforce rights against the state. Secondly, she argued that it was a task of socialist theory to enumerate the manner by which conflicts and disputes were to be resolved. This led to the elaboration of institutions, procedures and practices of a necessarily constitutional and representative kind, though at this stage Heller was insistent on at least some deliberative and participatory dimension to determine social policy. Some of her models of this time embrace the notion of a 'mixed' constitution with both representative and participatory mechanisms ensuring that the ritualistic aspects of democratic and communist 'governance' were avoided.

Thirdly, these schemes had to embrace the contingency of arrangements, laws and procedures. A self-governing community would be one where 'governance' was not restricted to housekeeping, but extended to the very terms and conditions of 'politics' itself. Heller was insistent that, in a socialist society, private property should be 'positively' abolished, which is to say displaced by the communal-collective governance over the means of production to ensure that social ends and goals could be realised.

The 'Great Republic', as she termed one of these normative experiments, thus fully embraces the demand for political discussion over the form and nature of all aspects of social functioning as opposed to ordering the latter on the basis of some unquestionable maxim of justice ('distribution according to needs') (Feher and Heller, 1987: 104ff., 87ff.). Indeed a major theme of Heller's attack on Marxism becomes the reduction or elimination of the political under the burden of satisfying needs, however expressed. For Heller, scarcity is part of the human condition. Our needs and wants will always outstrip whatever it is that we can collectively produce. In this sense we are condemned to having politics on a minimal specification of that term, which is to say we need to elaborate and refine the basis upon which goods are distributed according to agreed maxims of justice. There is no 'outside' or 'beyond' of justice, as there is for Marx. As she sees it the danger of allowing the pursuit of 'abundance' to guide radical activity is that it leads to an eternal 'transition', a state of affairs in which politics is 'postponed' pending the realisation of a society in which politics is rendered as 'administration'. On these terms the Marxian philosophy of 'super-enlightenment' becomes an ideology of de-enlightenment. The dream of absolute abundance, absolute freedom and absolute autonomy and a world beyond justice becomes 'schlaraffenland', 'a negative utopia: a nightmare' (Heller, 1982: 320). It becomes a mechanism justifying global enslavement rather than emancipation.

Towards a (humanist) Post-Marxism

As should be evident, Heller's embrace of utopian socialism was intended to show up the paradoxical quality of Marx's own project: a philosophy of history that was itself built on utopian expectations concerning the nature of the revolution to come. Her idea of utopia was 'reasonable' and 'realistic' as opposed to the hyper-rationalism of Marx's. In the work of the 1980s Heller challenged the anthropological assumptions as much as the productivist ones that underpinned Marx's position. If it can be said to be built from any particular insight or contention then it was the idea of the inevitability of contestation and pluralism. The problem with Marx's outlook is that it collapses the gap between subject and object. It makes the goal of social life the elimination of contestation, and thus of the possibility of different views and subject positions. It did so out of the belief that such contestation was contingent and based on scarcities that could be swept away in the advance of technology and industrial production. What would there be to argue over once everyone's needs were satisfied?

In a sense what Heller aimed at was a re-politicisation and re-valorisation of radical politics. It was to celebrate the diversity of human life whilst at the same time elaborating mechanisms by which individuality could be protected and promoted. If Marxism ultimately succumbed to the lure of an image of life 'after' politics then Heller returned to the classical image of politics as the site of the good life, of the *civitas* and of the engaged individual. This was as much 'conflict management' as 'self-management' – providing the means by which a diversity of positions and beliefs could be accommodated within a form of society dedicated to keeping hierarchy and subordination at bay. This radical ambition had two distinct iterations in Heller's work of this period: the first associated with *Radical Philosophy* involved the elaboration of a system of deliberation not unlike that of the early Habermas; the second, announced in *Beyond Justice*, sought a radicalisation of the presuppositions of liberal egalitarian theory to uphold a collective commitment to a deep egalitarianism of the kind found in nineteenth-century radical writings. How do they work?

In *Radical Philosophy*, a major work written in the 1970s, Heller articulates her distinct approach to ethical and moral contestation by insisting that disagreement – if not antagonism – is part of the human condition. We cannot – and should not seek to – escape contestation. The attempt to do so is fatal to the project of embracing and celebrating what it means to be an individual. Yet this observation alone should not be taken to imply that Heller simply abandons Marx's position for that of liberal thinkers such as Mill and Berlin who insist that all value positions are of equal value. They are not. As in earlier work, Heller insists that it is clear that some values are in fact more rational than others, and some *interpretations* of those values are more rational than others. For example, justice and equality are values that every modern individual recognises as valid. The problem is that we do not agree on what is required to 'realise' them. People differ as to what kind of arrangements are just or which kinds of equality are important. But this is where Heller's radical humanism is affirmed: unlike the Berlinian liberal, she does not regard all interpretations of core values such as these to be equally valid. A facet of modern consciousness is, she thinks, the progressive universalisation of values. Thus in any contest between conceptions of equality (say), it will be the view that universalises or generalises equality to the greatest degree that will 'win' (Heller, 1984b: 96). Such a conception may not win today or tomorrow, but – as Hegel implies – since universalisation *is* modern consciousness, such a development is at some level implicit in the way we conceive ourselves and others. In this sense contestation has meaning and legitimacy in so far as it pushes universal values in the direction of radical universality, radical equality and radical democracy. Institutions and practices that do not allow of universalisation will eventually find themselves in contradiction with the *ratio* of modernity itself. Today it is an anachronism to hold that some men are natural slaves or that women are inferior to men. Tomorrow it will be an anachronism to believe that some people should hold more power or influence than others in setting the political agenda. We should all have 'power' – this is what the radicalisation of democracy *means* (Heller, 1984b: 157).

It is this latter point that provides the basis of Heller's critique of bourgeois institutions in this iteration of her Post-Marxism. Heller agrees with Weber and Habermas that under capitalist conditions the function of parliamentary debate is not to permit the opening up of a fully-fledged discourse on the value rationality of social practices and procedures, but its *containment* on terms dictated by the functioning of the system. Thus public–political discourse had the character of an administrative allocation of tasks and procedures rather than a fundamental contestation on the ends of social production. Such a contestation would be essentially participatory in nature rather than representative. It would be far-reaching and involve all aspects of social and economic functioning. It would be one that fosters and promotes an active form of citizenship as opposed to that of the passive periodic voter found in present systems. It would be one that 'abolishes' all forms of domination and dependence so that the crude and impoverished variant of equality of contemporary society would be replaced by a deep equality that promoted genuine engagement in social life (Heller, 1984b: 157). This in turn implied that formal equality has to be matched by substantive equality if the discussion is not to be distorted in the Habermasian sense by the exercise of economic or any other kind of power. As she was to reiterate, a *radical* democracy presupposes the 'positive' abolition of private property and the collective-communal ownership of the means of production (Heller, 1984b: 157). Existing liberal-democracy, characterised as it is by the formal distinction between public and private realms, fell short of the radical republican model of the kind promoted by Rousseau, a world in which politics has no limits, and where the citizen sees in collective life the means by which her own individuality can come to fruition.

The schema outlined in *Beyond Justice* retains the radical thrust of earlier schemes but it is one that is posed in opposition to liberal egalitarianism, which by the early 1980s had become the dominant mode of discourse in political philosophy. Heller wanted in particular to address the disparity between the desire to redress the chronic inequalities that attend advanced capitalism and the affirmation of a free-market order, one that marked the work of Rawls and his followers. Retaining the radical thrust of her earlier approach, Heller notes that liberal egalitarians privilege the view of the individual inherited from earlier 'inegalitarians'. They maintain the idea of the individual as a discrete 'atom' with differential needs, talents and abilities. For egalitarians some of these talents and abilities are 'arbitrary' from a moral point of view and thus undeserving of the rewards that the operation of the market and rules of just acquisition will otherwise bestow on them. Here then the desirability of the state to ensure that what we receive is from the point of view of justice fully deserved. The state needs to intervene to ensure a redistribution of goods in accordance with accepted or 'intuitive' understandings of how society should 'look'. It should guarantee a certain pattern or outcome in conformity with our understanding of what is owed to individuals as opposed to what the market determines we are 'worth' (Heller, 1987: 182).

Quite apart from agreeing with Nozick's point that such schemas involve a conflict between the upholding of liberal rights and the desire to redistribute in accordance with maxims of justice, Heller attacks the underlying presupposition of such accounts. This is that equality should be defined in terms of the distribution of 'goods' as opposed to the kind of life chances and opportunities that are presented to us. If we were really serious about equality, she argues, we would encourage human excellence in whatever way it manifests itself (Heller, 1987: 191). We would be neutral as between the value of artistic production and the value of medical research. This in turn would necessitate a reversal of the liberal starting point. Society would be regarded as the repository of social wealth and each individual would be treated as a genuine equal irrespective of the particular talents and abilities they display. Since each individual's 'ipseity' is unique and all expressions of human excellence are of equal merit, every person should receive what they need to develop their talents and abilities irrespective of the gain to be had for society generally. Once her individuality has been so recognised, each would then receive an equal amount from the social pot, the respective contribution of each being on this view irrelevant from the point of view of determining who should get what. The desire to develop a true 'equality of life chances' would determine distribution, not market-based criteria. Such a plan would cut against the grain of liberal 'intuitions' concerning the necessity for 'incentives', measures to ensure the smooth functioning of the economy. But this is Heller's point: if we are really serious about equality then it must be as equality of life chances; if it is equality of life chances, then we cannot allow the market to determine how and which conditions each individual is to develop her own talents and abilities. As for Castoriadis, so for Heller equality of outcome was the logical basis of a system of justice attuned to parity of esteem and worth.

Although *Radical Philosophy* and *Beyond Justice* set out quite different normative arguments, the radicalism of each suggestion is striking, notwithstanding the 'abandonment' of Marxism as their guiding force. Both still depend on 'the positive abolition of private property', that is the transfer of all the productive resources of society into social ownership. They also depend to a high degree on an active citizenry committed to the development and maintenance of the 'Man rich in needs', as opposed to the impoverished subject of bourgeois liberal society. This is mediated by a distinctly Post-Marxian take on what is required to prevent such schemas degenerating into the 'dictatorship over needs' she saw lurking within the Marxian project – or at least the Marxism of the Second International and beyond. There is here a formal separation of private and public realms, of state and civil society, even if the model of the state is the Rousseauian participatory polity as opposed to that of liberal-democracy. There is an ever-present stress on the necessity for rights and constitutional guarantees against abuses by the state or the community that controls it. There is also a concern with heterodoxy and the possibility of conflict that emits of the need for institutionalised mechanisms of conflict resolution. These are, in short, 'realistic' utopias; normatively derived visions that retain a certain scepticism as to the possibility and desirability of moving 'beyond justice' in the manner described by Marx.

What is also evident in the works of this period is a deep hostility towards 'Jacobinism' and the putschist schemes of the kind associated with Leninist politics. Heller was insistent: without a *'consensus omnium'* there could be no transition to socialism, nor could a socialist society maintain itself for long without descending into tyranny (Feher and Heller, 1987: 229). What Heller offered was a revolutionary vision (or set of visions), but without the revolution – at least as far as that term has been thought about and practised for the past two centuries. What sustained Heller's politics was, on the contrary, an almost Hegelian faith in the necessary radicalisation of universal values to emit of an immanent critique of liberal–capitalism. The radicalisation of the values of freedom and equality did not have to be *fought* for so much as *argued* for. Radical universalism is in this sense the embodiment of the modern: it defines the modern in a manner that makes resistance to it as anachronistic as resistance to the idea of the equality of women, or the equality of peoples and races. This is not to say that everyone will agree that women or ethnicities are equal; it means that modernity contains its own logic of 'unfolding' that can be expected to make the radicalisation of values appear rational and progressive. In short, what sustained Heller's radicalism at this time is a belief in the autotelic unfolding of radical interpretations of justice, equality and freedom. What, arguably, was missing was the *subject* of the unfolding – a paradoxical lack for one who berated Marxism for its reduction of the human subject to a mere bearer of historical logic.

Radical politics and the postmodern political condition

In the wake of the victory of neo-liberalism around the globe in the 1980s and 1990s the expectation that, left to its own devices, modernity would happily evolve in the direction of the kind of normative schemas she advocated were confounded, at least in the short term. Faith in the universalising tendencies of the modern gave way to a kind of pessimism of what

Heller and Feher termed 'the postmodern political condition'. The postmodern was a distinct 'mood' or stance in relation to the modern, as opposed to a distinct time or place 'after' the modern (Heller and Feher, 1988: 3). It was marked in particular by a wariness to all redemptive schemas and particularly those associated with 'meta-narratives' such as Marxism. In terms of normative theory, this meant giving up the belief articulated above: that socialism represented the transcendence of liberal-capitalism, as opposed to the expansion of the possibilities and potentials contained *within* liberal modernity (Heller and Feher, 1988: 117). For postmoderns there would be no 'transcendence' of the given – no dramatic break of the kind hoped for by generations of radicals, not just Marxists. 'Socialism' would not after all be something markedly different to capitalism, but rather a kind of remodelling of the modern in conformity with a radicalised interpretation of the values of equality and freedom. In this sense the politics of redemption – of a world beyond justice – had to give way to a form of politics relevant to a world in which class identity and the class politics associated with both communism and socialism was giving way to various forms of self-identity and self-definition. The politics of emancipation, to which her earlier work spoke, was in some definitive sense over. How could this be?

An important aspect of Heller's later work is her stance on the nature of modernity which is now revealed as the site of 'symmetry', as opposed to a site of exploitation and exclusion as implied in her earlier work. With modernity comes 'symmetrical' relations in the sense that the spirit of the modern is closely bound up with the displacement of the idea of predestination according to the norms of stratification extent in earlier periods such as feudalism and slave society by the contingency of the functional division of labour (Heller, 1990a: 152; 1993: Ch. 3; 1999: 59). Modern societies *are* still hierarchical, but the hierarchy is, with increasing social mobility, one that is itself contingent. Whether one gets to the top of the 'pile' is less a question of birth or lineage, but of one's ability to acquire marketable skills. In turn whether one gets to be a lawyer or doctor is a question of education and opportunity. The greater the equality of opportunity, the more merit comes to determine who is at the top and who is at the bottom. As for Lyotard, the key battles of 'postmodern' society are not, then, aimed at the revolutionary transformation of society, but with increasing opportunity and access to education – among the many other 'services' that aids social mobility. These struggles are far from over; and in some places in the world have only just begun. But the point is the desire for far-reaching change underpinning the creation of mass socialist parties has been displaced by a social democratic concern to ensure that as many people as possible benefit from the opening up of social status and reward to merit.

If all this implies that Heller feels that 'left radicalism' is a redundant position politically then a note of caution is required. As Heller recognises, the battle for equality and self-determination is a long way from having been 'won' even in the most 'advanced' societies. The terrain of such struggles is now local rather than world historical. These struggles are, as Deleuze and Guattari might say, 'micro-political'. They concern the applicability and interpretation of values that are generally accepted as valid. Gone is the large-scale conflict over fundamentally different conceptions of how we should live. As Lyotard might put it, progressive politics has ceased being a politics of the *differend*, and has become one constructed around the constant and immediate amelioration of the 'present'. Nor is power so entrenched that it cannot be challenged or resisted by those affected by the decisions and policies of government. What is needed therefore is concerted action by individuals acting on a number of fronts, not by 'masses' seeking to over-turn 'the system'.

What such an analysis suggested is that liberal-capitalism is open or at least amenable to critique and reconfiguration, a point Heller doubted in earlier work where 'actually existing democracy' was regarded with almost as much suspicion as 'actually existing socialism'. In *Radical Philosophy*, for example, democracy was seen as a realm of instrumental action and admin-istrative decision-making. It was a form of containment of the value ratio-nal and far-reaching discussion of the kind that she felt to be immanent to the notion of a fully-fledged democratic community. In her work of the 1980s and 1990s, however, liberal democracy emerges as the ground of possibility – not of closure or containment as it appeared in earlier work. Since nothing is in formal terms ruled out in democratic discourse, it follows that all visions of how society should look can be discussed and their merits debated (Feher and Heller, 1987: 229). As Heller puts it, a democratic state can be transformed into a socialist one 'without being altered one iota'. As she makes clear elsewhere, '[t]he principles of formal democracy do regu-late our way of proceeding in social affairs, the manner of delivering our conflicts, but they do not impose any limitation on the content of our social objectives' (Heller, 1978: 869). It follows that the demand to overthrow such a system would be tantamount to the demand to replace an open, contin-gent set of relationships with one that is closed to debate. It is to forsake the possibility of progress towards more rational or enlightened ways of living with the certainty of regression to some pre-modern and stratified model such as the 'dictatorship over needs'. It thus follows that the subject of left radical thought and action is not a revolutionary subject, one who will over-throw liberal-capitalism; but one who will work within liberal-capitalism to enlarge the sphere of possibility for those within. The progressive subject is a citizen, not a revolutionary. Such a citizen is led by a set of ethical com-mitments to oppose injustice and to open up otherwise closed processes and institutions to equality of opportunity and access. This implies valuing 'rad-ical tolerance', that is intolerance towards all forms of discrimination; 'civic courage', or a preparedness to act in the name of left radical ideals even where this may disadvantage oneself. Finally it means acting in 'solidarity' with others, being prepared to act with and for those in need.

As becomes clear, then, Heller wants to stress that progressive politics represents an orientation to the 'here and now' rather to some far off 'Tomorrow'. The 'good life' is not a project that has to be formulated and campaigned for. It is a practice and even more an *ethics* that should and can permeate all our relations with others and that can be a guide for life. Here, of course, the strong Kantian emphasis that marks her later work even more than the earlier. To be 'on the left' is to have a particular comportment to the world. In preferring 'to suffer wrong than inflict it', in seeking to treat others as ends in themselves, in confronting injustice, the individual 'embodies utopia' rather working for the realisation of a utopian or ideal world (Heller, 1990b: 221). Thus even the individual acting alone can and does make a difference. As she puts it:

> I choose the world in which I live since I can act only in a world in which I live. My freedom is my gesture of 'turning around', of accepting that challenge of contingency, of life, in contributing to the actualization of such-and-such a possibility and not others. Freedom then is pre-eminently practical. It is praxis. (Heller, 1990b: 127)

Perhaps ironically, Heller's recent work thus returns us to some of her earliest meditations on the role of the individual in generating critiques of the system and an exemplary comportment to the world. This in turn highlights the essentially individualistic basis of her work. What counts is in the end the life and struggles of individuals acting together or acting alone. The important point for Heller was and always has been to *act* and not to have others act on your behalf or in your name.

Towards a 'postmodern' radicalism?

As should be evident, Heller's position strongly resembles others looked at here despite the lack of direct engagement with theorists such as Laclau and Mouffe. Her brand of 'personal thinking' meant a strong attachment to engaging with classical positions rather than with contemporary debates in social and political theory. The one exception would be in the context of this work the contribution of Habermas whose approach looms large over much of Heller's work of the 1970s and 1980s. Yet her work shares certain preoccupations with Laclau and Mouffe in particular. Like the latter, her work is animated by the 'disappearance' or perhaps non-appearance of the revolutionary subject, the proletariat, and its displacement by a profusion of subject positions and identities some of them given, others self-chosen. The politics of the New Social Movements was taken by all three to be a sign of the dissipation of the possibility of a universal 'project' able to countermand the centrifugal forces found in modern societies. There is also the concern with demonstrating the radical and emancipatory potential of a form of politics that was avowedly not revolutionary. Indeed there is a shared sense in which only by abandoning the rhetoric of traditional revolutionary politics that left radicalism could uncouple itself from the totalitarian dead end in which many such experiments ended. Most pertinently, they share the sense in which contemporary democracy offers the possibility of incremental transformation as opposed to the putschist strategies of the insurrectionary wing of radical thought. It was, so they argued, not merely possible but also necessary to work within the existing framework of democratic institutions and practices to secure the universalisation of equality and freedom. On this reading, radical democracy means a radical democratisation of present arrangements, not their supplanting or displacement by some other model. This is to say that the critique of liberal-capitalism is posited as an immanent critique of modernity rather than one that is posed from 'outside' the logic of the modern itself. Whereas Marx and the early Heller advance the case for a 'total social revolution', in her Post-Marxian phase critique is advanced as universalisation of the present. There is no rupture in the present, merely a continuation and elongation of present trends and tendencies.

We can of course go on to examine Heller's affinities with others in this book. There is the shared 'incredulity' at meta-narratives associated with the work of Lyotard with its attendant politics of incremental change in the face of the *differend*. But there are also glimmers of a *rapprochement* with the more radical conclusions of Castoriadis. As we have noted, Heller shared the hope that generalised self-management could provide the model needed to animate social movements who lacked a faith in the redeeming qualities of Marxian revolutionary practice. Even Castoriadis's later 'turn' to the model of the *polis* as a basis for thinking through communal self-definition is mirrored in some of Heller's own writings of the 1970s and 1980s, particularly *Radical Philosophy* and *Beyond Justice*. Nevertheless there are substantively novel or idiosyncratic aspects of Heller's 'Post-Marxism' which we should not lose sight of. These could be summarised as follows.

1 Much of her work is concerned with the attempt to recuperate the ethical thrust of Marxian 'humanism'. This meant acknowledging the pernicious nature of all forms of social stratification and the necessity for the development of relations of 'symmetric reciprocity'. Whereas in

her work up to the 1990s this translates into a need for the 'positive' abolition of private property, with her reworking of the concept of modernity comes the notion that modernity equates to the 'flattening' of social structures and relations to the point where the only kind of hierarchy tolerated is that based on norms of merit or desert. As we noted above, a key consideration in Heller's rethinking of her position is thus her growing reluctance to think in terms of a confrontation with the logic of modernity. Modernity represents – or is equivalent to – the drive towards the universalisation of the values of equality and liberty. The desire to extend and radicalise these values is one that takes place within liberal-democracy, the political form of the modern.

2   She argued for the growing displacement of a collective left radical *politics* with an individualised left radical *ethics*. The subject of political change and transformation is no longer the class or the larger aggregate subject, but the unencumbered individual. In Heller's view the macro-political aspects of left radical politics had to give way to a micro-politics of concrete activity in the everyday. The point is not to defer action for some far-off point in the name of Utopia, but to bring utopia to bear in the present. Another way of reading this transition is to say that Heller argued that in a sense the radical or revolutionary aspects of left radicalism had already been achieved with 'the democratic revolution' announced in the early modern period (1689, 1776, 1789). Under modern conditions there are no institutional or structural obstacles to self-definition or self-advancement. Thus the point of political action is not some transcendence of the given, but its continual opening out so as to embrace greater possibility for individual and social self-definition.

3   In her view the dichotomy between socialism – or 'left radicalism' – and capitalism has become an irrelevance. The contingency and openness of democratic procedure means that any socio-economic model can be argued for and created as long as enough fellow citizens agree with it. This in turn means that a political strategy based on the notion that such institutions and procedures should be by-passed or transcended is by definition illegitimate as well as potentially despotic. This further illustrates the importance of exemplary acts and an engagement with the 'everyday' as the terrain of left radical practice. Progressives need to show in their activity the nature of the world they wish to see created. This means displaying civic courage, solidarity with others and radical tolerance. It also means acting with others to achieve shared goals; but this is acting on the basis of alliance and affinity, not as representatives of the interests of the class or humanity or any other collective agent. To act is to take responsibility for acting which in turn can only make sense if the individual sees herself as a fully moral actor.

Heller's Post-Marxism: an asessment

Looking at the above, the distance from most variants of Marxism is strik-ing. But then Heller set little store by the appellation 'Marxist'. As we remarked above, once it became clear to her that little was to be gained by trying to rescue 'Marx' from the 'Marxists' she was quick to drop it. Heller's Post-Marxism is not one framed on the basis of a regret, but on the basis of perceived necessity. To be radical meant 'forgetting Marx'. But of course this gesture does not of itself ensure a radical position, and there are reasons for thinking that it does not.

First, as with Laclau and Mouffe, Lyotard and others it is pivotal for everything Heller says about the nature of a progressive politics that liberal-democracy offers an open and contingent realm of possibility. Assuming liberal-democracy can be so described, then the rest of what she says in relation to the nature of progressive thought and action follows. In particu-lar if all outcomes really are possible under democracy, then not to be 'democratic' on this reading is to show contempt for the very values and beliefs that have animated left radicals for the past three centuries at least. Yet this description of possibility might be thought to come up against both the theory and the practice of liberal-democratic politics, which is and was preoccupied with *preventing* majoritarian rule. The example of the United States is perhaps instructive here. The doctrine of the separation of powers between executive, legislative and judicial branches of government was devised to make it difficult, if not impossible, to advance a radical agenda. The same rationale led to the vesting of sovereignty in the Constitution rather than the people. It is not the voice of the *people* that counts in the final instance, but the voice of the *judges* who are appointed with the express purpose of 'protecting' the Constitution. We can add that the idea of federation was also designed to disperse power and by extension make it more difficult to supplant the liberal-capitalist given with an alternative social or economic logic.

Looking more closely at democratic theory Castoriadis and Deleuze and Guattari offer a critique of representation claiming that it was designed to keep power at one remove from those being represented. As J.S. Mill argued in his famous *Essay on Representative Government*, the purpose of represen-tation is not to allow people to govern, 'but to prevent them from being misgoverned' (Mill, 1972: 291). It is for this reason that left radicals, not least Heller herself, have been almost united in voicing the complaint that representative government is elite government. Since elites do not generally act in ways detrimental to their own interests, it can be expected that any further 'expansion' of equality and liberty will be achieved on the same laborious and grudging basis as it has been to date. The idea that liberal-democracy offers a space of unlimited possibility is thus one that would come as a surprise to those who designed it, who have offered a defence of it, as well as those who sternly criticise it for the reason that it offers a narrowness of political choices heavily mediated by the needs and interests of elites.

Even if it is accepted that the intention of those who created and defended earlier incarnations of liberal-democracy was to contain 'contingency', it might still be objected that contemporary democratic practice has broken out of this narrow range of possibility. Suffrage is now more or less universal, the range of interest groups is much larger and the political class is now itself more open and subject to the processes of social mobility that Heller is keen to acknowledge as the basis for her rethinking of the nature of modernity. Liberal-democracy might once have been constrained, but now it is more amenable to the views and wishes of all sections of society, offering not merely the possibility, but the prospect of meaningful change along lines associated with left radical critiques that once implied the need for confrontational means to advance. The difficulty with such a reading is that it relies on a view of democracy that is regarded with scepticism from across the political spectrum, as well as by marginalised electorates increasingly turned off by the spectacle of party politics. As Heller herself once argued, extreme economic inequality is corrosive of democracy since it loads outcomes in favour of those with the most money to spend (Heller, 1984b: 157; 1988: 134–8). If money were not essential to securing votes and influencing the behaviour of the political elites then businesses and wealthy individuals would keep their money to themselves instead of lavishing it on political parties and presidential campaigns. Left radical causes and groups have an in-built disadvantage in the increasing commodification of political life for the simple reason that they cannot afford to mount the kind of expensive campaigns that pro-business parties generate. This means exclusion from debate, from the media and 'the mainstream'.

More generally, the realities of global politics militate against regarding domestic liberal-democratic politics as a realm of 'contingency' and 'possibility'. It is not just Marxists after all who complain that global capitalism is not itself constrained by global political institutions that could offer a way in which 'contingency' and 'possibility' could be made meaningful (Held and McGrew, 2002). Those global institutions that do exist such as the IMF and World Bank do so expressly to advance the needs and interests of transnational capital and the Global North. They are not forums in which different models of development, different priorities, different political options can be debated and enabled. Even Bill Clinton lamented the fact that their role is to enforce a particular view ('the Washington Consensus'). Any challenges to that world-view are regarded as grounds for disinvestment, the imposition of fiscal penalties and structural adjustment policies. Far from a picture of openness and possibility, global politics offers the contrary image: a closed world where a numerically small group of 'masters' dictates the contours and content of the lives of the global majority. If modernity is indeed to be equated, as Heller argues, with the displacement of hierarchy and relations of dependence, then perhaps it would be accurate to describe global politics as 'pre-modern'. Indeed so extensive are the relations of bondage, serfdom and vassalage between North and South that it would perhaps be more accurate to describe them as 'feudal'.

So the notion that modernity equates to openness and contingency in political terms should probably be regarded as over-stating what is certainly true: that there are greater possibilities for individual self-advancement in advanced industrial society than there were under feudal societies. But this is a long way from implying that those inspired by progressive values and ideals should confine themselves to action aimed at expanding the opportunities available within the horizon of liberal-capitalism, particularly given the growing conviction that national and sub-national politics is becoming emptied of relevance to the lives of ordinary citizens. The nation state is much less the locus of political, social and economic life than it once was. The set of expectations to which Heller and to a certain extent Laclau and Mouffe are attached thus needs to be rethought. Whether this rethinking equates to a belief in the necessity for the elaboration of global political structures or the reining-in of the operation of transnational capitalism through, for example, alliances of supra-national 'blocs' such as the European Union and the Association of Southeast Asian Nations is a matter that need not detain us here. What we should note is that such observations point to the crisis of state-centric normative thought that posits the nation state as the primary unit of social and political life. It is no irony to note that Marx was well aware of such developments, and indeed of the coming redundancy of the state as the site of 'justice', however defined. Marx never discusses in detail the form and nature of 'global governance', but in a sense he did not need to. The idea of communism as an internationalist movement tacitly confirms that for him any solution to the problem of overcoming capitalism had to begin from a recognition of the international or 'global' dimension of the political, however defined. Whatever one thinks of Marx's characterisation of such a movement and the chains of causality that underpin it, his belief in the necessarily global character of the struggle between capital and labour is one that is arguably more compelling as 'globalisation' intensifies and the battle over its effects moves into 'global civil society'.

Where, on the other hand, Heller might be thought to be on firmer ground is in her rejection of the teleological imperative that some have read into Marx's work in favour of one that prefers the development of an ethics which can act as a guide for concerned individuals. It is a hotly debated point as to whether Marx can be said to have an ethics as such; yet the mere fact that there is a debate should alert us to what is at stake. It is not clear that Marx extolled an *ethic* of left radical practice as opposed to a notion of how changes in the material base would be reflected in openings and possibilities for the advancement of the class struggle. One of the features of life in advanced industrial society over the past thirty or more years is the ebbing of a class-based politics and thus of a politics of the kind that Marx documented. Of course, one response could be to lament the fact and urge greater efforts to generate increased class consciousness. Another response would be to develop alternative ways of seeking to develop and broaden left radical activity through engagement with progressive groups and causes in society. It is this latter kind of activism that interests Heller, one based on a common concern with all those who are struggling against oppression, in other words with New Social Movements. It is one that seeks alliances and allegiances to alleviate suffering in whatever form it takes – not just that which can be understood in terms of class oppression. It is one that starts from the humanist admonition to regard every person and their oppressions as of equal 'value'. It is one that says matters can be improved in the here-and-now, as opposed to after the much promised 'revolution'. From this point of view it is a position that emphasises that being 'active' is less about building parties or movements which will themselves take power in some moment of 'transcendence'. It means working on myriad fronts, for myriad causes with myriad groupings, individuals and organisations.

This is surely not an irrelevant characterisation of the possibilities of 'activism' given the complexity and multifaceted nature of the struggles and oppressions extant in the contemporary world. Thinking about recent examples, the Seattle protests of 1999 which led many to talk about the birth of a global anti-capitalist or anti-corporate movement was characterised as one involving 'Turtles and Teamsters', or environmentalists and trade unionists. This was followed by other protests that gave witness to the enormous diversity of struggles in the world, as well as diverse views on what kind of world should be created. It was also followed by the creation of the World Social Forum in 2001, an event that led to the proliferation of regional, national and local social forums mirroring the original in giving witness to the diverse nature of oppressions and the plurality of means by which they might be countered. The notion that all of this could be subsumed within an overarching narrative of class struggle is probably naïve, as Heller's critique implies. On the other hand, what unites these various struggles is a shared sense of the futility of working *within* existing constraints and definitions of 'possibility', highlighting the paradox of Heller's schema. Whilst the kinds of activisms of which her work speaks seem to be proliferating, many of those struggles are either by necessity or by design outside 'mainstream' political processes. They are DIY or unofficial responses to the lack of ways in which people can meaningfully participate and as such symptomatic of a widespread and well-documented process of disengagement from liberal-democratic politics. It is not a case of an expansion or radicalisation of liberal-democracy, but its rejection by those whose views, identities or politics are systematically or informally excluded from consideration (Tormey, 2004: Ch. 2).

So Heller's response to the crisis of Marxism is ambivalent. On the one hand, there is a clear sense that rejecting an historicised and deterministic Marx allowed her to develop varieties of normative theorising that were very much in keeping with what many libertarian-minded Marxists thought was indispensable in Marx in the first place: a commitment to a radically participatory, democratic conception of self-management. That she had to 'leave' Marx in order to develop these interlocking visions perhaps tells us more about what 'Marxism' had become over the latter half of the twentieth century than about Heller's idiosyncrasy as a thinker. On the other hand, her work of the 1990s shows a clear determination to escape the contortions of left radical thought altogether. At one level this can be understood as a personal gesture. Heller was evidently ready in her professional life to commit to moral philosophy and ethics as opposed to *political* philosophy. But on the other it could be read as part of the 'exhaustion of utopian energies' lamented by Habermas, amongst others. Yet this reading would only at best be partially accurate.

More to the point Heller latched on to two trends that were to become staple in the Post-Marxist analysis of contemporary society: the death of ideology and the post-industrial revolution. The latter in particular seemed to erase the problematic underpinning Marx's work: the growing polarisation of classes in advanced industrial society. Her resort to an ethics of responsibility was the response of someone who wished to maintain the ethical core of the left humanist position whilst acknowledging that the terrain of struggle had shifted from the collective struggles of classes to the discrete struggles of unencumbered individuals. As seems clearer today, the bipolar struggle has not 'disappeared'; it has been exported on to the terrain of global politics, as predicted by Marx. If there was a thought here that a politics informed by crisis and the travails of the working class had become redundant then the re-emergence of industrial militancy in the global periphery and semiperiphery over the course of the 1990s was a valuable corrective.

On the other hand, as Heller's analysis implies, Marx did not account for 'post-industrial' society at the 'core' and nor did his political strategy. Heller's response, which is to accentuate the possibility for those in wealthy countries to act, to make a difference, to suffer wrong rather than commit it, is one that should not therefore be dismissed as another form of 'resignation', but the logical working out of her own analysis of widely remarked-upon trends. Equally, such an individualised and individualistic conception of active 'citizenship' requires a recognition that one of the struggles taking place is that over the very parameters of 'possibility' and 'contingency' itself. To struggle against 'sweatshops' is to embark on a form of 'ethical' activism to which Heller's thought clearly speaks; but it is *also* to insist that it is possible to contemplate a world without sweatshops, without exploitation, without the erasure of the dignity and respect for the individual which was once such a ringing refrain of Heller's own critique of liberal-capitalism. It is to insist that possibility and contingency lie not in the debating chambers of national parliaments or amongst elite-driven political processes generally, but in the resistances and interactions of those 'everyday' individuals who have always been at the heart of Heller's analysis.

Summary

- *Heller's aim*: initially to develop a variant of humanist Marxism combining elements of Marx's early work with categories developed by the later Lukacs. This project was enriched by the promotion of explicitly utopian and republican sentiments to develop an account of radical democracy. Latterly, Heller broke explicitly with the method and substance of Marx's work, drawing on a variety of sources to develop a post-Kantian position that stresses the centrality of responsibility and autonomy.
- *Background*: Heller was a founder member of the Budapest School of humanist Marxism, the heyday of which was the 1960s. In the wake of 1968 and the Prague Spring, the School was broken up and the members forced into exile. Heller's humanist Marxism developed as a critique of Althusserian structural Marxism and vulgar Soviet Marxism.
- After the break-up of the School in 1976 Heller re-evaluates Marxism and seeks to develop an approach addressed to certain weaknesses in his approach. This included a normative commitment to radical democracy as communal-collective deliberation. It also included the reintegration of ethics and moral philosophy based on an understanding of history as open and contingent.
- Develops a variety of republican models that stress the necessity for collective participation in the life of the community; and ongoing deliberation concerning appropriate needs and wants to be satisfied; public ownership over the means of production. These socialist utopias are combined with an approach that resolutely rejects all forms of revolutionary politics along the Leninist or Jacobin line. Liberal-democracy is seen as a means to the achievement of radical democracy.
- Analysis of modernity leads Heller towards a more sceptical stance concerning the prospect of developing an overarching emancipatory position. The postmodern condition represents the rejection of meta-narratives

and thus the rejection of large-scale schemes for social transformation. All change would have to come about from within the framework of 'modernity', or liberal-capitalism.

Assessment

- *Strengths*: Heller's work is marked by a non-dogmatic approach that is creative in relation to theory as opposed to merely applying it or positing it as 'true' in some fundamental sense. The fact that ethics and politics are at the core of her concerns is a strength given the neglect of these matters by Marx himself, leading to a default utilitarianism in the approach of many of his followers ('whatever serves the interest of the class ...'). Her work is methodologically and politically individualistic which can be seen as a strength in terms of her commitment to understanding how complex processes impact on choice, responsibility and the centrality of solidarity and affinity in social struggles.
- *Weaknesses*: despite the force of her earlier critique of liberal-democracy her later work evinces a perhaps naïve optimism concerning the potential afforded for acting within liberal-democratic processes and procedures. This has a disabling impact on social movements who stand outside the mainstream of political discourse or who lack the means to engage in conventional politics. It is also disabling in respect to global politics where even the meagre basis for participation found in liberal-democracy is missing. Heller also dismisses the exclusionary and emasculating character of contemporary capitalism, asserting that modernity represents the inexorable unfolding of opportunities for great mobility and self-advancement. This ignores the reality of life in many parts of the world.

Sources and Further Reading

Burnheim, P. (1994) *The Social Philosophy of Agnes Heller*, Amsterdam: Rodopi.

Feher, F. and Heller, A. (1987) *Eastern Left, Western Left: Totalitarianism, Freedom, and Democracy*, Cambridge: Polity Press.

Feher, F., Heller, A. and Markus, G. (1983) *Dictatorship over Needs*, Oxford: Blackwell.

Gardiner, M. (2000) *Critiques of Everyday Life*, London: Routledge.

Grumley, J. (2004) *Agnes Heller: A Moralist in the Vortex of History*, London: Pluto.

Held, D. and McGrew, A. (2002) *Globalization/Anti-Globalization*, Cambridge: Polity Press.

Heller, A. (1972) 'Towards a Marxist Theory of Value', *Kinesis*, 5: 7–76.

Heller, A. (1976) *The Theory of Need in Marx*, trans. G. Feltrinelli, London: Allison & Busby.

Heller, A. (1978) 'Past, Present and Future of Democracy', *Social Research*, 45: 866–89.

Heller, A. (1982) *A Theory of History*, London: Routledge & Kegan Paul.

Heller, A. (1984a) *Everyday Life*, London: Routledge & Kegan Paul.

Heller, A. (1984b) *Radical Philosophy*, Oxford: Blackwell.

Heller, A. (1987) *Beyond Justice*, Oxford: Blackwell.

Heller, A. (1988) 'On Formal Democracy', in J. Keane (ed.), *Civil Society and the State: New European Perspectives*, London: Verso.

Heller, A. (1990a) *Can Modernity Survive?*, Cambridge: Polity Press.

Heller, A. (1990b) *A Philosophy of Morals*, Oxford: Blackwell.

Heller, A. (1993) *A Philosophy of History in Fragments*, Oxford: Blackwell.

Heller, A. (1999) *A Theory of Modernity*, Oxford: Blackwell.

Heller, A. and Feher, F. (1988) *The Postmodern Political Condition*, Cambridge: Polity Press.

Mill, J.S. (1972). 'Considerations on Representative Government', *Three Essays*, Oxford: Oxford University Press.

Tormey, S. (2001) *Agnes Heller: Socialism, Autonomy and the Postmodern*, Manchester: Manchester University Press.

Tormey, S. (2004) *Anti-Capitalism: A Beginner's Guide*, Oxford: Oneworld.

7

Jürgen Habermas: Reconciling Modernity, Autonomy and Solidarity

I have been a reformist all my life, and maybe I have been a bit more so in recent years. Nevertheless, I mostly feel that I am the last Marxist. (Habermas, 1992b: 469)

Habermas's theoretical enterprise effectively made Marx into a pioneer of contemporary emancipatory theory, rather than its prophet. The very breadth and systematicity of his project exposed some limitations of Marx's thought, limitations that at the very least stem from his historical location at the birth-pangs of industrial capitalism (Habermas, 1990: 11). Marx could not have witnessed capitalism's longevity, its ability to stabilise itself through different forms of state intervention, and become more socially, politically and economically complex, especially as a result of an ever increasing division of labour. Moreover, Marx had far more limited theoretical resources to draw on, principally Hegel, Smith, Ricardo and the French utopian socialists. Habermas (b. 1929), however, could and did stand on many more intellectual shoulders, some of whom were also 'giants': Weber, Freud, Parsons, Piaget, Kohlberg, Durkheim, Mead, Schutz, Austin, Peirce, Dewey, Arendt, Polanyi, Lukacs, Luhmann and others – plus Kant and Hegel. And not to forget Marx and Marxism in assisting his vision: he used Marxist concepts and problematics to construct his own theoretical edifice and retained Marxian sensibilities concerning the limitations of traditional ('first') philosophy in achieving human emancipation (the theory and practice link).

Habermas would probably raise his eyebrows at the thought of being labelled a 'Post-Marxist' if only because on a number of occasions, as the quotation above illustrates, he described himself as 'the last Marxist' (cf. Habermas, 1992c: 67, 81). Moreover, he scorned the seemingly Nietszchean-inspired attack on the Enlightenment by the other 'posts' (post-structuralists and postmodernists) in *The Philosophical Discourse of Modernity*. Thus, in defence of the 'unfinished project of modernity' he attacked Foucault and also thinkers whom we have associated with 'Post-Marxism' in this volume, namely, Derrida and Castoriadis. Yet, given the overall categorisation of 'Post-Marxism' in this book, his earlier work can certainly be portrayed as Marxism 'plus', since he was firmly rooted in the Frankfurt School that had no qualms in linking Marx and Freud. In addition, as the above quotation illustrates, he wanted to be both a Marxist and a 'reformist', which suggests that he aimed to bring something a little alien into standard Marxism. Indeed, in many respects this 'reformist' impulse, as he himself suggests, became uppermost in his long and productive career, as he evolved from a 'strong' Post-Marxist into a 'weak' one, moving from a constructive, critical engagement with Marxism in an attempt to overcome its theoretical deficits and holding out the possibility of profound social transformation, to a position where Marxist problematics and concepts have a far more residual presence.

Before looking in more detail at how Habermas aimed to improve upon Marxism's various deficits, we shall in summary form consider the political and intellectual purpose and political/intellectual context of his project that forms the backbone of his theoretical enterprise, and helps to throw his 'Post-Marxism' into sharp relief.

Purpose and context

Habermas described his 'motivating thought' as

> the reconciliation of a modernity which has fallen apart, the idea that without surrendering the differentiation that modernity has made possible in the cultural, the social and economic spheres, one can find forms of living together in which autonomy and dependency can truly enter into a non-antagonistic relation, that one can walk tall in a collectivity that does not have the dubious quality of backward looking substantial forms of community. (Habermas, 1992c: 125)

This 'reconciliation' involved monumental erudition and theoretical sophistication on Habermas's part. He balanced between, and synthesised, different political and intellectual traditions and academic disciplines: liberalism and socialism, Kant and Hegel, Weber and Marx, psychology, linguistics, systems theory (structure and function, differentiation, process and adaptation) and action theory (meaning, intentionality, roles, norms, beliefs and values), instrumental and 'communicative' rationality, and so on.

The synthetic nature of his overall project, whatever his personal Hegelian-style predilection for grand theorising, was the product of time and circumstance, of post-1945 Germany, traumatised by war and the social/political conflict of the inter-war period (Chambers, 2002: 168). He took stock of where the radical nationalist intellect had taken Germany (Nazism), as well as assessing the consequences of radical egalitarianism (Stalinism). His worry was that in post-1945 Germany the great moral wrongs of the Nazi period were not fully recognised, especially as the leading intellectual figures such as Heidegger refused to disassociate themselves from their pre-war, pro-Nazi views (Habermas, 1992c: 77–9, 192). Thus, he was in effect seeking an intellectual 'denazification' of German culture without making any concessions to a version of Marxism that was democracy 'lite'(Habermas, 1992c: 188). For Habermas 'bourgeois' democracy was better than no democracy at all, and was in Germany a tender plant that needed much intellectual watering. As he was later to say: in West Germany 'we know just how important bourgeois freedoms are. For when things go wrong it is those on the Left who become the first victims' (Habermas, 1992c: 50). Indeed, these freedoms were not merely 'bourgeois', according to Habermas, but reflected the progressive Enlightenment and modern impulse for the principles of human co-operation to become universal, rather than remain particular, or class specific. What emerges in Habermas's thought is an argument for democratic political stability and the rule of law based on a reasoned consensus, that is neither conservative nor repressive, and that accepts cautious and well-thought-out change, provided none of the material and moral gains of modernity are sacrificed (Habermas, 1992c: 183).[1]

This balance/synthesis approach can be put another way: he sought to create a *via media* between reality and utopia – as suggested by the title of one of his later works, *Between Facts and Norms*. Following in the footsteps of Hegel and Marx he wanted to make the 'real' rational and the rational 'real'. If Hegel aimed to *prove* that existing (early nineteenth-century Prussian) reality was rational, and if Marx aimed practically to *make* existing reality rational (if with a good deal of help from 'reality' itself), Habermas thought he could do a bit of both. In Giddens's apt phrase Habermas wanted to facilitate 'reason without revolution' (Giddens, 1982: 95–121). This involved a theoretical analysis of where 'we' *are*, where 'we' *ought* to go, and how far 'we' can go without either losing modernity's material advantages or going against a democratically organised consensus. Habermas's fundamental moves in making the real rational and the rational real, was firstly to show that modernity was moving in a rational direction, and secondly that unlike his Frankfurt School forerunners another kind of rationality apart from nihilistic, instrumental reason could predominate. Moreover, he not only embraced the

Frankfurt School's critique of positivistic Marxism, whether Second International, or Soviet, but challenged positivist orthodoxy in the 1950s and 1960s in the Anglophone world: science could not claim to be the only 'true' form of knowledge. Thus, he sought to escape from the 'scientism' of different kinds of positivism, and from the pessimistic leanings of Adorno and Horkheimer, for whom a substantive, emancipatory, non-instrumental reason was fated to become marginalised in such activities as modern art and music. This cultural vanguard was even more important as a result of Adorno and Horkheimer's identification of the new, commodified 'culture industry', such as film, popular music and sport, which was socially uncritical.

Habermas also aimed to rework the German philosophical tradition of Kant, Hegel and Marx to counter the Frankfurt School's Weberian-inspired pessimism about the nature of modernity, with its instrumental reason and bureaucratic 'iron cage'. Kant, Marx and Hegel in their different ways firmly believed that freedom and reason could – and would – triumph in the world. Habermas too believed some of this and adopted some of their methods and arguments. Thus, he shared Kant's moral universalism, use of a transcendental, grounding, 'conditions-of-possibility' style of argument and taxonomic mapping, usually in threes (e.g. theoretical, practical and aesthetic worlds, or science, morality, art). He followed Hegel in wanting to embody freedom and reason in institutions and in seeking to reconcile seeming opposites within some kind of concrete and meta-theoretical totality ('system' and 'lifeworld'). He adopted Marx's insight that, unlike Hegel, the quest for human liberation was of necessity an incomplete project, because the material conditions upon which it was based are themselves subject to change as well as conceptions of freedom and reason (within the transcending rules of discursive practice). Moreover, as already indicated, he shared with Marx an understanding of the *limits* of philosophy as *the* instrument of human emancipation. Other forms of knowledge within the human sciences were equally relevant.

Although he sought to counter the Frankfurt School's pessimism, Habermas's intellectual roots were firmly within its 'critical theory' framework. Critical theory combines explanation with normative and practical thinking to make the world a better – freer – place as opposed to what Horkheimer described as 'traditional' thinking which merely sought to describe and explain the world from an 'objective', detached viewpoint. As James Bohman (1999) puts it:

> Critical social theory has always sought to combine reflexive theory with intellectual and moral responsibility within a well-integrated interpretative and explanatory framework and in a political practice aimed at human emancipation. More than any other social theorist Habermas has furthered this endeavour.

Habermas defined critical theory as an attempt to eliminate 'man-made' suffering intimately built into the social structures necessary for the reproduction of human life (Habermas, 1992c: 194). However, the 'critical theory' of the Frankfurt School was originally another term for Marxism. Thus, its aims were universal human emancipation through the knowledge-empowerment of the working class. The form of knowledge was 'critical' in the sense that it sought to expose the contradictions or limitations of capitalism in delivering universal freedom and prosperity, but more importantly it endeavoured to expose the ideas that masked capitalist domination and exploitation. Famously, they used Lukacs's concept of 'reification', building on Marx's concept of 'commodity fetishism'. Seeing society in terms of 'thingification' concealed the fact that the exchange relations of commodities also included living labour and thus involved *social* relations of domination between capitalist and worker. The Frankfurt School saw the prevailing form of reification as 'scientism' or 'positivism', which held that the only 'true' knowledge was scientific knowledge, and was instrumental/technical, concerned initially with the domination of nature. By the 1950s this 'technocratic' methodology was also seen as the only 'true' one for the human sciences, thereby inviting a very different form of domination, of humans over humans. What also needs stressing is that following Marx the 'critical' theorist must not theorise for its own sake, as in 'first' philosophy that leaves the world as it is. Rather s/he should theorise with 'practical intent', have a firm eye on the goal of human liberation.

The Frankfurt School took their cue from the anti-positivist, Hegelian turn in Marxist theory after the First World War initiated by Karl Korsch and Georg Lukacs. What both these thinkers opposed was the prevalent interpretation of Marxism as a materialist science, as a form of economic determinism that gave little scope for the conscious, creative will in making history. This emphasis on consciousness in bringing about fundamental historical change was inspired by the Russian Revolution with its socialist goals. According to Second International orthodoxy such a revolution with *socialist* goals was not possible. The prevailing socio-economic conditions determined that only a *bourgeois* revolution was possible. Korsch and Lukacs, rather than abandon Marxism, sought to demonstrate that Second International Marxism in its scientism had been one-sided and sought to demonstrate this through highlighting Marx's debt to Hegel, who stressed the active role of consciousness in making history, the human capacity to reflect on their circumstances and the causes of their suffering in order to make the 'rational' 'real', whatever Hegel's ultimately conservative inferences. Thus, the stress was not merely on mental activity, but practical activity, on praxis. On this question Korsch and Lukacs (as did Gramsci) turned to Marx's writings, especially his aphoristic fragment, *Theses on Feuerbach*, which sought to integrate both philosophic idealism and materialism through historically grounded, collective, 'sensuous' 'practical activity'. Thus, 'the' dialectic of history was not solely an objective one, the outcome of the interplay of the forces and relations of production as outlined in Marx's 'Preface to a Contribution to a Critique of Political Economy'. Rather it contained an irreducibly subjective, cultural, political and creative element.

Yet the Frankfurt School, Horkheimer in particular, disliked Lukacs's praxis-oriented dialectic because it privileged to the proletariat's role in the overcoming of the subject/object dichotomy. This was not merely because the world-shaping, revolutionary role of the working class in the Soviet Union and in Western Europe was increasingly called into question in the two decades after the First World War, witnessed by the triumph of Stalinism and Nazism/fascism. But also because this version of the dialectic became a 'totalising' one ('history' = proletarian self-emancipation) that ultimately seemed to efface all freedom and contingency in understanding the historical process. This led members of the School to move away from what they termed the 'philosophy of consciousness' or of 'identity' (of subject and object). Nevertheless, they still wanted to cling, if rather pessimistically in the face of the instrumental rationality of technocratic, 'expert' ideology and in the absence of a distinctly emancipatory agent, to the ideals of what they termed 'critical theory'. As already suggested, this theory aimed to criticise existing capitalist society from the point of view of its ideals of freedom and reason by uncovering their bogus embodiment, especially in their cultural/ideological forms. They were engaged in 'immanent critique', pointing out the gap between declaration and deed in liberal-capitalist democracies. However, this critical strategy in the 1950s seemed to lose its force as a result of the growing hegemony of managerialist, 'scientific' and technocratic ideologies that stressed the 'efficiency' of means (e.g. in attaining economic growth), taking the ends for granted (that is, 'purposive-rational action'). Thus, the contradiction between the means and universally endorsed (rational) ends was not so obvious. This led Habermas in the late 1960s and early 1970s to establish a new grounding for critical theory – combining the 'is' and the 'ought' – in his theory of communicative action, hoping to establish a less contrived form of progressive hope, in contrast to his immediate Frankfurt predecessors, who had rejected Lukacs's Marxist, proletarian revolution solution.

Making good Marxism's theoretical deficits

Before looking more closely at Habermas's relationship to Marx and Marxism we ought to note that in intent and in effect it underwent some subtle and not-so-subtle shifts. We have to remember that from his earliest published work – *The Structural Transformation of the Public Sphere* – to his later – *Between*

Facts and Norms – there is a central concern with the public sphere and the quality of practical deliberation within a modern, liberal democratic, capitalist setting, and that his attitude towards Marx(ism) has always been coloured by this overall consideration. Yet over time his radicalism (albeit never revolutionary) and his Marxist sensibilities became more muted. His work in the 1960s revealed an interest in creating the conditions for undistorted communication and communicative control over the 'subsystem' of purposive-rational action, which certainly had radical, anti-capitalist implications. As he said famously:

> Our first sentence expresses unequivocally the intention of universal and unconstrained consensus. Taken together, autonomy and responsibility constitute the only Idea that we possess a priori ... only in an emancipated society, whose members' autonomy and responsibility had been realized, would communication have developed into the non-authoritarian and universally practical dialogue from which both our model of reciprocally constituted ego identity and our idea of true consensus are always implicitly derived. To this extent the truth of statements is based on anticipating the realization of the good life. (Habermas, 1978: 314; see also Habermas, 1987b: 118–19)

In other words there is still the use of the trademark Frankfurt School and Marxist 'immanent critique', and a seeming desire for fundamental social transformation. In contrast, his work from the 1980s onwards witnesses a far more accommodating view of capitalism (as part of the 'system' and a differentiated modernity) and liberal democracy, where the public sphere of communicative action merely offers suggestions or creates legitimating kinds of argument for parliamentary assemblies. Further, Habermas by the mid-1980s seemed to have given up on trying to overcome Marxism's theoretical deficits, when he talked of the 'obsolescence' of the 'production paradigm' (Habermas, 1987a: 74–82), in contrast to his earlier desire, in the form of immanent critique, to 'reconstruct' historical materialism in the sense of taking it apart and putting it back together again in a new form, 'in order to attain more fully the goal it has set for itself' (Habermas, 1984: 95). Finally, there is far less use of Marxist language (although 'reification' still remains), such as 'crisis'. Nevertheless, many of his criticisms of Marx and Marxism remained fairly constant over time.

Habermas's critical and constructive engagement with Marxism's weaknesses as an emancipatory theory can be subsumed under three headings:

1   The inadequacy of its two basic 'meta-theoretical' categories. First, historical materialism, used to explain human social and economic organisation and historical development, offered a one-sided productive force/relation theory of history, prioritising productive forces at the expense of production relations ('work' over 'interaction'). This inadequacy also

had implications for the validity of the concepts of 'base' and 'super-structure'. Secondly, following from this lack of attention to 'interaction', Marxism, in Habermas's opinion, was unable to provide an adequate normative grounding for an emancipated society, because it had no convincing theory of democracy (Habermas, 1992c: 188–9).

2   Habermas questioned the contemporary relevance of Marx's analysis and critique of modern capitalism, not merely as a result of his conceptual inadequacies, but also because capitalism itself had changed since the nineteenth century from a 'liberal' to a state, 'organised' form, resulting in a fundamental change in the nature of social conflict.

3   Not surprisingly his querying of orthodox, (aspirationally) anti-statist Marxist solutions and strategies for achieving human emancipation, led him to justify his 'reformist', as opposed to revolutionary stance.

Meta-theoretical level: historical materialism

We must remember that Habermas starts from some fundamental, Marxist-inspired questions: how *does* the human species constitute itself, how does it reproduce itself materially and symbolically, and how *ought* it to? And how do the answers to these questions inter-relate? In terms of the explanatory and empirical aspect, Habermas held that Marx at the most general level developed his theory of species self-constitution one-sidedly. Although in his empirical work Marx acknowledged the importance of critical species' self-reflection, the theory/practice relation and the need to abolish ideologies, his own philosophical self-understanding restricted species self-reflection to 'work alone': he reduces the 'self-generative act' of the human species to labour' (Habermas, 1978: 42). Thus, Marx's notion of species self-constitution was fundamentally instrumentalist and productivist. Although Marx recognised the importance of production relations, these were not built into his overall theory, and it is this sphere which allows for a broader conception of self-reflection, reflection on the principles of human co-operation. More concretely, although Marx distinguished between 'labour' and 'interaction', he did, in a manner of speaking, make 'labour' do all the work.

This one-sidedness had crucial negative ramifications for his theory of history, because this positivistic and productivist model produced a rigid determinism, that ignored the significance of human contingency in a double sense. In terms of political practice, it encouraged vanguardism, because, apart from being a form of totalising knowledge, the notion of inevitable progress eliminated any sense of risk involved for those bearing the consequences of an action (Habermas, 1990: 12). Secondly, it led to a faulty analysis of productive formations. Productive forces were *necessarily* embedded in production relations, which were culturally and normatively constructed, and were in pre-capitalist societies based on kinship relations, thereby making production relations a subset of broader social relations. Humans not only distinguish themselves in producing their means of subsistence (Marx), but also reproduce themselves through a family structure, based on language and facilitating a sophisticated division of labour (production relations) (Habermas, 1984: 137–9). In a sense Habermas was reiterating the Weberian thesis that in historical–dynamic terms the 'culture' of Protestantism was crucial to the rise of capitalism. Thus, Habermas questioned the productive force/relation causal ordering. Building on Piaget's theory of individual learning, he held – if problematically – that societal evolution depended on society's problem-solving capacity, that is to say its capacity to learn in a collective sense. Marx narrowly confined this learning capacity to technical or organisational knowledge, of an instrumental or purposive sort associated with developing productive forces (Habermas, 1984: 97). Habermas's conception of learning was far broader, involving 'moral insight, practical knowledge, communicative action, and consensual regulation of action conflicts ... that in turn first make possible the introduction of new productive forces' (Habermas, 1984: 97–8). Without new organisational principles of social organisation there could not be new forms of social integration, which enable new productive forces to be utilised or existing ones to be further developed. Indeed, as Habermas famously said, the development of normative structures constituted the 'pacemaker' of social evolution (Habermas, 1984: 120, 160; 1991b: 313), for example the development of law that led to social stability (Habermas, 1984: 162). Thus, a socialist transition would be bound up with the normative processes of democratisation of the formerly (capitalist) 'private setting of ends' (Habermas, 1984: 124). Nevertheless, the creation of social problems to be resolved stemmed from the material 'system' if its 'steering capacity', that is, ability for co-ordination, became overloaded (Habermas, 1984: 125). Another implication of making 'interaction' an important explanatory factor was that it conceptually allowed for a far greater variety of productive systems to exist, and called into question Marx's stages theory of developing productive epochs. Yet, Habermas did not object in principle to the idea of historical directionality, akin to a form of teleology. Rather, he did not endorse its Marxist form. In keeping with his Weberian/Parsonian-inspired understanding of modernity, this learning process, which enabled system adaptation, meant that there was growing system differentiation and new forms of integration at a higher level, and therefore a growing level of complexity (Habermas, 1984: 141).

Marx, therefore, was unable to appreciate the evolutionary advantages of the 'systemic interconnection between the capitalist economy and the modern state administration' (Habermas, 1991b: 339). Thus, Habermas was questioning whether the orthodox Marxist assumption that base/superstructure distinction was a permanent feature of capitalist society. In the contemporary era of 'organised' capitalism, in contrast to liberal capitalism, the state through intervening in the dynamics of the market demonstrated that the 'superstructure' was no longer determined by the economic 'base' (see e.g. Habermas, 1974: 195). Furthermore, he suggested that such a distinction could not be applied to pre-capitalist societies, where kinship ('interaction') relations were often crucial in deciding the distribution of work and its rewards, rather than a distinct, market 'base'. The formal distinction between economic production relations and cultural ideological relations was, he held, specific to capitalism (Habermas, 1984: 144).

Meta-theoretical level: communicative action (rationality)

Moving to the is/ought element of human species self-constitution, Habermas was as concerned as Marx with existing and ideal principles of human co-operation (or more precisely 'co-ordination' (e.g. Habermas, 1991b: 397), and their interconnection. Thus, his theory of communicative action has to be understood within the backdrop of these empirico-practico-normative questions. Habermas's theory of communicative action, which he began to develop seriously in the late 1960s,[2] was the product of his long search to overcome two problems that arose in critical theory. The first was the 'ought', value problem, because the original Marxist position was based upon an immanent critique of capitalism, the contradiction between what it promised to deliver in terms of human freedom and material fulfilment and what it actually achieved. With the triumph of instrumental reason, of technocratic science as an ideology, that contradiction had been effaced, and the (meagre) sources of ideological opposition had to be looked for outside the 'system'. Habermas thought that he had found a new basis for immanent critique in linguistic practice (Habermas, 1978: 314) – the values of autonomy and responsibility were embedded in this practice – in the sense that people in their linguistic practice were unwittingly willing the conditions for 'undistorted' speaking. The second problem was to surmount the pessimism of Horkheimer and Adorno, who had been persuaded by Weber's argument that modernity consisted of the triumph of instrumental rationality. Habermas in *Knowledge and Human Interests* (see also Habermas, 1992c: 193) had introduced an optimistic note by talking about different types of knowledge (or 'interests' arising from everyday life, involving the self-reproduction of the human species) – scientific–technical–empirical (control of nature, 'labour'), practical (understanding of others – hermeneutic, 'interaction') and emancipatory (self-reflective, critical, anti-ideological, 'power').

Thus, to each form of human activity he ascribed a 'proper' or legitimate form of knowledge. He later came to see this as a dead-end, because he was still working within the 'philosophy of consciousness' problematic, of the (monologic) individual and their (subjective) relation to the (objective) world, and therefore had not fully escaped from the primacy of instrumental reason. Although he did not reject instrumental reason as such, through utilising the philosophy of language (the speech act theory of Austin, and the pragmatism of Dewey) and theories of intersubjectivity derived from Mead and others, he developed a theory of 'communicative reason', uncovering the rationality inherent and implicit in speech. Communicative reason, in a sense arriving at the 'truth' together, became the foundation of his theory of communicative action, and what was later to become his theory of deliberative democracy, which focuses on the procedures necessary for consensual agreement (see e.g. Habermas, 1998: Ch. 9 *passim*).

In his first significant published attempt at theorisation 'What is Universal Pragmatics?' (Habermas, 1984: 68) he discussed what it meant for speakers to reach an agreement that 'terminates in intersubjective mutuality of reciprocal understanding, shared knowledge, mutual trust, and accord with one another' (Habermas, 1984: 3).[3] Such an agreement normally involved 'validity' claims of comprehensibility, truth, truthfulness and rightness. Clearly, what was excluded from such a consensus were different kinds of instrumental rationality based on deception, manipulation and coercion, and what was central was the expectation that reasons had to be provided for agreement and disagreement, reasons for 'yes' or 'no' (see also Habermas, 1991a: 287). Although in reality avoiding coercion and deception might be difficult, built into speech acts was an 'anticipation' of an ideal speech situation. He was adopting what he termed a 'quasi-transcendental' analysis, looking at the pragmatic conditions that made agreement possible, whilst allowing speakers themselves to reach agreements whose content was not based upon external, 'true' absolute principles.

His theory of communicative action managed to achieve a number of objectives simultaneously. Not merely did it point concretely to another form of human rationality that was not instrumental, and avoid the 'monologic', 'philosophy of consciousness', it enabled him to overcome some of Marxism's normative deficiencies, especially its democratic deficit. The prescriptions of the radical intellect could not be authorised by 'scientific' insight into 'history', and would have to be submitted to democratic deliberation for agreement. Lastly, at one level he could claim to have focused on the theory/practice, a central concern of classical Marxism, because mutual understanding achieved through language was crucial to the co-ordination of human action.

Analysis and critique of contemporary capitalism

His direct engagement with Marxist problematics and concepts weakened during the 1970s as he followed through the logic of his theory of communicative action and as a consequence of his growing attachment to the systems theory of Parsons and Luhmann (although he saw his theory of communicative action as an optimistic alternative to Luhmann's pessimistic notion of 'cybernetic society'). This change can be seen by contrasting his two explanatory critiques of contemporary (capitalist) society in *Legitimation Crisis* and *The Theory of Communicative Action*, despite their common concern with the reproduction of stable forms of 'interaction' or 'social integration', and references to highly significant terms 'system' and 'lifeworld' in both works (Habermas, 1976: 8; e.g. 1991b: 153–4). At the most superficial level this change can be attested to by the use of language: the earlier text refers to 'contradiction' and 'crisis' (albeit that they are only 'tendencies'), whilst the latter is littered with the term 'pathologies', and 'contradiction' is used more sparingly. In *Legitimation Crisis* there were even hints at the idea of socialist transition (Habermas, 1976: 93–4).

Although Habermas had previously challenged some of the basic concepts of Marxist political economy – the labour theory of value (Habermas, 1974: 227–31; 1987b: 104) and the falling rate of profit (Habermas, 1974: 222–7), in *Legitimation Crisis* he had not totally rejected the political economy perspective. Thus, he still embraced the Marxist view that a fundamental contradiction existed at the heart of capitalism, between socially, co-operatively created wealth and its private appropriation, a contradiction that constantly had to be suppressed or legitimated (Habermas, 1976: 48, 93). Further, he held that the capitalist *'class structure'* (Habermas's emphasis) was the 'source of the legitimation deficit' (Habermas, 1976: 43). Nevertheless, in keeping with his 'reconstructed' historical materialism, which stressed 'interaction' and the learning capacities of societies to overcome their problems, especially in an era of modernity, he argued that capitalism had changed from its 'liberal' (base/superstructure) to its 'organised' form. Whilst Marx may have been correct in his analysis of the economic problems of liberal capitalism, 'organised capitalism' was different, rendering class conflict more latent than manifest (Habermas, 1976: 38). The state not only could control economic fluctuations (more or less), but also could through income redistribution dampen down the class struggle through encouraging a system of class compromise. Indeed, unlike as in Marx's day, wages (as well as prices) were not strictly governed by the law of value, as a result of state regulation and union–employer agreements. Thus, in a sense production relations were 'repoliticised' (Habermas, 1976: 36). The contemporary state as well as the monetary system had a steering capacity to ensure that the capitalist form of material production was smoothly co-ordinated. Habermas's crucial point was that the economic crises of capitalism had been displaced under 'organised' capitalism by various forms of crises. An administrative, 'rationality' crisis could, he postulated, arise from budgetary difficulties, either because of the demands of countercyclical management, or because of the rising expectations, resulting from electoral competition between different political parties (Habermas, 1976: 74). He acknowledged the possibility that an economic crisis could lead to the 'systematic overloading of the public budget', causing a withdrawal of mass loyalty (Habermas, 1976: 69).

Habermas, however, focused more on problems of 'legitimation' and motivation, associated with social integration, issues surrounding the destabilisation of normative structures relating to work or the 'achievement' ethic and political participation. Hitherto modern capitalism's political stability was based upon a depoliticisation of the public sphere through the 'civil privatism' of a familial and vocational culture (career, leisure and consumption). This was, however, being undermined because among other things of the growing mismatch between the expansion of the educational system and the occupational structure, so that educational achievement would not necessarily be met by appropriate financial rewards (Habermas, 1976: 81). In addition, there was little motivation in low-paid and monotonous jobs. Culturally, nonmaterialist values were emerging as there was more emphasis on the values of leisure in contrast to the monetary rewards of work. Further, an antibourgeois counter-culture and a 'communicative ethic' inspired by modern art had emerged, fostering a youth culture of opposition or withdrawal (Habermas, 1976: 90–2). To add to these crisis tendencies, the achievement orientation in bourgeois culture, which relied on pre-bourgeois, often religious cultures, was undermined by 'scientism', rendering beliefs criticisable (Habermas, 1976: 80). Ideological erosion was also manifest in the challenge to the culture of possessive individualism – the product of a risk culture that produced individual striving – by development of collective goods such as transport and health (Habermas, 1976: 83). Other destabilising factors included the rise of a 'universal morality' that called into question loyalty to a particular state, and interference by the state in the educational curriculum, early schooling, family planning, marriage laws and the like, undermining traditional cultures. This led to the politicisation of the private sphere, as well as the loss of 'meaning' and the possibility that the state could not sustain loyalty through 'consumable values', because this loss of meaning gave rise to 'exorbitant demands' (Habermas, 1976: 93).

We can see from all this that Habermas was attempting to give a complex account of the 'legitimation crisis' that involved both spheres of material and symbolic reproduction, and their intermeshing. Yet, he had not at this stage given up on the idea that the capitalist system – effectively its 'contradictions' – was key to understanding this phenomenon.

Although Habermas continued with the basic idea of capitalism as either suppressing or legitimating its contradictions, especially between the social production and private appropriation of wealth in *The Theory of Communicative Action* (Habermas, 1991b: 343–56, 391–2) the Marxist language of 'crisis' and 'contradiction' became less evident. Most significantly, we do not get a sense of Habermas attempting to sustain an immanent critique of capitalism in a socially transformative sense that was characteristic of his earlier works. Developing the concepts of 'system' and 'lifeworld' announced in *Legitimation Crisis*, he now saw the central fault-line in contemporary capitalism to be the conflict between 'system' and 'lifeworld'. In *The Theory of Communicative Action* he characterised this conflict as the 'colonisation' or 'mediatisation' of the 'lifeworld' by the 'system'. Briefly put, by 'system' Habermas meant the sphere of human co-operation associated primarily with *material* production and reproduction (of 'work' and instrumental activity). The 'system' was co-ordinated (or 'integrated') by the 'steering media' of power (administration) and money (the economy). The 'system' co-ordinated the 'consequences' of people's productive actions, whatever their motives and intentions. The 'lifeworld' (a term borrowed from Husserl and Schutz), on the other hand, referred to the arena of *symbolic* (linguistic) production and reproduction, and the underlying, taken-for-granted assumptions, values and world-views needed to enable people to reach a mutual understanding, forming the basis of communicative action. The 'lifeworld', Habermas held, provided the 'context-forming background of processes of reaching understanding' (Habermas, 1991b: 204). This was the area of social 'integration', of cultural reproduction and socialisation (Habermas, 1991b: 137–8). In the private sphere the 'lifeworld' was embodied in such institutions, as the family, and in the public realm it included the voluntary associations of civil society (e.g. neighbourhood associations; Habermas, 1991b: 309), and ultimately the processes that made the democratic state accountable such as the mass media.

Borrowing from Parson's functionalism, Habermas saw that in the modern world the 'system' had become separated, or 'uncoupled', from the 'lifeworld', which was characteristic of a differentiating modernity. In pre-modern times both spheres were united through kinship relations in particular, but with the development of market relations and capitalist ownership relations, the family as such ceased to be a productive unit. Habermas made it clear that this differentiation of 'lifeworld' and 'system' was not an inherently 'bad' thing, because it enhanced human productivity, and through money and power made decision-making much more time-efficient (Habermas, 1991b: 321), as well as helping to 'rationalise' the lifeworld by encouraging procedurally based agreement. He also endorsed the differentiation of the value spheres, and their corresponding discursive practices, of science, morality and art, loosely connected with the 'everyday' 'cognitive-instrumental', 'moral-practical' and 'expressive' 'moments' (Habermas, 1991b: 329). What he objected to was the 'system' taking on, or 'colonising', those activities which were proper to the 'lifeworld', rendering them dysfunctional or 'pathological' (personality), producing 'anomie' (social integration) and the loss of meaning (cultural reproduction) (Habermas, 1991b: 143), as well as cultural impoverishment (Habermas, 1991b: 327–30). It led to the commodification or reification (ends/means rationality) of private life and the 'juridification' of family relations through increased welfare state regulations, citizens becoming clients (Habermas, 1991b: 322) with the social services becoming a 'therapeutocracy' (Habermas, 1991b: 363) all of which encouraged an instrumental-strategic attitude, undermining a sense of social solidarity. The public sphere of the lifeworld became colonised by the 'culture industry', the press and later the mass media.

Solving the problems of modernity

The job of the critical theorist was not to liberate the lifeworld from the 'system', which would incur the loss of all the productive benefits that modernity had brought. Rather it was, as he said later, to 'erect a democratic dam against the colonisation of the lifeworld' (Habermas, 1992a: 444). Unlike his Frankfurt School forebears this colonisation did not represent doom and gloom. The New Social Movements, preoccupied with defending non-materialist values, were resisting this colonising process. And unlike Marx this type of conflict was neither principally based on class, nor about material redistribution. What was emerging was a 'new politics' in West Germany, of new middle classes, younger generations and the more educated, who were concerned with the effects of economic growth (environment), nuclear issues, alternative lifestyles, minority rights and gender equality (Habermas, 1991b: 392–3). Moreover, supranational political institutions, such as the European Union, properly democratised, offered some hope.

Habermas's own proposals to keep the 'system' in check relied on the use of democratically constituted legal regulation. Unlike the Marxist view of law as a superstructural reflection of the economic base, for him it was a category and social relation where the 'system' and 'lifeworld' rubbed up against each other (Habermas, 1991b: 309). It was a necessary part of the economic and administrative 'system', but in democracies it could be consensually lifeworld based. In *Between Facts and Norms* we see Habermas returning to his earliest preoccupations with the public sphere, with public deliberation, and the relation between communicative action and the 'system'. He held that in modern societies the 'law can fulfil the function of stabilising behavioural expectations only if it preserves an internal connection with the socially integrating force of communicative action' (Habermas,

1996: 84). He wanted the 'lifeworld' to have an input into the formulation of law, but as in so much of his writing we see him as wanting to have every category and institution in its proper place, if only because an essential ingredient of modernity is the growth of functional differentiation, or 'complexity'. Thus, the deliberative process under modern conditions could not take the form of direct democracy of a face-to-face society, with a 'macrosocial subject' owing to the existence of different types of discourse as well as differing interests. Rather, this process had to be institutionalised, yet allow for the interplay of 'informally developed public opinions' (Habermas, 1996: 298–9). For Habermas, the role of legislatures is to formulate and authorise laws, whilst informal, 'communicative power' is to be exercised in the manner of a 'siege'. It 'influences the premises of judgement and decision making in the political system without intending to conquer the system itself ... it takes responsibility for the pool of reasons that administrative power can handle instrumentally, but cannot ignore, given its juridical nature' (Habermas, 1996: 486–7; 1992a: 452). Elsewhere he stated that the influence of communicative power ought to be limited to the 'procurement and withdrawal of legitimation' (Habermas, 1992a: 452).

For him, 'radical democratisation' meant that there had to be a '"separation of powers"', with the 'democratic dam' preventing 'system imperatives' encroaching upon the lifeworld (Habermas, 1992a: 444). For a 'rational political will', the 'rationalised lifeworld' had to meet the political system 'halfway' (Habermas, 1996: 488, 358). In effect, he was arguing for what he termed a 'self-limiting' democracy, and for the idea of a '"weak" public' (Habermas, 1996: 306–7; 1989: 67). This 'weak' sphere was not meant to encroach upon the actual functions of the 'strong' sphere. Although he acknowledged that parliament (part of the 'strong' sphere) might not be responsive to 'autonomous ["weak"] public spheres', they could be made to be if these spheres – the mass media, political parties, trade unions, and other associations – were influenced by a 'liberal-egalitarian political culture sensitive to problems affecting society as a whole' (Habermas, 1996: 488). Many of Habermas's later writings have been concerned with how to build this 'democratic dam' within the public sphere – indeed within the cosmopolitan global public sphere in the face of the legitimation problems that the global 'system' has created (e.g. Habermas, 2001a; 2001b).

An important consequence of his overall position is his rejection of Marx's idea of revolution, of thinking that the 'system' could be brought under the control of the lifeworld. The idea of a free association of producers democratically organising the economic system was 'nostalgic' (Habermas, 1990: 15; 1991b: 340), and inefficient (Habermas, 1992c: 72, 94) and had proved unrealistic as demonstrated by the political and economic failure of state socialism (Habermas, 1996: 479). Such a conception was symptomatic of holistic thinking, of thinking in terms of an 'ethical totality' (Habermas, 1990: 11; 1992a:

443–4, 452; 1989: 52–3, 67), of concrete life forms, à la Hegel, as evidenced by Marx and Engels's championing of the Paris Commune (Habermas, 1996: 478). This 'substantive' perspective was always open to totalitarian abuse. This was at the expense of proceduralism that enabled proper democratic deliberation that would genuinely combine solidarity and autonomy. Habermas declared that one could only theorise about the 'conditions' of the emancipated life. Actual decision-making and its structures was up to the participants of such emancipated societies (Habermas, 1990: 12; 1996: 478).

Marx's problem, according to Habermas, was that the alienation perspective, the basis of the normative 'need' for revolution, was faulty. It underpinned Marx's value theory, and meant that he could not accept that the operation of exchange value (to co-ordinate different productive spheres) was here to stay, and because he condemned it *in toto* he was unable to differentiate between its role in the destruction of traditional life-forms and types of reification in post-traditional societies (Habermas, 1991b: 340–1). For Habermas his notion of lifeworld colonisation as described above, stemming from his theory of communicative action was better suited as a critique of the different malfunctioning aspects of modernity (Habermas, 1991b: 342). Habermas's 'reformism' then manifested itself mainly in his concern to create far more democratic procedures through constitutional changes in order to ensure that the 'system' did what it was best at, the reproduction of material values, and not attempt the reproduction of communicatively based symbolic values of the lifeworld.

Appraising Habermas's Post-Marxism

There is little doubt that Habermas's attempt to fill Marxism's various deficits and go beyond them has been a skilful, serious and thoughtful exercise, and that in both the meta-theoretical and critique-of-capitalism areas he has exposed some basic weaknesses. These include Marxism's general failure to integrate systematically the 'labour' and 'interaction' categories in accounting for historical development and the facile elision of normative and explanatory/descriptive ('ought'/'is') dimensions through a positivistic, deterministic historical teleology, which meant that Marxism has been unable to develop a well-thought-out normative democratic theory. Moreover, Marx did not investigate the complex issues surrounding the cultural reproduction of society. And in terms of its critique of capitalism and the construction of a plausible alternative to it, Habermas's point has to be endorsed: Marxists have generally failed to see the importance of Weberian insights into modernity concerning its ever increasing division of labour and attendant forms of economic, social and political differentiation and the need for their co-ordination. Nevertheless, leaving aside the accuracy of Habermas's critique of Marx and Marxism,[4] we can ask whether his own thinking suffers from its own 'deficits', indeed whether the old Marxist questions and insights have totally gone away. The underlying thrust of much of this appraisal – which focuses mainly on the later, post-1960s writings, after he had effectively dropped the immanent critique principle of his Frankfurt forebears – is that Habermas's attempt to reconcile 'reason' with modernity, with every human activity (nearly) fitting into a neatly constructed theoretical (especially 'instrumental' and 'communicative' rationality) category, does not wholly convince.

Turning first to his discussion of Marx and Marxism's meta-theoretical deficits. In stressing the 'interaction' side of historical development and the obsolescence not merely of the 'production paradigm', but also of the base/superstructure distinction in order to open a space for democratic deliberation, and lay the basis for a reformist strategy Habermas runs the risk of generating his own form of one-sidedness. Merely because the 'production paradigm' cannot explain *everything*, this does not mean that it cannot explain *something*, especially if we add the prefix 'capitalist'. Many of the 'old' political issues generated by capitalism have not gone away, whether they are unemployment, economic inequality and welfare spending, and of course it has created new ones especially connected to environmental devastation, alluded to by Habermas in *The Legitimation Crisis*, and genetic engineering. Many of these issues are now affected in different ways by the phenomenon known as 'globalisation', a term that designates another phase in capitalist development, and has intensified pressures on welfare spending and created more obstacles for egalitarian projects. In other words, the 'needs' of capital accumulation still constitute an important explanatory factor in contemporary politics. This has implications for the validity of the base/superstructure distinction, which Habermas argues is no longer relevant. Although the contemporary state in capitalist societies may be more involved in the concerns of the economic 'base' in terms of economic management (although this is less so under the neo-liberal dispensation), it is still managing the 'base' on behalf of the 'base', that is, representing the dominant interests of the 'base'. Moreover, the distinction serves to highlight the fact that although formal equal political and legal rights are 'real', class and other forms of asymmetric distinction still impact upon the question of how equally effective they are for all citizens. The upshot of the argument presented here is that Habermas is correct in questioning that viability of historical materialism as a theory of *history*. Nevertheless, he is less compelling in assuming that important elements of the theory cannot be applied in a nuanced way to the politics of contemporary capitalism.

The problem with Habermas's one-sided stress on 'interaction' (that later became his theory of communicative action) at the expense of 'labour', and his desire to efface the base/superstructure distinction, can be viewed in another way. Although Marx may have overemphasised labour, especially industrial labour, as an explanatory (and in effect a normative) postulate, Habermas himself becomes too one-sided in his own categorisation of labour almost exclusively as an instrumental (human/nature) activity – as part of the 'system' to be 'steered' especially through the 'medium' of money (cf. Giddens, 1982; Honneth, 1982). Habermas felt that he could separate the spheres of 'labour' and 'interaction' (Habermas, 1974: 169), because in the contemporary world it was *technically* (emphasis added) possible for hunger and misery to be overcome (in the 'labour' sphere), but this 'liberation' did not necessarily converge with liberation from 'servitude' and misery (in the 'interaction' sphere). This narrow definition of labour excludes its embeddedness in human (production) relations, and ignores the fact it is regulated by a capitalist modernity, of a capitalist-driven division of labour, and market-driven benefits and burdens, that are not collectively and democratically legitimated, but at best the outcome of workers making individual preferences in a situation of unequal power relations *vis-à-vis t*he employer. Thus in complaining that Marx was 'nostalgic' about non-alienated labour, Habermas does not provide a space that allows the loss of expressivity through capitalist, wage labour to be balanced against the gains of efficiency and a possible dialogic (as opposed to individuated) compromise between these two values. This downplaying of the category of alienated labour because he sees labour mainly in instrumental terms may be because, for Habermas, human universalism exhibited itself primarily through language rather than through the need to develop and exercise self-directed energies.

Moreover, these market norms are not 'natural' (that is, the legitimate outcome of modernity), but embedded and legitimated through the 'superstructure' that upholds the rights of the private ownership of productive assets. Habermas rules out the possibility that the instrumental activities involved in material production should be mediated through some sort of deliberation. Thus, unsurprisingly he thinks that the question of property relations is a dead issue. He asserted that the argument about 'forms of ownership has lost its doctrinal significance' (Habermas, 1990: 17). His unstated assumption is that this issue has become settled as a result of a rationalising modernity. Furthermore, in factual terms whether the argument about forms of ownership has in fact lost its 'doctrinal significance' is questionable when we think about the almost global neo-liberal drive to privatise state assets.

Habermas's intellectual difficulties stem in part from his desire to portray modernity, in contrast to his critical theory forerunners, in positive terms. Thus the capitalist context of modernity becomes obfuscated by his use of the category 'system' (= instrumental rationality), representing the human activity of material reproduction. He morally neutralises capitalist relations through giving them a functionalist gloss by referring to the needs of co-ordination by the 'steering media' of money and power. Habermas therefore evades the fact that for the 'system' to function smoothly, enormous economic and political power resides in the hands of a capitalist and administrative elite, whether in terms of law-making, policy-making or in making day-to-day decisions. In other words, Habermas obscures the fact that the 'system' systematically disempowers a majority of the population. Moreover, it is a moot point as to whether it is possible to distinguish between 'money' and 'power' when analysing capitalist/worker relations – another example of Habermas being too categorially neat. Even if the Marxist notion of 'exploitation' as 'unpaid' labour is not endorsed, the capitalist takes advantage of the fact that workers have no alternative but to accept asymmetric power relations in the workplace, because for most a work 'opt out' is not an option (see Sitton, 2003: 130). Thus whatever Marx's over-enthusiastic prognoses were about capitalism's downfall, his spelling out of the A, B and C of capitalism as a functioning productive system, which at both the macro and micro levels exploits and disempowers, is hard to ignore.

The capitalist context of decision-making in the public sphere also tends to become obscure, especially in Habermas's later works. The regulation of 'system'/'lifeworld' relations through law, as already indicated, involves both 'weak' and 'strong' publics. At least two problems are raised by this position. The first is that Habermas makes light of the systematic bias, both in the procedures themselves that universally in liberal-'capitalist' democracies give the executive arm of government not merely power to make decisions (which of course Habermas would argue is functionally proper), but also to set political agendas, however much the 'weak' public might be able to do so in theory. This is not to say that 'weak' publics *never* impact upon 'strong' publics. Merely, that their impact, especially between elections, is indeed 'weak' because the bias of political initiative goes from core to periphery, rather than the reverse. Thus, in effect Habermas seems to be espousing a model of democratic elitism, somewhat in the manner of John Stuart Mill in *Considerations on Representative Government* (1861) (cf. Habermas, 1996: 171). The second problem relates to one of the decisive instruments of will-formation – the mass media. True, in his early work on the public sphere, *The Structural Transformation of the Public Sphere*, he has a far more pessimistic view of its role,[5] but in *Between Facts and Norms* he seems to be less worried about its capacity to influence. In 'crisis' situations, 'in critical moments of an accelerated history' actors at the periphery can 'reverse the normal circuits of communication', presumably in the light of what happened in Eastern Europe in 1989 (Habermas, 1996: 380–1). Yet, in terms of a *model* of political/legal legitimacy, he is conceding that in reality it is *abnormal* for genuine, undistorted communicative power to spring from the lifeworld (cf. Chambers, 2002: 184). Thus, if there is such systematic, communicative bias, which favours political and economic stability, this is certainly to the advantage of 'money' and 'power' elites who 'steer' the 'system', and brings into question the legitimacy of the 'system', whether within the context of liberal-capitalist democracy the 'rational political will' of the 'rationalised lifeworld' can really meet the political system 'halfway' (see Cook, 2001: 141).

All these problems underline the difficulties that Habermas has in reconciling 'reason' and 'reality'. His idea of 'reason' consists of communicative action, which in a rationalising lifeworld means a growing plurality of arenas that enable public issues to be debated between free and equal citizens, who are free to debate anything they choose. In a situation of a functionally differentiating modernity this means that there will be different types of discursive, communicative rationality that have to have their appropriate procedural expression (Habermas, 1996: 180). Yet at the same time his version of 'reality' is a legally regulated 'system', the prize achievement of this increasingly complex and functionally differentiated modernity, whose enactments in liberal-democracies ultimately express the 'communicative' wishes of the lifeworld. The problem, as already suggested, is that if 'reason' is systematically distorted by dominant interests in the 'system', except in abnormal times, then the 'system' can hardly be legitimate.

The strategy of the later Habermas to get around this problem is in effect to wear two 'hats', the normative, procedural, deliberative 'hat' in which citizens freely and equally debate whatever they choose, and the modernity 'hat' that advises the democratic deliberators that substantive interference with the causes of lifeworld colonisation can only undermine the material benefits of modernity. Thus, Habermas is involved in his own 'performative contradiction' in that he castigates Marx and his followers for thinking about utopia as a substantive (non-procedural) life-form, yet invokes his own 'substantive' arguments when defending (in effect) modern, liberal-democratic capitalism. In other words, in contrast to the younger Habermas, there seems to be an unwillingness to will the *conditions* for an ideal speech situation, which would involve large-scale economic and social transformation. At one level this could be viewed as an unrealistic prospect from the point of view of 2006, yet we cannot rule it out as a matter of principle, because in certain conditions a form of democracy that extends into the heart of humanity's productive energies may be not only possible but 'rational' in an ethical sense. Such a scenario could arise, for example, if for ecological reasons, such as climate change, important sections of the world's population had to be less oriented towards material consumption. Thus, a question mark remains concerning the extent to which Habermas is helping us to 'walk tall' in the 'modern' era. His earlier 'strong' Post-Marxist position, although it relies far too heavily on the use of linguistic practice as a form of immanent critique (at the expense of material interests/conditions), at least serves as a criterion to measure the extent to which the ideological sources of public decision-making affecting the lives of all citizens in liberal (capitalist) democracies flows downwards rather than upwards.

Conclusion

Habermas can be seen as a fertile thinker for radical democrats, despite his functional, 'system'-theoretic loyalties, who has not fully developed the radical implications of his own democratic commitments, which could make for a 'strong' Post-Marxism rather than his preferred 'weak' Post-Marxism. Moreover, his highlighting of many of late modernity's 'pathologies' would also suggest the need for fundamental social transformation. Perhaps ultimately Habermas wanted to make the 'real' too 'rational', in the spirit of Hegel, rather than Marx (Anderson, 1992: 331). Although he is on strong ground in assuming that the clock of modernity with the growth of different kinds of political, economic and social differentiation requiring different forms of integration could and should not be put back, we do not have to adopt his 'categorial' strategy that rules out communicative action making democratic inroads into the 'system', seeking more obviously to eliminate the 'pathological' consequences of modernity without abandoning its substantial gains (see Cannon, 2001: 181). There appears to be little space in his thought to contemplate the relation between democratic planning and markets (see e.g. Devine, 1988). Moreover, a 'strong' Post-Marxist position would not confine, as Habermas does, the conditions of democratic possibility to the procedural. The democratic context also has to include a good deal of social and economic equality before a genuine, undistorted consensus is possible (Scheuerman, 1999). Thus, in a sense, Habermas's thought can itself be radicalised, perhaps paralleling the footsteps of the Young Hegelians who wanted to radicalise the dialectical side of Hegel's thought and play down his 'system', which Hegel held had reconciled the 'rational' and the 'real'.

In many respects Habermas followed, if in a far grander way, the intellectual trajectory of Michèle Barrett and Ernesto Laclau in moving from a 'strong' Post-Marxist position to a 'weak' one, from a Marxism 'plus' to a body of theory where only the faint echoes of Marx are to be found, despite his many assertions that he remained a 'Marxist' (at least until 1992). In moving from wanting to make up for Marxism's theoretical and political deficits he developed a position not too dissimilar from Laclau and Mouffe (and Lyotard) in seeking to deepen the representational aspects of existing liberal democracy. Thus, although there was a huge theoretical gulf between Habermas and many of the 'Post-Marxists' considered in this volume, *politically* any utopian energy (although never strong) concerning a major socio/economic/political transformation seems to have become well and truly exhausted. And if we were to seek more historical parallels, the position of the famous 'revisionist' Eduard Bernstein and the Marxian 'renegade' Karl Kautsky, come to mind. Bernstein, at the turn of the twentieth century, sought to revise Marxism in the light of contemporary theory (neo-Kantianism and marginalist economics) and current social, economic and political developments. Albeit in a far less sophisticated version than Habermas's, Bernstein's revision celebrated the virtues of liberal democracy and citizenship, the attenuation of class conflict under modern capitalism, the inability of the working class to act as a potentially hegemonic subject, the undesirability and unlikeliness of profound historical ruptures. This rendered the identification of capitalist and 'socialist' historical stages as meaningless, especially because history could be characterised as the development of human co-operation in all its forms and because even under capitalism the human capacity to learn meant that the natural and social environments could be increasingly controlled. And thus social, economic and political change could be brought about by moral suasion rather than through class conflict. And a final parallel: both still proclaimed to be 'Marxist'. The parallel with Kautsky is that, although he did not use the term 'modernity', he was unwittingly a conceptual modernist in the Habermasian–Weberian mode, stressing the importance and advantages of an ever-increasing division of labour, commending political change in a rupture-free manner through parliamentary democracy and opposing violent revolution as an idea whose time had passed. Thus, despite Habermas's undoubted erudition and intellectual sophistication and his urging of radicals to be forward-looking, when it comes to political practice there is something rather familiar, something rather *déjà vu*.

Summary

- Habermas as a Post-Marxist?
- *Habermas's overall project*: reconciliation of modernity with autonomy and solidarity through democracy.
- *Intellectual framework*: synthesis of German philosophy (Kant, Hegel, Marx) with contemporary Anglo-American philosophy and social theory. *Critical theory*: combination of factual, explanatory and normative postulates.
- *Context*: post-war Germany with memory of Nazism and aware of dangers of Stalinist Marxism. Wants democratic stability and autonomy

within a prosperous society. A reformist rather than revolutionary thinker.

- Reaction to Frankfurt School's pessimism about future of modern world, especially with the rise of instrumental rationality.
- Intellectual/political evolution from 'strong' Post-Marxist to 'weak' Post-Marxist.
- *Making good Marxism's theoretical deficits*: meta-theoretical (historical materialism), communicative action, analysis and critique of contemporary capitalism (from 'legitimation crisis' to 'system/lifeworld'), solving the problems of modernity (creating a 'democratic dam').
- *Appraising Habermas's Post-Marxism*: most of Marxist categories irrelevant in understanding contemporary society? Are Habermas's better? Problem with demonstrating the 'real' as 'rational' in a communicative action sense. Radical implications of Habermas's thought.

Sources and Further Reading

Anderson, P. (1992) *A Zone of Engagement*, London: Verso.

Bernstein, R.J. (ed.) (1985) *Habermas and Modernity*, Cambridge: Polity Press.

Bohman, J. (1999) 'Habermas, Marxism and Social Theory: The Case for Pluralism in Critical Social Science', in P. Dews (ed.), *Habermas: A Critical Reader*, Oxford: Blackwell.

Cannon, B. (2001) *Rethinking the Normative Content of Critical Theory, Marx, Habermas and Beyond*, Basingstoke: Palgrave.

Chambers, S. (2002) 'Can Procedural Democracy be Radical?', in D. Ingram (ed.), *The Political*, Oxford: Blackwell.

Cook, D. (2001) 'The Talking Cure in Habermas' Republic', *New Left Review*, 12 (second series): 135–51.

Devine, P. (1988) *Democracy and Economic Planning*, Cambridge: Polity Press.

Dews, P. (ed.) (1999) *Habermas: A Critical Reader*, Oxford: Blackwell.

Giddens, A. (1982) 'Labour and Interaction', in J.B. Thompson and D. Held (eds), *Habermas, The Critical Debates*, London: Macmillan.

Giddens, A. (1985) 'Reason without Revolution? Habermas's *Theorie des kommunikativen Handeins*', in R.J. Bernstein (ed.), *Habermas and Modernity*, Cambridge: Polity Press.

Habermas, J. (1974 [1971]) *Theory and Practice*, trans. J. Vierel, London: Heinemann.

Habermas, J. (1976 [1973]) *Legitimation Crisis*, trans. T. McCarthy, London: Heinemann.

Habermas, J. (1978 [1968]) *Knowledge and Human Interests*, trans. J.J. Shapiro, London: Heinemann.

Habermas, J. (1981) 'Modernity versus Postmodernity', *New German Critique*, 22: 3–14.

Habermas, J. (1984 [1976]) *Communication and the Evolution of Society*, trans. T. McCarthy, Cambridge: Polity Press.

Habermas, J. (1987a [1985]) *The Philosophical Discourse of Modernity*, trans. F. Lawrence, Cambridge: Polity Press.

Habermas, J. (1987b [1969]) *Toward a Rational Society*, trans. J.J. Shapiro, Cambridge: Polity Press.

Habermas, J. (1989 [1985]) *The New Conservatism*, trans. S.W. Nicholson, Cambridge: Polity Press.

Habermas, J. (1990) 'What Does Socialism Mean Today? The Rectifying Revolution and the Need for New Thinking on the Left', *New Left Review*, 17(183): 3–31.

Habermas, J. (1991a [1981]) *The Theory of Communicative Action*, Vol. 1, trans. T. McCarthy, Cambridge: Polity Press.

Habermas, J. (1991b [1981]) *The Theory of Communicative Action*, Vol. 2, trans. T. McCarthy, Cambridge: Polity Press.

Habermas, J. (1992a) 'Further Reflections on the Public Sphere', in C. Calhoun (ed.), *Habermas and the Public Sphere*, Cambridge, MA: MIT Press, pp. 421–61.

Habermas, J. (1992b) 'Concluding Remarks', in C. Calhoun (ed.), *Habermas and the Public Sphere*, Cambridge, MA: MIT Press, pp. 462–79.

Habermas, J. (1992c [1986]) *Autonomy and Solidarity, Interviews with Jurgen Habermas*, ed. P. Dews, London: Verso.

Habermas, J. (1992d [1962]) *The Structural Transformation of the Public Sphere*, trans. T. Burger, Cambridge: Polity Press.

Habermas, J. (1996 [1992]) *Between Facts and Norms*, trans. W. Rehg, Cambridge: Polity Press.

Habermas, J. (1998 [1996]) *The Inclusion of the Other*, Cambridge: Polity Press.

Habermas, J. (2001a) *Postnational Constellations*, trans. M. Pensky, Cambridge, MA: MIT Press.

Habermas, J. (2001b) 'Why Europe Needs a Constitution', *New Left Review*, 11 (second series): 5–26.

Held, D. (1980) *Introduction to Critical Theory*, London: Hutchinson.

Honneth, A. (1982) 'Work and Instrumental Action', *New German Critique*, 26: 31–54.

Marx, K. (1971) *The Grundrisse*, ed. and trans. D. McLellan, New York: Harper Torchbacks.

McCarthy, T. (1984) *The Critical Theory of Jurgen Habermas*, Cambridge: Polity Press.

Rasmussen, D. (ed.) (1999) *The Handbook of Critical Theory*, Oxford: Blackwell.

Rockmore, T. (1989) *Habermas on Historical Materialism*, Bloomington, IN: Indiana University Press.

Scheuerman, W.E. (1999) 'Between Radicalism and Resignation: Democratic Theory in Habermas's Between Facts and Norms', in P. Dews (ed.), *Habermas: A Critical Reader*, Oxford: Blackwell.

Sitton, J.F. (2003) *Habermas and Contemporary Society*, Basingstoke: Palgrave.

Thompson, J.B. and Held, D. (eds) (1982) *Habermas, The Critical Debates*, Basingstoke: Macmillan.

Townshend, J. (1999) 'Lenin's *State and Revolution*: An Innocent Reading', *Science and Society*, 63: 63–82.

White, S.K. (1988) *The Recent Work of Jurgen Habermas*, Cambridge: Cambridge University Press.

Endnotes

1   Not surprisingly, he was uncomfortable about what he saw as the non-dialogical student militancy in the 1960s.

2   We should note that the timing of some 'later' intellectual shifts can be exaggerated. The so-called 'linguistic turn' started in the late 1960s in Habermas (1978: 314),

as did his interest in the idea of communicative action (Habermas, 1987b: 92), although he stated that he had the germ of this idea as early as 1954 (Habermas, 1992c: 187).

3 Pragmatics is a form of linguistics dealing with contexts in which people use language, as well as the behaviour of speakers and listeners in relation to the process of communication.

4 Many issues could be raised here, but the overall point has to be that although Habermas is not totally wrong, he does not sufficiently underscore the complexities, and perhaps tensions, in Marx's thought. Thus, his attitude towards the division of labour, crucial to a functionally differentiating modernity, is far more complex than Habermas allows, and changes over time (see Townshend, 1999: 63–82). One can also query Habermas's portrayal of the concept of alienation as 'nostalgic' on Marx's part. Far from wanting to turn the clock back, Marx in his later writings in the *Grundrisse* for example, in making the distinction between 'socially necessary labour' and 'surplus labour' time is clearly recognising that not all work is going to be fun (Marx, 1971: 144–52). Furthermore, Habermas's critique of Marx's normative perspective as too concrete, as in the case of his analysis of the Paris Commune, shows a lack of understanding of Marx's position. It was based not on some concrete image of an ethical totality, but more on what workers themselves were doing to emancipate them against the tyranny of capital. Thus, he was open-minded about the precise form this liberation would take, and although he supported the Paris Commune (1871), only a year later he clearly endorsed the idea of workers' power through the parliamentary ballot box for countries such as the United States and Britain. In other words, Marx's strategic preferences in achieving the 'good life' were always condition-dependent, and it was up to those collectivities that were doing the self-emancipating to decide the procedures and processes of decision-making. Hence, he shared with Habermas the intention at least of the radical intellectual not dictating to a benighted multitude the precise form that human liberation would take.

5 He argued that under modern capitalist conditions, especially through the mass media, the 'bourgeois' public sphere had lost its influence in facilitating legislation in the general, public interest (p. xi).

8

Jacques Derrida:
Deconstructing Marxism(s)[1]

We would be tempted to distinguish this spirit of the Marxist critique, which seems to be more indispensable than ever today, at once from Marxism as ontology, philosophical or metaphysical system ... and from Marxism incorporated in the apparatuses of party, State or Workers' International. (Derrida, 1994)

Strictly, Derrida (1930–2004) could not be categorised as a 'Post–Marxist'. He never labelled himself as such. And he never *was* a Marxist. Yet he demands inclusion here, not merely because of his enormous influence on the 'Post-Marxist' canon, especially on Laclau and Post-Marxist feminism, but also because the 'event' that many sympathetic and not-so-sympathetic to the Post-Marxist idiom had been waiting for finally arrived: Derrida's explicit settling of accounts with Marx and Marxism (or: 'Deconstruction finally meets Marxism'!). The 'event' happened in April 1993 when Derrida gave two lectures at the University of California, Riverside, entitled 'Specters of Marx: The State of the Debt, the Work of Mourning and the New International'. This provided him with an opportunity to showcase his deconstructionist approach and clarify his relationship with Marx (and Marxism) – to demonstrate how these two theoretical (and perhaps practical) registers overlap, yet remain distinct. He held that 'deconstruction has never been Marxist, no more than it has ever been non-Marxist, although it has remained faithful to a certain spirit of Marxism, to at least one of its spirits ...' (Derrida, 1994: 75; see also Derrida, 1987: 63; 1989: 221). After outlining precisely to which 'spirit(s)' he remained faithful, we examine the most critical Marxist responses, and his reply to them.

Apart from demonstrating how an author is unwittingly implicated in the very thing they are trying to exclude (in this case Marx and ghosts), Derrida's deconstructionism manifested itself at an obvious level in looking closely at the structures and processes of language and meaning, to demonstrate how unstable they are, how they mutate and how supposedly clear distinctions are far from clear. Among other things Derrida constantly shows in *Specters of Marx* (Derrida, 1994) how even translations of Marx's works into different languages often involve slippages of meaning. What also becomes quickly apparent in the process of reading *Specters* is that the title of the text itself is set up for deconstruction: 'Specters of Marx' – most obviously the word 'specters' evokes the opening line of the *Communist Manifesto*: the 'specter' of communism 'haunting Europe'. More than this: the whole phrase refers to the images of, and feelings/attitudes towards, Marx(ism) evident in Fukuyama's *End of History and the Last Man* (Fukuyama, 1992) which celebrates the 'death' of Marx(ism), as well as raising the question of how progessives ought to 'receive' the Marx(ist) inheritance through the 'work' of mourning, deciding which of Marx's 'spirits' to avow or disavow. And this in turn involves exploring the semiotic permutations of the term 'spirit' itself, ranging from the living dead or the dead living of the ghost and its constant returning, from virtual representations created by 'tele-technology', from false images of the present and future (derived from Marx's teleological conception of history), to 'truer' incarnations of ideals in the present and future encapsulated in the notion of a 'promise'. 'Specter' also refers to the spectral dimension in Marx's writings, often overlooked by Marx's commentators, involving not merely an evaluation of his treatment of spectrality in the broadest sense, but also speculations about his feelings towards matters spectral, especially ghosts.

The name 'Marx' too can be deconstructed, especially in terms of what it means to be a 'Marxist'. In 'The State of the Debt' Derrida discusses not only 'our' indebtedness to Marx, what 'we' should choose to inherit from Marx, but also the nature of the contemporary state and issue of Third World debt. 'The Work of Mourning': this refers not only to work itself, central to Marx's preoccupations, but also to the activity of mourning, especially in relation to the supposed 'death' of Marx and Marxism. Lastly, the 'New International': this term is in one sense the least ambiguous in that Derrida does not explicitly deconstruct it (although the 'old' International of International Communism is at least gesturally deconstructed). Yet precisely what it might mean concretely remains far from clear, perhaps deliberately so, summoning 'us' to invest it with meaning.

Derrida gives added force to the multiplicity of meanings in *Specters* by weaving into it many allusions to Shakespearean texts, especially *Hamlet* as well as *Timon of Athens*. He does so partly in order to introduce his own philosophical preoccupations, especially with the concept of time and the role of metaphors in the constitution of concepts. This is encapsulated in Specters' post-face: 'time is out of joint' (Hamlet) – a concept/metaphor susceptible to much deconstruction (Derrida, 1994: 16–19). But partly in order to point up parallel, spectral themes in Shakespeare and Marx (perhaps not surprising in the light of Marx's well-known love of Shakespeare's writings), which in their ghostly form well and truly put time out of joint. Moreover, Derrida wants to draw a symbolic parallel between the dead, murdered father of Hamlet and the 'death' of Marx(ism), which raise questions of inheritance and mourning. Perhaps more importantly, *Specters* alludes to a rich and dense theoretical undergrowth that marks the whole deconstructionist enterprise as developed by Derrida, which can only be telegraphed here, yet constantly informs the text.

Briefly put, Derrida's version of deconstruction, following Heidegger, aimed to explore and assess the presuppositions underpinning the whole Western philosophical tradition, from Plato to Husserl, by demonstrating that its founding assumption and aspiration, its 'metaphysics of presence', was deeply flawed. Plato's model of truth consisted of a 'soul' in silent 'dialogue' with itself, of a pure, self-identical 'presence'. The object of this dialogue was the pursuit of eternal, timeless truths, or 'transcendental signifieds', based upon such things as essence, reason and spirit. Such a dialogue, of course, could only include others through speech. Yet 'presence' persisted because the speaker could hear him/herself speak and spoke what s/he had on their mind. For Derrida this notion of 'presence' was doubly problematic. In terms of time, 'nowness' is hard to pin down, since it is somewhere between the 'otherness' of past and future, or between such mental states as memory and desire. And just as important: language is used to represent 'present' thoughts, inscriptions supposedly identical with them. Yet words or 'signifiers' assume their meanings through difference, that is, by what they are not, as do indeed, the concepts or 'signifieds'. Meaning, then, involves not just the 'present' identity of signifier and signified, but the absent 'other' ones of difference. Thus, for Derrida, language as an expression of 'present', 'pure' subjectivity was impossible, and an 'ontology' that supposed a 'pure' being could be identical with itself was illusory. He therefore wanted to blur the distinction between 'being' (as presence) and non-being (as absence, difference, as past or future). Such distinction blurring was central to his political project: to expose the violence of institutional categorisation, whether linguistic (the act of naming), or phenomenological (the perceiving of the 'other').

The term 'spectrality' helped capture his objections to the notion of ontology-as-presence, since it referred to something that was neither being, nor non-being, neither body nor 'soul', associated the whole gamut of human sensibilities, imaginings, memories, hopes, fears, desires, repressed traumas and so on, all those things that are both present and absent. And the term 'differance' (combining to differ and defer), a neologism coined by him and sounding the same as pronounced in French, summed up his argument that meanings of signifiers were unstable in the sense that they could always mean something else in another linguistic juxtaposition or historical context. Finally, we should note that the term 'presence' does not in Derrida's writings simply refer to epistemology as perception, but is connected to ontology, especially in its psychoanalytically conceived form involving different kinds of repression that affect the 'present', and lastly to ethics in terms of our obligations to absent 'others'.

'Specters': the key themes

Derrida places his deconstruction of Marx(ism) within a wider framework of what it means to 'learn' to live 'finally' and the role of what it means to be a scholar within this process (Derrida, 1994: xix–xx, 176). Crucially for Derrida this means learning to live with ghosts and spectrality in general, which he terms 'hauntology' – all things that are neither fully present nor fully absent, neither living nor dead, that occupy the borderland between the perceptible and imperceptible (which for him includes almost everything!) (Derrida, 1994: 51). This form of 'learning' entailed an analysis of interweaving what we might term 'psycho-ontological', epistemological and ethical themes, especially in relation to time (as if there could ever be a 'finally'!) – *psycho-ontological*, because ghosts and spectrality in general are part of our 'being' – who we are, particularly in the face of death, (either our own or what or whom we might hold dear – or hate), or stemming from other fears or hopes for the future or as a result of the things we repress (the product of trauma); *epistemological*, because these feelings (along with external ideological mechanisms) generate perceptions/representations/apparitions of things non-substantial (for example, the living dead or the dead living); and *ethical* because 'we' have a responsibility (justice) to those not present: the dead and the not yet living. Spectrality in its many guises serves to disjoint time, by making the very category of the 'present', or 'now' or contemporaneity slippery (e.g. 'living in the past' or 'living in the future', or both) and by reminding us of our obligations to past and future generations. Derrida held that scholars in general, with their analytical propensities, sharply distinguishing between real and unreal, being and non-being, did not 'do' time and spectrality (Derrida, 1994: 11). On this score Marx fared better than most, but still fell short. And of course to 'do' time and spectrality properly you needed to be a deconstructionist, which was still one of Marx(ism)'s (self)critical 'spirits' (Derrida, 1994: 92)! learning to live with ghosts (= 'hauntology').

Within this broad, 'hauntological' framework *Specters* can be broken down into three elements:[2] first, Derrida's avowal of a 'certain' spirit(s) of Marx(ism); secondly, his rejection of certain 'spirits' in this 'work' of mourning, involving a critique of Marx's treatment of spectrality; and thirdly, his affirmation of his deconstructionist project which could at least affiliate to Marx(ism)'s self-critical spirit, and help in the 'repoliticisation' of Marxism.

Always a little suspicious of naming, Derrida declared that he was not a 'Marxist', as indeed Marx himself had stated (Derrida, 1994: 88). Still, now that the Marxist 'dogma machine' was disappearing, he held that there was no excuse not to read (and reread) Marx in such a way that goes beyond scholarly discussion. Not to do so amounted to theoretical, philosophical and political irresponsibility. 'Not without Marx, no future without Marx, without the memory and inheritance of Marx: in any case of a certain Marx, of his genius, of at least one of his spirits' (Derrida, 1994: 13). What emerges is Derrida's preparedness to endorse quite a few of Marx(ism)'s spirits, although he is fully aware of the possibility that he might offend some Marxists because he has no wish to license a seek-and-destroy mission of *all* specters. We need to recognise, he says, 'untimely specters that one must not chase away but sort out, critique, keep close by, and allow to come back' (Derrida, 1994: 87).

He most obviously affirmed Marx(ism)'s analysis and critique of capitalism in all its forms, its superstructures and its self-justifying ideology (Fukuyama's being the most recent). For example, the non-dogmatic Marxist tradition could usefully analyse the contemporary problems, of international trade wars, overproduction and Third World debt (Derrida, 1994: 63) (just some of the ten 'plagues' of the New World Order; Derrida, 1994: 81–4). At the superstructural level Marxism would be important in re-elaborating the concept of the state, national sovereignty and citizenship, as well as exposing the limitations of 'juridical formality' in relation to national and international law. In particular, one can find inspiration in the Marxist 'spirit' to criticise the 'presumed autonomy of the juridical and to denounce endlessly the *de facto* take-over of international authorities by powerful Nation-States, by concentration of techno-scientific capital, symbolic capital, and financial capital, of State capital and private capital' (Derrida, 1994: 85, 58–9, 94). All in all, capitalist political and economic institutions had caused sufferings unparalleled in human history (Derrida, 1994: 85). In other words, the Marxist critique could demonstrate how liberal-capitalist democracy is unable to live up to its ideals. Equally, it could usefully question these ideals themselves, which would include an economic analysis of the market, the laws of capital, of types of capital, financial or symbolic (therefore spectral), liberal parliamentary democracy, modes of representation and suffrage, the determining content of human rights, women's and children's rights, the current concepts of equality, liberty, especially fraternity (the most problematic of all), dignity, the relation between man and citizen (Derrida, 1994: 87). Furthermore, one could in the 'spirit' of Marxism analyse the novel, spectral effects of 'techno-mediatic power' which was allied to the 'political class' and involved academics and which severely restricted the democratic space (Derrida, 1994: 52–3).

More significantly, however, he enthusiastically approved of Marx(ism)'s self-critical spirit, as a result of the 'irreducible historicity' of Marx's 'theses' in the *Communist Manifesto* the inevitable by-product of unpredictable 'new knowledge, new techniques and political givens' (Derrida, 1994: 64, 88–9). Marx(ism) was able to recognise the need for its own self-transformation. At the most general level this form of self-criticism involved breaking with *'almost everything'* (Derrida's emphasis) in orthodox Marxism associated with its systemic, metaphysical, or ontological totality, especially its dialectical method and materialism, as well as its concepts of labour, mode of production, social class, all of which in turn underpinned its political organisation of internationals, proletarian dictatorship, single party and the state (Derrida, 1994: 88). In others words it had to break with its usual account of, what we could term, the 'onto-political' relation. More specifically, the 'new techniques and political givens' that Marxism had self-critically to adapt to stemmed from the emergence of a new political landscape shaped by the 'tele-techno-media' that made the traditional political party less effective and which had implications also for traditional conceptions of the state and the role of trade – all of which demanded *'new* modes of representation' and new forms of struggle (Derrida, 1994: 102; original emphasis).

More significantly, the 'new knowledge' – deconstruction – that Marx(ism) had to self-critically embrace involved an analysis of Marx's treatment of spectrality. Derrida argues that Marx reduces spectrality to a specific religious model, to mysticism, and is explained (and explained away) by socio-economic factors (e.g. commodity fetishism), thereby ignoring psychological factors (Derrida, 1994: 148, 173). Marx both believed in and wanted to abolish all spectrality through the creation of a communist polity. This simplistic approach to spectrality stemmed from a fundamental theoretical inadequacy: Marx assumed that spectrality was merely a problem of the ontology of 'presence', as 'actual reality and as objectivity' (Derrida, 1994: 170, 105). Although Derrida did not dismiss this 'pre-deconstructive' approach to spectrality out of hand, he held that it ignored the historicity of 'man's' being – the relation between being and time – the instability of presence or 'nowness', the product of past and future creating an 'out-of-jointness' or lack of contemporaneity. And if we add the impulses uncovered by psychoanalysis that help structure human experience – fear (especially of death), trauma, repression, conscience of the super-ego, the spectral effect of feeling watched by the father (Derrida, 1994: 7) – and less fear-driven ethical impulses, then the only conclusion we can reach is that spectrality in one form or another is here to stay (p. 164). We have to learn to live with 'certain spirits' (pp. 174, 176). This desire to eliminate spectrality in general, according to Derrida, was the product of his own fear of ghosts, something with which he was obsessed (p. 105):

> Marx does not like ghosts ... He does not want to believe in them. But he thinks of nothing else. He believes rather in what is supposed to distinguish them from actual reality, living effectivity. He believes he can oppose them, like life to death, like vain appearances of the simulacrum to real presence. (Derrida, 1994: 46–7)

Thus, Marx could be deconstructed: he was unwittingly implicated in the very thing that he was trying to exclude. His obsession with ghosts entailed their constant conjuration (Derrida, 1994: 140).

Derrida demonstrated in a number of Marx's texts just how obsessed he was with chasing ghosts away, beginning with his doctoral dissertation, his discussion of money or ideologies (Derrida, 1994: 45–6), and in his sparring with Stirner in the *German Ideology*. In his confrontation with Stirner Marx argued that Stirnerian methods of exorcism would be ineffective and that Stirner himself was still haunted. Derrida proposed that Marx himself was wrestling with his own specters and that Stirner in effect became a 'bad brother' because he was a 'bad son of Hegel' (Derrida, 1994: 122–32). Ghost-chasing also revealed itself in his discussion of the nature of a communist revolution that would be a revolution in the revolution itself, no longer hiding its revolutionary (socio-economic) content in the trappings of the past (Derrida, 1994: 113–19). Finally, Derrida highlighted how Marx in *Capital* hypothesised that commodity fetishism would vanish as soon as objects and activities lost their exchange value (Derrida, 1994: 113–15). Derrida attempted to show in deconstructive fashion how the use/exchange-value distinction is not *necessarily* clear-cut, that transition from use to exchange value is an 'impure' one, and that use values were 'haunted' by the possibility of exchange at some future time. This 'impurity' stemmed from the ever-present possibility that a good (object or labour) will be exchanged because of its very usefulness. This 'corruption' was even more likely because of the possibility of different types of exchange other than money.[3] Both use- and exchange-value *concepts* are 'haunted' by each other, although he did not reject the analytic usefulness of this distinction as such (Derrida, 1994: 160–2).

Crucially, this strong desire to chase ghosts away had harmful effects on the Marxist political tradition and was in part responsible for the creation of totalitarianism in the 1930s in the Soviet Union and in Germany and Italy that led to the Second World War. Both sides in this period were 'equally terrorized by the ghost, the ghost of the other, and its own ghost as the ghost of the other' (Derrida, 1994: 105). Moreover, this 'ontological' belief that ghosts could be chased away meant that Marxists mistakenly believed that a fully transparent, 'present' society could be established which would eliminate that need for the 'political' altogether (Derrida, 1994: 84, 171).

What also had to be deconstructed was Marx(ism)'s ethico-political dimension. He insisted on remaining faithful to, heir to, its emancipatory aspirations Although the Holy Alliance of 'old Europe' attempted to banish the 'specter of communism' (as did Fukuyama), communism, Derrida invoking the 'messianic', like democracy and justice, could not be erased because these values were part of the 'universal structure' of human experience (Derrida, 1994: 167). Communism, like democracy and justice, was always 'to come', always subject to 'différance' (Derrida, 1994: 28, 64–5, 99–100). Marx(ism) represented, 'a certain emancipatory and *messianic* affirmation' (Derrida, 1994: 89; original emphasis), which meant that we should not 'give up every form of practical or effective organisation' however poor Marxist practice had been in the past, and that we should work for a 'new international' (Derrida, 1994: 89).

In effect the value of deconstruction, which involved a 'radicalisation' and 're-politicisation' of Marxism, for progressive/radicals lay in the fact that the emancipatory project would not end up in a totalitarian cul-de-sac. 'Differance' always meant, echoing Walter Benjamin's reflections on the bleak prospects for revolution in the 1930s, that the 'messianic' 'promise' of democracy, justice and communism to 'come' recognised that both the past, present and future could always be invested with unpredictable and new meanings. The emancipatory road by definition always had to be an open one – full of aporias, whose resolution/irresolution could not be predicted in advance. The lack of a 'hauntological' avowal in Marxism, the corollary of its 'binary' (being/non-being) ontological approach, meant that in establishing a new society it did not leave room for uncertainty and openness to further 'events', new forms of justice, democracy, communism. These terms represented the 'messianic' in general 'that other ghost which we cannot, ought not to do without' (Derrida, 1994: 168) – a 'weak' or quasi-transcendental messianism, a non-deconstructible category that through time can undergo infinite mutations, but presumably increasingly 'enlightened' ones. The messianic appeal belongs

> properly to a universal structure, to that irreducible movement of the historical opening to the future, therefore to experience itself and to its language (expectation, promise, commitment to the event of what is coming, imminence, urgency, demand for salvation and for justice beyond law, pledge given to the other inasmuch as he or she is not present, presently present or living, and so forth) ... (Derrida, 1994: 167, 59)

Justice, Derrida held, was non-destructible-associated with 'desert-like messianism' without content and non-identifiable – and based upon a necessary 'disjointure', which was a 'de-totalising' condition because of the need to be open to 'alterity', 'singularity' and so on (Derrida, 1994: 28). There was the need for a 'real' historicity, allowing for an opening to 'event-ness' that was not possible within the orthodox Marxist historical framework of 'onto-theological or teleo-eschatological program or design' (Derrida, 1994: 75, 59). Indeed, the teleological and eschatological elements had to be separated in order to employ the latter element in a deconstructive fashion (Derrida, 1994: 90). Such predictability embodied in the teleological account of history denied openness to 'alterity', and therefore in effect denied the 'emancipatory promise', grounded on undecidability and responsibility.

Although Marxist internationalism, from Derrida's viewpoint, had been a failure, it crucially signalled the unfulfilled 'promise' of world-wide forms of social organisation (Derrida, 1994: 91), which could presumably attempt to solve the major issues facing humankind outlined by Derrida as: unemployment, immigration, trade wars, problems of free markets (cheap labour/ deteriorating social welfare), foreign debt, arms trade, nuclear weapons, inter-ethnic wars, international gangsterism, weaknesses of international law, especially in its enforcement (Derrida, 1994: 81–2). Thus, he called for a 'New International' which would transform international law, its concepts and scope of intervention, consistent with democracy and human rights, and applied to the socio-economic sphere, beyond the control of nation states (Derrida, 1994: 84). He conjured up the idea of an international alliance 'without coordination, without party, without country, without national community ... without co-citizenship, without common belonging to a class' (Derrida, 1994: 85), which should be involved in a theoretical and practical critique, especially of international law, and the concepts of the state and nation (Derrida, 1994: 85–6). We should note that his idea of a critique involved a 'messianic' affirmation and a 'promise' that entailed the production of 'events' and 'new effective forms of action, practice, organization, and so forth' (Derrida, 1994: 89). Breaking with party or state forms did not mean that we should 'give up on every form of practical or effective organization' (Derrida, 1994: 89).

In sum, we can see how Derrida as an 'heir' to Marx(ism) in his work of 'mourning' put it through its deconstructive paces, which enabled him to remain 'faithful' to, and yet consistent with, its self-critical spirit. We are now in a position to review the Marxist response to these deconstructive attentions.

Marxists respond

Although there were different reactions from the Left to *Specters*, we focus on the sharpest points of disagreement between self-proclaimed Marxists (Ahmad, 1999; Eagleton, 1999; Lewis, 1999) or those who had strong Marxist affiliations (Spivak, 1995) and Derrida's explicit response to them.[4] We should note that both Eagleton and Ahmad's animus against Derrida's overtures

199

towards Marx(ism) partly stemmed from the anti-Marxism of his academic deconstructionist followers, especially in the United States, and also perhaps from his unwillingness – as a man of the Left – to disassociate himself from them (a demand for a 'responsible' decision'?) (Eagleton, p. 84; Ahmad, p. 102). Common to all these Marxist critics was an explicit or implicit defence of Marx(ism)'s account of what we have called the 'onto-political' relation of full 'presence'. As noted earlier, Derrida's deconstruction involved breaking with *'almost everything'* (Derrida, 1994: 89; original emphasis) in orthodox Marxism associated with its

> supposed systemic, metaphysical, or ontological totality ['dialectical method' and 'dialectical materialism'], ... its fundamental concepts of labour, mode of production, social class ... the whole history of its apparatuses [the Internationals of the labour movement, dictatorship of the proletariat, the single party, the State]. (Derrida, 1994: 88)

In other words, Derrida seemed to reject everything associated with the Marxist 'onto-political' theory/practice couplet. Thus, although Eagleton noted that Derrida was prepared to use Marxism as a critique, he was unwilling to identify with its 'positivity', its demand for an 'effective' socialism that stemmed from its materialist analysis (Eagleton, p. 86). In effect, Derrida's ethical stance, divorced from any kind of Marxist-informed ontology, produced an 'empty, formalistic messianism' that had little concrete to offer in terms of political action and organisation (Eagleton, p. 87).

Similarly, Lewis complained that Derrida dismissed out of hand Marx(ism)'s claims to 'provide a viable knowledge of history capable of grounding an adequate practice of social transformation' (Lewis, p. 139). All Marxist concepts are disavowed, especially class as an analytical instrument and agency (Lewis, p. 149), as are important illustrations of the theory/practice tradition in Marxism, such as the role of Bolshevism in 1917, Luxemburg on the mass strike, Lenin on the national question, and so on. Indeed, apart from failing to make any theoretico-practical distinctions *within* Marxist tradition (Lewis, p. 137; Eagleton, p. 87), he buried 'every core concept of Marxist theory and practice', except the spirit of self-critique (Lewis, p. 139). Couching this argument slightly differently, Ahmad queried Derrida's separation of the teleological (the aim of history) from the eschatological (the victory of 'good' – communism – over 'bad' – capitalism) in order to rescue the 'messianic' element in Marxism. Hence, socialism had no material grounding. Derrida had renounced the idea of socialism 'as a logical possibility arising out of the contradictions of capitalism itself, and push[ed] it into the voluntaristic domain of acts of faith' (Ahmad, p. 95). Thus, Derrida's attempt to 'reconcile' Marxism and deconstruction was deeply problematic.

From the absence of this Marxist 'onto-political' position in *Specters*, that strongly linked socio-economic structures and processes to political action in order to achieve the 'good', Lewis in particular drew more specific conclusions concerning the rise of totalitarianism in the Soviet Union. He rejected Derrida's psychological argument that Stalinism arose from Marx(ism)'s 'ontological' fear of ghosts in general (Derrida, 1994: 104–6), and offered a socio-economic and political explanation based on Tony Cliff's theory of 'bureaucratic state capitalism' (Lewis, pp. 145–6, 153–7). From Derrida's interpretation of Stalin, Lewis deduced that he was attempting to 'discredit *revolution* both as a political strategy for the present and as a social aspiration for the future' (Lewis, p. 145; original emphasis). Spivak too had problems that implicitly derived from Derrida's onto-political stance, which, first, impinged upon his ignoring women's issues in general. Thus, he did not discuss the effect of Post-Fordist global homeworking on 'subaltern' women, nor new forms of socialisation of women's reproductive labour, relating to such things as population control and surrogacy (Spivak, 1995: 66–7). Further, he did not use Marxist methodology (presumably a 'political economy' approach) to make any systematic connexions between the 'ten plagues' that affected the New World Order (Spivak, p. 68). Finally, Derrida's own notion of the 'onto-political' meant that he failed to spot how Marx in *Capital*, in his analysis of value, is attempting to show 'rationally' for the worker the socialist 'ghost' in the capitalist present of commodified labour (Spivak, pp. 75–7).

Different conceptions of the 'onto-political' also led his Marxist critics to take exception to Derrida's idea of the composition and function of a 'New International', 'without party, ... without class' and the like (Derrida, 1994: 85; cf. Macdonald, 1999: 165). Ahmad wondered about the precise form that his called-for critiques of nation, state and international law would take, and who apart from the writers of these critiques would be in this International (Ahmad, pp. 104–5). Moreover, since it was 'anonymous' and without 'community' it seemed to be composed of 'monadic individuals' (Ahmad, p. 105). And if we add the 'religious cadences of 'desert-like experience' and 'waiting for the other and for the event' this International seemed more like a 'Masonic order' (Ahmad, pp. 105–6). Lewis objected to Derrida's New International in a slightly different if predictable way. It was a manifestation of a new 'true socialism' criticised by Marx in the *German Ideology*, which separated politics and ideology from economics and socialism from class needs and interests at a particular time. Thus, instead of 'class-struggle socialism', we have a struggle of universal, abstract human rights, involving cross-class alliances and leadership by 'intellectual elites' (Lewis, p. 149). Such rights, whilst desirable, could only be achieved, Lewis argued, through proletarian revolution. All this indicated that Derrida was pessimistic about the working class's capacity to fight for a better society (Lewis, p. 157), and was a 'reformist' rather than a revolutionary (Lewis, p. 158).

There were three other specific criticisms that did not spring directly from different conceptions of the 'onto-political'. Ahmad wondered what exactly Derrida was mourning, given that he had despised Stalinism in all its manifestations and had been critical of Althusser's recasting of Marxist theory (Ahmad, p. 92). In effect, Derrida seemed to be mourning not the death of the 'Father', but the fact the 'kingdom' had been inherited by right-wing usurpers, rather than deconstructionists (p. 93). And Lewis questioned whether the Marx/Stirner debate should be framed exclusively in psychological terms. Derrida took little account of its context. Stirner's *The Ego and His Own*, emblematic of the Young Hegelian movement, was published (1845) just when Marx (and Engels) were working out their new, materialist conception of history. Finally, Spivak suggested that Derrida, in focusing on the treatment of money in *Capital,* had failed to notice Marx's distinction between commercial and industrial capital (p. 65). This point served as a back-drop to her general theme that Derrida ignored the 'ghostly' significance of the commodified labour process and especially how it impacted on contemporary women.

Derrida replies

Derrida's retort, 'Marx and Sons' (although it is not clear where this puts Spivak!) (Derrida, 1999) sees him keeping his deconstructionist theme running in its psychoanalytic register. He continued to probe these self-proclaimed Marxists about what it meant to be a 'Marxist', or at least what Marx(ism) meant to them. He stated that he had always had an explicit indifference to preoccupations with 'legitimate descent', and had analysed this 'fantasy' in its phallogocentric mode in order to 'throw it into crisis' (Derrida, 1999: 232–3). This, he hoped to do 'performatively' by challenging the value of 'full presence' of one 'true' interpretation of Marx(ism) (Derrida, 1999: 224).[5] This 'descent' in its inheritance/proprietorial form raised more questions than it answered: where are the 'presumptive property deeds'? Has their title deed been 'duly authenticated'? 'Who ever authenticated this property right'? (Derrida, 1999: 222). Indeed, the suggestion that hovers over his response is that their very proprietoriality about Marx, as the 'true' heirs, or the rightful or 'proper' inheritors of Marx's 'legacy' led them to misunderstand, misread and mislabel Derrida (and what does it mean to 'inherit? And how *ought* we to inherit, by being faithfully unfaithful or unfaithfully faithful?) (Derrida, 1999: 219).

This misunderstanding as already suggested was, Derrida argued, at the basic level of not comprehending his intention, which was not to claim the right to be the 'true' heir of Marx. More substantively, his concern was with the Marxist conception of what we have termed the 'onto-political', which in one of its 'spirits' called for a deconstructive 'repoliticisation'. The standard Marxist theory/practice version 'welded' the 'political' to the 'onto-logical', that is, to a notion of the 'present-being' of the universal as the state, and cosmopolitan citizenship, or the International as the Party. This conception of the 'onto-political' relation led, Derrida suggested, to Marxism's *disastrous historical failures* (Derrida, 1999: 221; original emphasis). What Derrida seemed to be saying was that an acknowledgement of what we might term the 'haunto-political' relation would enable self-proclaimed Marxists to avoid driving up the totalitarian cul-de-sac by resisting giving single, 'true' political meanings to the 'being' of the 'universal' and the like. His Marxist critics failed to respond to his attempt to articulate psycho-analysis and politics in a 'new way' involving the spectralisation of death and mourning, along with fetishism and narcissism. He wanted to develop a 'new logic' of the relations between the unconscious and politics (Derrida, 1999: 259). Marxists hitherto had failed to deal with the psychoanalytic dimension in a 'convincing and rigorous manner' (p. 235). And contra Lewis this approach would enable a better understanding of the Gulag (rather than the state capitalist substitution of the bureaucracy for the bourgeoisie) and political assassination, as well as the 'spectral' causes of bureaucracy (Derrida, 1999: 243, 235).

Yet, his critics were wrong, Derrida held, in concluding that this 'haunto-political' perspective meant that he had done with the 'ontology' of class (and class struggle). He had taken 'very seriously' the existence of some 'thing' called 'social classes' and their struggles (Derrida, 1999: 237). Rather he had problems with orthodox Marxist analysis in this area which applied concepts in an undifferentiated manner, and more importantly identified class as 'homogenous, present and identical to itself'. Nevertheless, this lack of heterogeneity did not exclude social struggles and antagonisms. Seemingly, his quarrel with the orthodox Marxist base/superstructure approach was its presumption that a 'simple opposition of dominant and dominated' existed, or that the ideas of the economically dominant class transparently aware of its interests always ultimately prevailed, or that 'force' was always stronger than weakness (presumably because this excluded the moral dimension from politics) (p. 238). He maintained that theories of class and class strug-gle had to go back to the 'drawing board', which would also have to take account of the 'new realities of the techno-scientifico-capitalist "modernity" of world society' (Derrida, 1999: 239).

Derrida's call for a 'New International' not based upon class solidarity also led his critics to think that he had abandoned class as a significant polit-ical consideration. His response was to say that he was concerned with 'another dimension of analysis and commitment ... that cuts across social differences and oppositions of social forces' (Derrida, 1999: 239). He had no wish to deny or eliminate affiliations to class or party. Rather, he aimed to make 'an appeal for an International whose essential basis or motivating force would not be class, citizenship or party' (p. 252). And one could not determine, *a priori*, in '*singular* situations' what kind of 'decision' would be made in the light of different, 'undecidable' considerations of class, nation, party strategies, citizenship and so on (Derrida, 1999: 239–40; original emphasis), although he thought that class and party were ceasing to be 'dominant paradigm[s]' (p. 252). Moreover, there was nothing utopian about a 'New International' which was in the process of coming into existence. Lastly, his critics were not clear about whether they thought that international alliances could be forged *only* out of a 'common belonging to a class' (p. 240).

There were also other misunderstandings. In answer to Ahmad's question as to what Derrida was mourning, he replied that he himself was not mourning anything. *Specters* was more a study of mourning, especially the relation between the unconscious and politics (Derrida, 1999: 259). Moreover, it was not about 'reconciling' himself with Marx(ism), since he had never been in battle with Marxism. In any case, with which Marx(ism) was he meant to reconcile? One of the basic themes in *Specters* was to problematise the very process of identification, including self-identification, of what it means to be a 'Marxist' (pp. 226–7). Additionally, there was at least one elementary misreading of Derrida by Spivak, who held that Derrida was against 'repoliticising' Marxism (p. 223). Derrida also noted that Eagleton and Ahmad had failed to detect his playful and ironic tone (Derrida, 1999: 234). More seriously, he objected to Ahmad's charge that his writing had a 'quasi-religious' tone. He failed to note his messianic/messianism distinction. The first term was associated with a 'certain irreducible religiosity', which he held later in the text to be part of the 'universal structure of experience' (Derrida, 1999: 248), and which was a discourse about the promise and justice and included the revolutionary commitment of Marxists. The second term he associated with religion and presumably superstition, which was not consistent with his call for a 'New Enlightenment'. He did, though, admit that this distinction was not always clear-cut.

As for being mislabelled by his Marxist critics, although he did not give explicit reasons, he claimed that he was not a 'post-structuralist', nor a 'post-modernist', nor opposed to 'meta-narratives' (Derrida, 1999: 228–9). He also held, contra Lewis, that he was not a 'pessimist', whatever his wish to complexify issues of class. Rather, his notion of 'messianicity', like the 'experience of the impossible', involved a pessimist/optimist composite, a necessary requisite for a revolutionary approach to politics (Derrida, 1999: 245). Indeed, he claimed that his Marxist critics were the true pessimists in wanting to reproduce the 'obsolete forms of organisation' represented by the state, Party and International (p. 245). Relatedly, he did not wish to be categorised as either 'reformist' or 'revolutionary', because he did not want to be presented with an 'abstract choice' (p. 242).

Thus, Derrida insisted that his 'statutory' Marxist critics had by and large misread him, that in effect their 'proprietoriality' about Marx(ism) meant that they preferred not to listen to him and interrogate their own affiliations towards Marx(ism) as they understood it. Moreover, this 'proprietoriality' suggested that they were not prepared to acknowledge the significance that psychoanalysis might have not only for their own Marx-affiliation, but also for the Marxist theory of ideology based on an ontology of presence, or what we have called 'onto-hauntology'. Finally, in their quest to paint Derrida into a non-Marxist corner they wrongly interpreted him as disavowing *any* Marxist account of the 'onto-political' relation associated with class and class struggle.

Assessment

So what was the outcome of this meeting between Marxism and Deconstruction? We have to remember that although both sides were committed to democratic socialism in some form and wanted to see the end of liberal-democratic-capitalist hegemony, their starting points were different. Marxists began (and perhaps finished) with Marx. Derrida's intellectual layering, however, was far more complex and eclectic, embracing phenomenology, existentialism, psychoanalysis, ethics and linguistics as expressed in the writings of Husserl, Heidegger, Kant, Hegel, Freud, Saussure, Blanchot, Levinas and others, and his understanding of Marxism as a 'scientific', non-ethical theory seemed shaped by his close proximity to Althusser. Nevertheless, Derrida in his own way was reaching out to Marx(ism) – maybe as the 'other' of liberal-capitalist democracy – not only at a declaratory level. He also embraced some of Marx(ism)'s 'onto-political' motifs, especially in its understanding and critique of liberal-capitalist democracy. Further, he did not reject such notions as class and class struggle, provided that they were in some way re-conceptualised (presumably making the link between objective, social location and consciousness far more problematic). Additionally, in 'onto-political' terms he wanted to attach far more significance to the spectralising role of what he termed the 'tele-techno-media', its effects on consciousness ('presence') and its encroachment upon the democratic space (presumably its role in opinion formation at the expense of political parties). Yet, there could be few compromises concerning his deconstructionist stance, which worked at different levels in order to destabilise meaning, create doubt and uncertainty.

On the other side the Marxists were unwilling to enter into the deconstructionist game, although they did so inadvertently, acknowledging that there were a variety of Marxisms – wrongly assuming that this was a point against Derrida! Thus they were not prepared to discuss the nature of political commitment generally or their particular Marxist affiliation except in purely theoretical, or 'onto-political' terms. Could they have made any concessions without abandoning any of their core tenets ? They could at least have recognised the significance of psychoanalysis, not only for their own political beliefs, which may be ethically and theoretically grounded, but nevertheless may be an expression of a 'singular' subjectivity with all sorts of 'spectral' resonances. They could also have admitted that psychoanalysis might be important for understanding systems of power (especially [male] 'leadership' and the need for 'security'), something which the Right have always instinctively grasped. And within these systems rhetoric often has a crucial role. Here a couple of crude examples might suffice: during the Cold War the US Right in effect held that the Communists were preventing the full realisation of the American Dream, and now it is the Terrorists. The question of the structural impossibility of *everyone* becoming affluent under *any* capitalist system is thereby evaded. We might also raise the question whether the emerging Soviet ruling class in the 1920s could have consolidated its power without playing on the fear of invasion from the West. Admitting the importance of what we might term the 'affective' dimension of politics does not mean that the rationalist, 'interest' account has to be jettisoned, since political decisions may require both kinds of explanation. One final point on the significance of psychoanalysis and its analysis of human instinctual drives: Marxists from the Frankfurt School, especially Erich Fromm, Marcuse, Wilhelm Reich and Habermas embraced this mode of human understanding to help explain such things as Nazism/fascism and the (pathological) internalisation of cultural norms. In other words, psychoanalysis has not always been an alien paradigm for Marxists.

Then there is the ethical angle which is at the centre of Derrida's preoccupations. Even if they wished to reject his ethical position (cf. Soper, 1996) they could have at least admitted that the ethical issue at least had 'haunted' Marxism, that it was 'repressed' in Marx's works (Geras, 1985). So, for example, although Marx held that he was giving a 'scientific' account of 'exploitation' by analysing the labour process that produced surplus value, the term 'exploitation' itself carries unmistakable ethical weight. And of course Marx's communist ideal was nothing but ethical, however historically 'inevitable'. Yet at a deeper level we could say that although Marxists could admit that capitalism could be denounced in ethical terms, they might also have to admit that their *own* motivation – their commitment to constructing a society which they will not see or benefit from, and which involves all sorts of personal sacrifices – is profoundly ethical. And although Derrida in order to maintain an 'openness' to the 'other' was loath to endow his notion of justice or democracy with any content, there is in a sense a common notion of justice as a 'gift', that in the struggle for socialism nothing is expected in return.

Marxists might also have to admit that Derrida, in remarking that their standard notion of the 'political' was in need of some criticism, was not far off the mark. The classical Marxist view was that the essence of the 'political' could be reduced to class struggle. Hence, a classless society meant the 'end' of politics. Yet to embrace Derrida's notion of 'differance' and its democratic-political implications does not mean the 'end' of Marxism. Conflict within a classless society could be admitted without in any way conceding that the need for economic, social and political equality remains an over-riding goal. Indeed, at this point we might even say that the 'political' and the 'ethical' conjoin in the sense that arriving at the 'truth' together, at the heart of the democratic principle, often involves the deconstructionist 'doubt' ethic associated with the instability of meanings. 'Différance' might also help various Marxist parties to remain democratically honest. Further-more, on the question of the rise of Stalinism, although there is much to be said for the structural/historical explanation offered by Lewis, we still have to ask the question as to whether there was a democratic deficit in the thinking of the 'best' Marxist Bolsheviks in the pre-Stalin period, who understood themselves to be fully armed with the certainty that 'history' was on their side. This suggests the need for a powerful check against so-called 'substitutionist' tendencies, with the Marxist Party, or its Central Committee, or its leader claiming the right to speak on behalf of the whole proletariat (and 'history'). Thus, whatever 'dirty-handedness' might be involved in real politics it should be made much clearer when democratic lines are crossed.

Yet even if these Marxists could have regarded Derrida more favourably this does not mean that his answers to all their objections, both large and small, were completely satisfactory. Although there seemed to be a space for some kind of Marxist version of the 'onto-political' with the suggestion that the Marxist analysis of class and class struggle ought to go back to the 'drawing board' and that he had no wish to deny class and party affiliations in relation to internationalism, we get little sense of how this might be cashed out in means/ends, strategic terms at the heart of the Marxist theory/practice concern. Indeed, whilst it is true that Marxists have not really explored the whole issue of how working-class interest becomes translated into something far more moral and universalistic at the internationalist level, we get little indication of how the 'universal' and 'particular' might be integrated. Although Derrida sees the need for 'practical and effective organization' (Derrida, 1994: 89), his own practical suggestions concerning Internationalism amounted to no more than a call to like-minded scholars to criticise the capitalist dispensation, especially its legal forms. This *de facto* undervaluing of concrete activity also seemed to be too hasty in his reluc-tance to commend Marxist forms of Internationalism which has included numerous successful anti-imperialist struggles (e.g. Vietnam, Cuba and Angola in the 1960s) and countless acts of international trade union solidarity. True, we might agree that the current anti-capitalist movement is not obviously class-based, but the big strategic question is whether in the long term such a movement can hold together without some kind of class anchoring, albeit on a contingent basis, and whether a movement that has no sense of itself as a class can ultimately overthrow capitalism. Of course we might want to endorse Derrida's criticisms of standard Marxist assumptions about classes being 'identical' with themselves, but anti-capitalist alliances without any recognition of the strategic significance of class, or party, may prove to be politically ineffective (Critchley, 1999: 166).

We might also want to query the value of Derrida's 'ad hominem' charge that these Marxists were 'proprietorial' about Marx. Even if this were true, does this necessarily invalidate the truth claims they are making about Marx(ism)? Interestingly, he did not enter into any further discussions of Marx's texts raised by these Marxists. So Lewis's point, politically and intellectually contextualising the *German Ideology*, is ignored, as is Spivak's about how *Capital*'s analysis of value seeks to demonstrate the socialist 'ghost' in the capitalist present of commodified labour. Although a deconstructive approach can show how difficult it is to separate exchange and use-value in practice, in one register at least the effects of the commodification of labour on the 'singularity' of the worker would be relevant even to a Derridean critique of capitalism. The 'abstract' labour that haunts 'living' labour has palpable effects. Indeed, although Derrida does not spell out what he means he does admit that 'we must grant this to Marx and take account of the analytic power this [use/exchange value] distinction gives us' (Derrida: 1994: 160–1).

We might wish to go further and ask how valuable, from an emancipatory viewpoint, is asking 'ad hominem' questions about Marx. True, he may have been obsessed with ghosts (aren't we all?), but the desire for transparency is surely part of a process of freeing ourselves from 'bad' ghosts, from William Blake's 'mind-forg'd manacles' – consistent with Derrida's call for a 'New Enlightenment'. And true, Marx's explanation of ideology might have ignored its psychoanalytic and phenomenological 'being/time' sources, yet this should not mean that he was wrong in focusing on the fetishising effects of commodity exchange that helps to 'naturalise' capitalism. Here again one could suggest that perhaps Derrida is 'supplementing' Marx. Thus, Derrida states that 'pre-deconstructive' defetishising through the ontology of 'actual reality' of 'presence' (labour, production and exchange) 'does not mean false, unnecessary, or illusory' (Derrida, 1994: 170). Rather, these insights are limited because they assume a stable knowledge, and cannot take into account 'seismic events that come from the future' the product of the 'unstable, chaotic, and dis-located ground of the times' (Derrida, 1994: 170).

This brings us finally perhaps to the most difficult issue of all. Derrida affirms a good deal of Marx(ism)'s 'pre-deconstructive', onto-political analysis (if not its political party/state incarnations), especially its critique of liberal-democratic capitalism. Yet, how do we combine it with his conception of the 'haunto-political', underpinned by an array of critical techniques that affirm his deconstructive ethic, which he hoped would 'repoliticise' Marxism? Although he seems to want some kind of theory/practice relation and calls for 'practical and effective organisation' (Derrida, 1994: 89), this remained gestural throughout his 'contretemps' with Marxist orthodoxy. Although he insisted that his notion of 'justice-to-come' was not justice deferred, his questioning stance at the heart of deconstruction seemed to suggest that in any practical incarnation of ideals there would always be something missing, and that 'something', that 'other', was somehow more important than anything that is 'present'. Yet maybe his message is far simpler: the democratic 'promise' means that a radical egalitarian's work (even that of 'mourning') is never done. Marx would have agreed. But for a different reason: he did not seek to question the Western metaphysics of 'presence' by demonstrating its congenital 'impurity'. Rather, his notion of 'impurity' stemmed from a notion of praxis always open to revision in the light of new kinds of experience (knowledge, material situation, needs, and the like). Derrida may have identified Marx as an anti-philosophical brother. Yet we may still ask: did Derrida really follow Marx in wanting to stop talking to philosophers? All the same: should not self-proclaimed Marxists avow at least one of Derrida's 'spirits'?[6]

Summary

- Deconstructing the book's title.
- The meaning of deconstruction.
- Key themes in *Specters*.
- Learning to live with ghosts (= 'hauntology').
- Affirmation of Marx(ism)'s analysis and critique of capitalism in all its forms, its analysis of the ten 'plagues' of the New World Order.
- Approved of Marx(ism)'s self-critical spirit.
- Deconstructs Marx's treatment of spectrality, Marx(ism)'s ethico-political dimension, and teleological and eschatological elements.
- Affirms the 'messianic' 'promise' of democracy, justice and communism to 'come'.
- Calls for a 'New International' which would transform international law.

Marxist criticisms

- Lack of relation between theory and concrete practice.
- Lack of material basis for socialism.
- Inadequate account of rise in totalitarianism in the Soviet Union.
- Question composition and function of Derrida's 'New International'.

Derrida replies

- Meaning of 'Marxist' and 'Marxism'.
- The value of the 'haunto-political' relation – avoidance of totalitarianism, and a 'new logic' of the relations between the unconscious and politics.
- Misunderstanding about class, and misread.
- Need for non-class-based International.

Assessment

- Their starting points different, shared anti-capitalist/anti-liberal democracy positions. Yet Marxists need to reconceptualise class and class struggle.
- Marxists need to explore nature of political commitment generally or their particular Marxist affiliation, and could admit that psychoanalysis might be important for understanding systems of power.
- Ethical issue has 'haunted' Marxism, and was 'repressed' in Marx's works.
- Justice as a 'gift'.
- Standard notion of the 'political' in Marxism in need of some criticism.
- Against Derrida, little strategic thinking, and superficial concern with theory/practice relation.
- Problem of integrating the 'universal' and 'particular', and big strategic question of whether transformative internationalism possible without some kind of class anchoring.
- Limitations of Derrida's 'ad hominem' charge that these Marxists were 'proprietorial' about Marx.
- But Derrida not opposed to 'pre-deconstructive', 'onto-political' analysis.
- Problem of combining the 'haunto-political' and the 'onto-political'.

Sources and Further Reading

Ahmad, A. (1999) 'Reconciling Derrida: "Specters of Marx" and Deconstructive Politics', in M. Sprinker (ed.), *Ghostly Demarcations, A Symposium on Jacques Derrida's Specters of Marx*, London: Verso.

Callinicos, A. (1996) 'Messianic Ruminations: Derrida, Stirner and Marx', *Radical Philosophy*, 75: 37–41.

Critchley, S. (1999) *Ethics, Politics and Subjectivity*, London: Verso.

Derrida, J. (1975) *Of Grammatology*, trans. G.C. Spivak, Baltimore, MD: Johns Hopkins University Press.

Derrida, J. (1987) *Positions*, trans. A. Bass, London: Athlone Press.

Derrida, J. (1989) 'Politics and Friendship', in E.A. Kaplan and M. Sprinker (eds), *The Althusserian Legacy*, London: Verso.

Derrida, J. (1994) *Specters of Marx, the State of the Debt, the Work of Mourning, and the New International*, trans. P. Kamuf; intro. B. Magnus and S. Cullenberg, London: Routledge.

Derrida, J. (1999) 'Marx & Sons', in M. Sprinker (ed.), *Ghostly Demarcations, A Symposium on Jacques Derrida's Specters of Marx*, London: Verso.

Eagleton, T. (1999) 'Marxism without Marxism', in M. Sprinker (ed.), *Ghostly Demarcations, A Symposium on Jacques Derrida's Specters of Marx*, London: Verso.

Eagleton, T. (2004) 'Don't Deride Derrida', *Guardian*, 15/10/2004, p. 27.

Fukuyama, F. (1992) *End of History and the Last Man*, London: Hamish Hamilton.

Geras, N. (1985) 'The Controversy about Marx and Justice', *New Left Review*, 150: 47–85.

Laclau, E. (1995) 'The Time is Out of Joint', *Diacritics*, 25: 85–6.

Lewis, T. (1999) 'The Politics of "Hauntology" in Derrida's Specters of Marx', in M. Sprinker (ed.), *Ghostly Demarcations, A Symposium on Jacques Derrida's Specters of Marx*, London: Verso.

MacDonald, E. (1999) 'Deconstruction's Promise: Derrida's Rethinking of Marxism', *Science and Society*, 63: 145–72.

Soper, K.(1996) 'The Limits of Hauntology', *Radical Philosophy*, 75: 26–31.

Spivak, G.C. (1995) 'Ghostwriting', *Diacritics*, 25: 64–84.

Sprinker, M. (ed.) (1999) *Ghostly Demarcations, A Symposium on Jacques Derrida's Specters of Marx*, London: Verso.

Endnotes

1 This bracketing of 'ism' as in Marx(ism) is our own bracketing, and not Derrida's, and is used to capture the idea that the discussion often slides between Marx, the relations between Marx and his followers, and Marxism as a fixed doctrine.

2 His coruscating deconstruction of Fukuyama will be omitted here, because as far as Marxists were concerned this was not a contentious area. In all probability they fully sympathised with Derrida's visceral rebuttal.

3 Elsewhere he seemed to speak favourably about this 'corruption' by exchange value: 'what would the Enlightenment be without the market? And who will ever make progress without exchange value?' (Derrida, 1994: 152).

4 Although other Marxists, or writers with strong Marxist sympathies, also criticised him: for example, Callinicos (1996), Soper (1996) and MacDonald (1999). Jameson's 'Marxist' discussion is not dealt with here mainly because his sympathetic, constructive criticism was something that Derrida broadly accepted. See also Laclau (1995).

5 Another version of 'performativity' consists of taking responsibility for changing the very thing that it interprets, that is presumably Marxism (Derrida, 1999: 219).

6 See Terry Eagleton's passionate defence of Derrida against his British detractors, upon Derrida's death, clearly affirming the progressive, political side of his version of deconstruction (Eagleton, 2004).

9

Conclusion: Whither Post-Marxism?

In the introduction we deferred offering a definition or indeed judgement on Post-Marxism, pending a discussion on the work and contribution of a number of critical theorists whose work has been discussed in relation to it. However, conclusions are occasions for drawing together the strands of the preceding argument in an effort to resolve outstanding issues. In our view there would seem to be at least two matters that we can and indeed should comment on in closing. This is firstly to what extent it is possible to identify a common position that is identifiably 'Post-Marxian'. Is it meaningful to talk of a Post-Marxian approach or a Post-Marxian politics? Is there anything that unites these figures beyond a deep scepticism about Marx's claim to be offering a genuinely emancipatory theory? Secondly, it is to ask whether and to what extent 'Post-Marxism' represents an advance in philosophical, theoretical and political terms over that which it was intended to query, problematise and indeed supplant, namely Marxism, or more particularly the work of Marx. Can we say with any certainty that the Post-Marxian detour – if such it be – represents an advance on any of these terms to Marx's own approach?

In surveying what has gone before we think it is possible to outline a core Post-Marxian problematic or starting point. This is not the same as saying that Post-Marxism is an ideology united by commitment to a shared vision or even shared ideals. Rather it is a set of positions united by the shared perception of the importance of tackling and addressing particular problems raised by Marx, as well as the more general problem of 'Marx' and 'Marxism' itself. This set of problematisations, which are in all manner of ways interconnected, can be summarised in the following way:

1 *The problem of history.* There is a common suspicion of the teleological narrative that is seen to underpin Marx's work. This is to say that a uniting feature is the rejection of that aspect of Marx's approach that seemed

to suggest a unilinear pattern of historical development positing the 'inevitability' (mechanical, ethical or political) of communism as the 'end of history'.

2 *The problem of revolutionary subjectivities.* All of these figures reject the identification that follows from Marx's account of the historical process identifying the proletariat as the sole or primary agent of change. This is either because of the perceived redundancy of the working class as a meaningful category of analysis, or because the empirical behaviour of the working class suggested the obverse, or because other kinds of subjectivity were becoming relevant in questions of social change (New Social Movements, affinity groups, students etc.), or because the focus of class was only one relevant co-ordinate in the description of the operation of domination.

3 *The problem of ethics.* Marx is seen as promoting an economic determinism that denied the centrality of agency and thus of singular agents in political struggle. This undermines the sense of the agent as in some sense responsible and in turn undermines the ethical and moral aspects of the political agent. Marxism is seen as a utilitarian doctrine and thus one promoting the possibility of 'breaking eggs' to make the communist 'omelette'.

4 *The problem of positivism.* Marxism, it is held, privileges scientific knowledge over kinds of knowledge, from aesthetics and ethics, to 'experience', and practical reason. It thus sees revolutionary change as a scientific enterprise and posits the need for clear analysis as opposed to an ethical or moral imperative as the basis for acting. The Party is seen as the repository of this knowledge to the detriment of discussion and deliberation in other processes or institutions.

5 *The problem of vanguardism.* Since knowledge is valorised by Marxists in the pursuit of revolutionary goals it follows that those in possession of knowledge are similarly valorised relative to all others. The Party is thus divided either expressly or tacitly into cadres and masses, intellectuals and functionaries. Given this emphasis, such a division is, it is held, likely to pass over into the structure of post-revolutionary society, with a division between the 'planners' and those whose lives are planned.

6 *The problem of democracy.* Whatever *The Communist Manifesto* had said about 'winning the battle of democracy', Marxist political practice has at best paid lip-service to the notion. How, it was asked, could critique become a genuinely democratic and inclusive form of practice, both in terms of revolutionary praxis and in terms of the institutional forms of the future post-capitalist society?

Let us look briefly at each problematic in order to probe further the degree to which this problematising of central features of the Marxian tradition suggests the development of an alternative Post-Marxian paradigm.

The problem of history

The most obvious point of departure from classical Marxism is the rejection of the teleological narrative that is held to characterise the latter, particularly in its more Hegelian moments and iterations. This is to say that all the figures here reject the view that it is possible let alone desirable to posit history as a process of 'unfolding' towards some known endpoint. Habermas seeks to reconstruct historical materialism along lines accommodating interactive communicative and collective problem-solving elements. Laclau and Mouffe emphasise the contingent discursive nature of identity and the primacy of those identities in political struggles and outcomes. Virtually all the figures seek to blur to a greater or lesser extent the boundary between economic base and ideological superstructure, emphasising how ideology can affect the base and how the development of the base is often determined by political battles and hegemonic struggles of an unknown and unknowable outcome. The impression we get is thus less of a historical process, teleological or otherwise, as of an historical 'terrain' or battleground with broad parameters and fixed elements – but no 'direction' or imperative underpinning it. Even less is there held to be a 'meta-narrative' or overarching story into which all human action fits. There had to be room for 'historicity', for the sense of the historical as opposed to Marx's 'teleo-eschatological programme or design', as Derrida characteristically puts it. In short, Post-Marxists urge us to reopen the sense of history as something open, contingent and unpredictable. If this means dismantling the explanatory power of the base–superstructure heuristic then all the figures here seem more than willing to undertake the task.

These objections seem well founded. Empirical evidence of the truth of Marx's historical narrative is far from compelling, if only because some of Marx's expectations have yet (so far) to translate into reality. Capitalism is still with us; the contradictions expected to explode it, or at least undermine it, have yet to do so; the working class has in Western countries remained largely unmoved by various appeals over the past century to mount the barricades or even to take power through non-violent means. One could go on. This is surely not, however, the end of the argument. What becomes apparent, for example, is that far from abandoning 'meta-narratives', many Post-Marxists are happy enough to offer their own, in turn allowing us to query the openness and contingency of their own approach. A number are committed to a periodisation that insists on the reality of 'postmodern times', and others are insistent on the progressive 'unfolding' of modernity, often echoing Fukuyama's 'end of history' narrative. With the benefit of hindsight the suggestion that modernity equates to the universal unfolding of equality, liberty and democracy has a curiously outmoded feel to it given the deep inequalities of wealth and power around the world.

Post-Marxism is often less an anti-teleological stance than one that displaces one variant of teleology with another: the triumphant march of liberal democracy. The irony is that with the rise of transnational corporations, the weakening of the nation state as the site of power and contestation and the remilitarisation of the process of global accumulation even liberal commentators are often happy to signal the increased relevance of Marx's analysis of globalisation in the first section of the *Manifesto*. Marx's meta-narrative is perhaps more relevant now than it ever was in the past. Yet the point remains: Post-Marxist commentary often invokes the very sense of history as something impelled by deep lying forces whether they be unconscious or tendentially rooted in 'modernity'. The result is, on the plane of the political, a pessimistic and, on occasion, conservative account of human possibility that sits uneasily alongside the oft-declared aim to open up 'history' to possibility and invention. A further irony is that whereas in Marx's work as a whole we find deterministic statements of the kind that suggests an unfolding of this kind (*The 1859 Preface*), we also find more nuanced appreciations of the role of individual and collective actors in shaping social development (*The 18th Brumaire of Louis Bonaparte*). It is in this sense quite possible to find the resources in Marx for mounting a thorough critique of determinism in all its guises, and in particular in the guise of the 'Whig' retelling of history from the point of view of human propensities, 'human nature' or primordial qualities supposedly held by 'contingent' individuals.

The problem of revolutionary subjectivities

Marx had one vision of radical subjectivity and this was embodied in the working class – not, of course, the actually existing working class – but the working class 'in the making', to deploy E.P. Thompson. The distinction made desirable the creation and maintenance of the Communist Party as the 'leading' element of the class and as the repository of its permanent interests. As many critics, not just Post-Marxists, argue, this sense of the Party as the articulation between empirically existing class and class-for-itself gives it a privileged position in relation to class struggle and, indeed, the class itself. As we noted, Post-Marxism is a largely post-1968 phenomenon and one of the key reasons for this is that the radical political activity occurring during that time rarely seemed to be proletarian in origin or substance, and even less so associated with or instigated by revolutionary parties of the classical Marxist kind. The year 1968 saw the emergence of students, civil rights activists, women and the non-denumerable 'outside' of advanced capitalist society.

What impressed Post-Marxists was the non-working-class nature of the participants in these various actions and the non-class nature of many of their demands. This was a different kind of militancy, one animated by 'post-materialist' values, discrete causes and injustices and the struggle of distinct identities for visibility and voice. Here was proof positive of the non-materialist 'causes' of militant political action and thus the limited utility of the Marxian 'meta-narrative'. This provided the key to many Post-Marxian investigations and the probing of all kinds of sites and sources of radical energies, from machinic desire, to unconscious magmas, libidinal intensity and the deep wells of sublimated life forces. All latched on to the essentially spontaneous and unpredictable nature of these flows, desires, intensities, meanings to hammer home the limited utility of an approach that stressed the necessity for capitalist crisis as the basis of radical politics and the necessity for political action against 'immiseration'. The desire to act became one more arbitrary, non-determined, non-causally rooted 'moment' demonstrating the capriciousness at the heart of the human condition.

What are we to make of these attempts to improve upon the Marxist account of radical subjectivity? The positives seem obvious enough. What '1968' and the re-emergence of New Social Movements tell us is that class is not the only basis of radical political action, and in many ways is becoming less significant as a means of analysing the rise of certain forms of struggle and the nature of many political demands. Post-Marxist perspectives have taken seriously the specificity of different kinds of oppressions, and the different locations in which oppressions take place. Rather than allowing them all to be marginalised by or subsumed under the discursive character of class struggle and proletarian emancipation, these 'minoritarian' oppressions were given centre-stage in Post-Marxist analysis. Struggles and resistances have a complex, diverse, plural nature to them under advanced capitalist conditions, and Post-Marxism takes seriously the idea that this plurality is in some sense constitutive. It tells us that the experience of oppression and domination is multi-causal, non-reducible and contextualised. Any attempt to reduce this complexity to the story of a given class will rightly be regarded as at best patronising and at worst exclusionary.

On the other hand, such accounts have their limitations. The first is that in emphasising the unpredictable and spontaneous character of human action the material causes of radical political action are too often underplayed. This is not to say that all meaningful resistance has a material cause; but it often does, often enough to suggest that poverty and material factors are at least as important as other variables in radicalising individuals. It would thus hardly be of surprise to a Marxist to find that many of the various resistances and protests witnessed since Fukuyama's declaration of the end of history (1989) are 'materialist' in character and orientation, often impressively so. Just to take Latin America, the Zapatista insurgency was sparked by the signing of the North American Free Trade Agreement in 1994 and by the general lack of resources and power of indigenous peoples. Hugo Chavez's coming to power in Venezuela was similarly caused by poverty and unemployment together with the desire of indigenous peasants to seek recognition. His programme focuses on the return of scarce natural resources and the redistribution of land to peasants. The fall of the Bolivian presidency in 2005 was directly caused by peasant resistance. Both the electoral success of the Brazilian Workers' Party (PT) in 2002 and the radical Left in Uruguay in 2004 have economic causes at heart. More generally the rise of an 'anti-capitalist movement' is at one level plausibly read in terms of Marx's analysis – as of course it is by a now newly confident Marxian Left. Such developments are not, in other words, just a case of 'desire' or an unruly magma from which the urge to resist evolves. These are, in terms of self-definition, revolts against 'neo-liberalism' and often explicitly in the name of specific or general 'interests' that have been neglected or ignored.

Of course many Post-Marxists rail against the idea of 'interests' and objective class conditions; but if hindsight can be of any service here it is in reminding us that the category of 'interest' is far from exhausted as a heuristic device. Asking 'who benefits?' is still a useful basis from which to gauge how and why the economically powerful behave in the way they do. It also allows us to offer the *Marxisant* conjecture that the era of New Social Movements and diverse and plural struggles was one tied up with a quiescent era of capitalist accumulation. With the oil crisis and the depression of the 1970s this quiescence gave way to the more strident politics of neo-liberalism and the assault on the 'overloaded state'. Gone the relative comfort and security which allowed these ideas of 'diversity' and 'plurality' to circulate and flourish. Post-Marxism born in this climate was very much a creature of it. As material conditions worsened, particularly at the periphery and semi-periphery over the course of the 1980s and 1990s, so political radicalism reverted to a more 'materialist' character. The result in these regions has been increasingly militant trade union activity, the rise of populist socialist leaders such as Chavez and the attempt to forge bonds of solidarity across the labour movement generally.

This above does not invalidate Post-Marxist findings, which remain pertinent in the most advanced industrial countries. It reminds us that just as Post-Marxism was a reaction to the failure of Communism in advanced industrial society, so it is very much a creature *of* advanced industrial society. It is a creature of Post-Fordism, of post-industrialism, postmodernism (even in reaction to it), of the perceived 'death of the working class'. But what recent events across the developing world remind us of is that much of the world's population lives under conditions all too familiar to the reader of *Capital*. They do not have the basic means enjoyed by many students and civil rights activists of the 1960s, but are rather locked into the weary battles familiar from Marx's accounts of the travails of the Chartists, of early trade unionists and the Working Men's Association. From the perspective of this world, Marx's analysis looks far from exhausted.

The problem of ethics

Many of the figures here did not seek to repair Marx's ethical deficit in overt philosophical terms (Heller is perhaps the exception). Yet recognition of the need to address the issue of the terms and conditions upon which the individual should, or could, act was a major preoccupation of many Post-Marxists. Foucault suggested that Deleuze and Guattari offered not a politics but an ethics centred on the necessity to resist incorporation into 'micro-fascist' structures and projects. Feminists lent towards an 'ethic of care'; Lyotard placed the problem of justice at the heart of his later work; and for Laclau and Mouffe toleration of the other became the ultimate value in their modelling of a radical democracy. In addition to this making room for choice and preference, Post-Marxists developed their own ethical systems and foundations. Habermas developed a 'discourse ethics' grounded in communication; Heller explicitly invoked the deontological ethics of Kant; and Derrida placed great emphasis on openness to others, invoking communism, justice and democracy as aspects of the 'universal structure' of human experience.

These accounts remind us that Marx could indeed be dismissive of ethics and morality as relics of the religious imaginary inherited from feudalism. A radical science did not need a radical ethics. Knowledge would guide action, not values. But there was also a more compelling reason for Marx's haughtiness in relation to individual responsibility, and this is that it invoked an artificially inflated sense of the importance of individual action, when the reality was that it was classes that mattered. Ethics was on this view condition-dependent, and in particular dependent on a world in which there were meaningful choices to be made by discrete individuals. The idea that under conditions of exploitation there are such choices was a key plank in Marx's critique of bourgeois ideology, one which posits the individual as 'chooser', 'actor' and designer of his or her own 'fate'. Such an image was one that kept alive the sense of having control over one's own life when the reality was, for Marx, quite different. This was a description of the condition of choice for the *bourgeois*, not for the great mass of men and women who were constrained by the material circumstances in which they found themselves. We can add that such a standpoint is hardly irrelevant for describing the dilemmas confronted even now by large swathes of the world's population. For those huddling in the *favelas*, *barrios*, ghettos, shanty towns and cardboard cities of the developing metropolis, the world of ethical dilemmas, of 'others' to be respected, of pluralisms to be entertained and tolerated, is far removed from the daily grind many encounter.

On the other hand, we can note that the character of recent struggles and resistances often has an overtly 'ethical' character to them. The sense of historical inevitability or necessity that helped the Bolsheviks fortify their supporters is clearly anachronistic, as is the notion that ethics could be decided in the heat of battle. The Zapatistas evoke explicitly the need to 'listen' to their constituency as opposed to 'leading' them; the PT's revolution is one understood in terms of the need to foster participation; and even the populist Chavez takes care to ensure that 'campaneros' are given their opportunity to speak and share experiences. More generally, a feature of the anti-capitalist movement is less the overthrowing of structures as much creating their own in the image of the world they would like to create. The World Social Forum, the institutional flag-bearer of the alter-globalist movement, characterises itself as an inclusive 'space', as a forum in which difference and plurality will be heard. All around are reminders of the need to adapt in accordance with shifting priorities, different interpretations and changing emphases.

So at one level Post-Marxists seem to be vindicated in their insistence on the inevitability of the ethical – but what is also noticeable is that under contemporary conditions this is ethics with a distinctly radical purpose: to combat the unethical regime of capitalism and the institutions that underpin it. It is an ethics that finds itself outside liberal democracy and thus outside the framework of possibility lauded by Heller, Lyotard, Laclau and Mouffe, and even Habermas. Plurality and diversity has not in this sense rendered transformative politics irrelevant as many such figures assumed it would. It has changed the nature and character of transformative politics from being built around structures of representation (party, congress, manifesto) to being built around shared affect and what Subcomandante Marcos of the Zapatistas terms the 'intuition' that dignity requires overcoming capital.

The problem of positivism

A major strand in the Post-Marxist case against Marxism is evidently the discontent with the positivist methods that underpinned the teleological narrative and aspirations of Marx and some of his later followers. The fact that it was Engels who lauded Marx in the spirit of Darwin is, it seems, easily forgotten, as is the fact that many of Marx's later followers such as Gramsci, Lukacs, Korsch and the Frankfurt School were stern critics of positivism, yet still Marxists. Nonetheless such declarations and expectations are doubted by Post-Marxists who almost universally stress the contingency of human action, radical and unique forms of human subjectivity, and the 'historicity' as opposed to determined character of the historical process. This has different sources and colourings, according to the intellectual 'language game' being played. The concern with the unconscious as evidenced in the work of Castoriadis, Deleuze and Guattari and the early Lyotard supplied one source of contingency in that the unconscious was seen as either undetermined and creative, or itself the source of social reality. For the more post-structuralist inclined, the priority of language was the key to reading contingency. Language did not mirror the world, so much as generate meaning through the internal play of *différance*. Given the difficulty of maintaining the stability of meaning, destabilisation and newness were constant threats to the overall integrity of the sign system and beyond that social life generally. For others such as Habermas, a key feature of the human condition is problem-solving capacity, which is inherently contingent and unpredictable. For these various reasons the attempt to predict the unpredictable at the heart of the positivist enterprise is at once incompatible with an emancipatory ethic and suffocating of it. As the history of communist regimes showed, the attempt to regularise and account for all possible outcomes was inevitably doomed to fail with literally fatal consequences. Lyotard was in this respect Marxism's harshest critic, equating the desire to account for the whole with the totalitarian impulse to control and suffocate newness. Although Habermas saw Lyotard and his followers as 'young conservatives', they were perhaps closer on this key matter than either cared to admit.

The case against Marx is well trodden and there are armies lined up on the other side to protest both the innocence and the guilt of the relevant parties. What is less remarked upon is the degree to which, notwithstanding these assaults, many Post-Marxists are themselves heavily committed, if not to positivist schemas, then to explanatory frameworks that evince predictions and hypotheses of a kind otherwise condemned as totalising. Deleuze and Guattari, for example, are committed to a strong ontological position that insists on our ability to read large-scale processes and effects such as fascism and capitalism with reference to desire and libidinal investment. We have noted that Lyotard substitutes one meta-narrative with another, namely that of the onward march of the postmodern condition. Even a figure such as Derrida, for all his aporias, slippages and plays of signs, erects an impressively totalising system, which in the hands of his many admirers can become just as suffocating and intolerant a practice as Marxism. The difference is that the ambition to translate explanatory schemas into political practice is signally absent in many of those who fly the flag for these approaches. What seems as difficult to ignore is, as we noted above, the durable nature of Marx's analysis of the structures of capitalism, if not the trajectory of capitalist society as such. Marxism may not be a science in the manner described by Comte; but it is one that seems still to inspire works of great interest and richness – as many Post-Marxists are happy to concede. The positivist charge may thus hide as much as it reveals, namely the degree to which Marx's work has at one level survived the test of time and been deployed to greatly augment our understanding of the world around us.

The problem of vanguardism

The Post-Marxist distaste for positivism was not merely intellectual in origin, but one that concerned the nature and role of intellectuals in theoretical and political practice. It is one, we can note, that was of considerable concern to Marx himself. As he insisted, the task of the emancipation of the proletariat was a task of *self*-emancipation. It was for these reasons that he opposed utopian schemes as 'recipes for the cookshops of the future'; and also the idea that the Communist Party was an entity that stood apart from the proletariat, as opposed to being merely the 'leading' element of it. The difficulty is that Marx is judged not only by what he wrote, but also by what Marxists did and do in his name. The examples to date hardly encourage the view that such a definition has been at the heart of Marxist attempts to generate radical trans-formation or, once in power, to put the needs, wants and interests of the class above the narrower needs of the party apparatus itself. As the litany of exam-ples from recent history demonstrate, all too often Communist Parties have found themselves at odds with those they are said to lead or represent, with the effect that the empirical wishes of ordinary men and women have often disappeared in the attempt to make reality fit the theory.

It is the ease with which Marx's writings were turned into recipes, if not for 'cookshops', then for what became known as 'substitutionism' that forms the strategic backdrop for Post-Marxist attempts to 'de-centre' the intellectual. Mouffe argues that the political philosopher's role should be to offer different interpretations of justice, equality and liberty, rather than 'true' ones. A similar line is implicit to Heller and Lyotard's critique of meta-narratives, with its attendant fetishisation of the role of the intellec-tual in bringing 'truth' to the hapless masses. More substantially, the point was often and repeatedly made, that since the goal of history was always-already known then this self-emancipation was always exclusionary in the manner by which it sifted out forms of emancipation that did not follow the lines outlined by Marx himself. The proletariat was only emancipating itself, in this sense when it was doing what Marxists told it do – which, of course, defeated the point in the first place. All this demonstrates the impor-tance of contingency and the unknowability of subjective preference and desire. If the how and why of human preference and language eluded map-ping along predictable and 'known' lines, then in a sense the role of the intellectual can be nothing more than the careful exploration and investigation of what a number termed the 'local' nature of resistances and struggles. There was no overarching cause of resistance and struggle and thus no overarching role for the intellectual to play in the channelling or shaping of them. The intellectual's wings were clipped by all manner of strategies. He or she descended from the status of Philosopher-King, to a modest figure of no great consequence or stature. The intellectual voice was one amongst a cacophony of rival voices – no more though no less valuable than anyone else's.

In relativist times such a stance is mainstream rather than revolutionary, which is perhaps the source of a certain difficulty, for such a stance undoubtedly enacts the kind of performative contradiction with which we have become familiar. In making claims as to the nature of the role of truth and the intellectual, theorists are doing more than merely adding their voices to the hubbub. They are saying how and in what circumstances particular voices and thus particular individuals *should* be regarded by everyone else. They are making claims of a traditionally 'intellectual' kind that look strangely like the claims of those they are criticising. They are speaking to those 'below' – shaping the contours of theoretical and political combat. As otherwise sympathetic critics such as Gayatri Spivak have argued, the 'local' nature of, for example, Foucault and Deleuze's intellectualism was essentially self-contradictory, involving a global claim about what it was and was not possible for intellectuals to say and think. In addition both were and are fêted in all manner of respects, not least by the hagiographical treatment of the kind Marx himself was deeply embarrassed about. Moreover, whatever their democratic intentions the often baroque, dense or otherwise opaque prose of the 'Post-Marxists' gives scant credence to the idea that they were able to escape the vicissitudes of vanguardism, albeit of a peculiarly academic kind.

By contrast Marx at least aspired to being the kind of intellectual that Gramsci would later term 'organic'. This is to say that he saw his own theoretical practice as being informed by, as well as informing, the actual political struggles with which he was daily involved. Contrast the clear prose of a work such as *The Communist Manifesto* with the elusive jargon of much Post-Marxist writing. The point is that critical thinkers do not evade intellectual vanguardism by retreating to the academy; but by seeking to connect to the lives and concerns of actual people engaged in real struggles. Marx knew this. His failure, if such it was, is not rooted in any lack of effort to connect to those struggles. It is surely better characterised as located in the tacit contradictions of an enterprise that sought to connect knowledge and action, knowing and doing. The claim to understand or explain a process is both a moment of 'vanguardism' and a moment of potential emancipation ('*I know the way; follow me*'). The only way to avoid the contradiction of analysis is either to drop the Kantian admonition to learn through knowledge ('*Sapere aude*'), or to drop emancipatory aims in the name of avoiding choosing between one form of life and another. Both positions might with justification be regarded as complicit in the maintenance of the status quo.

The problem of democracy

Ultimately many of the points raised above coalesced in terms of the critique of Marxian politics generally and its impoverished account of democracy in particular. Marx, it seems, thought the working-class movement was democratic in so far as it manifested the deep-rooted interests and/or needs of the working class to challenge wage labour. He assumed that with the intensification of class struggle and class consciousness that increased numbers would enter the movement, forming a counterweight to any sectarian or partial interests developing within it. And of course he expected the Communist Party to comport itself both as a part of this movement and as a leading element of it – both leader and led. There is a certain naïvety in the assumption that merely by positing itself as part of a broader movement this alone would guarantee that any such party would remain true to the wishes, hopes and interests of those who composed the latter. It shows that a large part of the work of 'democratic theory' was in fact being done by the trends and tendencies of capitalism, and with the idea of the inevitable intensification of class struggle. As capitalism became unsustainable so the options narrowed, to the point where Rosa Luxemburg could declare that the choice confronting the working class was black and white: 'socialism or barbarism'.

On the other hand, it is clear that Marx did have a theory of democracy if not a 'democratic theory'. He argued that parliamentary democracy was illusory and sectional; whilst organic forms of democratic self-organisation such as those developed in the course of the Paris Commune of 1871 prefigured the proletarian democracy to come. Nevertheless, as seems clear enough, Post-Marxism is at one level a complaint about the lack of a developed account of the conditions and operation of a post-capitalist-democratic order. There may be an account of democracy here, but it is too thin or undernourished to provide a meaningful counterweight to the determinism and positivism of Marx's overall approach. Beyond that, differences flow. There is a world of difference between, for example, Deleuze and Guattari's 'nomadic' post-democracy and the modest constitutionalism of the later Habermas. More fundamentally, Post-Marxism seems split between those who have decided that a progressive politics must involve the radicalisation – if not consolidation – of *existing* liberal-democratic capitalism, and those who see a necessary break between the democratic forms available now and those 'to come'. Thus Laclau and Mouffe, Heller, Habermas and

Lyotard are all in their ways insistent that liberal democracy is in some sense ambiguous or contingent enough to allow radicals the prospect of working for the extension of democracy from within. Heller, for example, was at pains to repeat there is nothing in the operation or practice of liberal democracy to rule out the extension or radicalisation of democratic practice. By contrast Deleuze and Guattari, Castoriadis and even Derrida are all to one degree or other more sceptical, seeing the operation of liberal democracy as in some key sense complementary to the operation of capitalism and private accumulation. All urged not merely the extension or radicalisation of democracy, but its displacement by forms of interaction that allowed for an authentic communal collective form of existence, such as found in the 'polis' or in some more elusive or abstract process of deliberation.

On the other hand, if there is a uniting theme here, then it is with the recognition – or assertion – of the constitutive nature of human difference and diversity, and thus the necessity for institutions, procedures and processes that allow these differences to shape collective outcomes. It is as much Marx's alleged indifference to difference that irked as much as his dismissal of the need for deliberation beyond 'the administration of things'. The point many Post-Marxists made is that there is a limit to representation, and to being represented – even by those with the very best interests of the community at heart. There is always something, some desire, some form of identity, some profound need or wish that 'escapes', making necessary deliberation as a 'political' act. The denial of this difference was the denial of the individual's 'individuality' on this reading. To embrace democracy was in this sense to embrace the idea of openness – openness to difference, to contingency, to collective self-creation. Hence the centrality of procedure, and the need to adhere to the outcomes of a properly democratic process. Hence too the notion, oft-heard, of democracy as a kind of 'empty place' or space in which the community can map its own future without regard to historical process of determination. In short, communism was seen as an anti-democratic ideal, one that limited the community to a given path of societal rationality.

If there is a drawback with the collective demand for 'democracy' of Post-Marxism then it is that they rarely analysed sufficiently the *conditions* for democracy, and thus radically underestimated the degree to which democratic procedures and outcomes can be shaped, manipulated and distorted by the actions of those with access to the media, to mechanisms of representation and political parties. This is of course particularly so in the case of those who insist that a radicalisation of democracy is possible within the liberal-capitalist framework that generations of earlier radicals, and not just Marxists, insisted was a major stumbling-block to permitting people's voices to be heard. Developments over recent decades have if anything sharpened rather than blunted the force of these critiques. The media has in most advanced democracies increasingly concentrated in the hands of a few magnates or corporations; the cost of entry into democratic participation has become increasingly prohibitive; the increase in police and military capacity in advanced democratic states makes 'radical' activity of any kind increasingly precarious or foolhardy. The Post-Marxist expectation that the 'unfolding' of the democratic revolution would equate to the unfolding of opportunities and occasions to radicalise existing structures looks, from the vantage point of contemporary democratic politics, naïve; but of course many Post-Marxists will always retort, and with some reason, that it is for these very reasons naïve to assume that radical change *could* come from without. As many of them argue with some justification, many such efforts have tended to worsen rather than improve the lot of ordinary men and women.

Nonetheless, a key factor in contemporary discussions of the 'democratic deficit' is rarely factored into the analysis of much Post-Marxist writing. This is that the nation state has become ever more denuded of sovereignty and power to alter states of affairs that are now the result of global forces and flows of money unhampered by national markets. 'Democracy' remains at the level of the nation state whereas power and influence are increasingly to be found at the global level (IMF, World Bank, G8 etc.). The irony is that 'globalisation' was long ago analysed on such terms by Marx in *The Communist Manifesto*. His conclusion that resistance at the local or national level had to be augmented and then intensified at the global level was certainly novel in 1848; now, however, it is the *sine qua non* for a meaningful democratic politics, whether social democratic or anti-capitalist. In short, the notion that existing democracy needs to be radicalised or extended loses sight of the key feature of political developments over the past three decades. There is no global 'democracy' to speak of – nor very much of a prospect of one developing under the global elites. Even the milder Post-Marxists thus find themselves in the position of Jacobins rather than the Victorian or liberal progressives they can sometimes sound like. Democracy of a meaningful kind has first to be created; and this in turn means confronting those who oppose the dilution of their power in favour of a global *Estates General*. Marx understood this, but then he was standing closer to the 'democratic revolution' sweeping Europe than are today's radicals. On the other hand, this still leaves the 'problem of democracy' – of how it is to be constituted, of who is to be heard. Today's anti-capitalists have shown in their taste for 'horizontal' and non-hierarchical structures, for 'disorganisation' and 'rhizomatic' self-organisation, an awareness of the perils of vanguardism that earlier generations of radicals were perhaps less aware of, or prepared to confront at face value. For the former there can be no assumption of 'interest' of a representable kind. Voice, presence and difference are, as Post-Marxists have long advised, intrinsic to the prefiguration of radical alternatives. The politics of the New Social Movements and their more recent progeny are testament to the relevance of the observation.

So what are we to make of Post-Marxism? What remains significant and worth commenting on is the vastly different nature of the enterprises associated with the latter and Marxism. In one sense all the thinkers considered in this volume could be considered practice-'lite', fitting neatly into Perry Anderson's characterisation of 'Western Marxism' as a body of knowledge that had ceased to work within the theory/practice tension. Nearly all the thinkers considered here, although they often had strong political affiliations at some stage of their career, could be considered as philosophers of one stripe or another, many drawing regular stipends from academia (Guattari and Castoriadis are the obvious exceptions). In sharp contrast with the Marxists of the early decades of the twentieth century – Kautsky, Lenin, Luxemburg, Trotsky and Gramsci – all of whom could be considered as 'organic' intellectuals firmly embedded in workers' movements committed to social transformation. The academic and philosophical platform of Post-Marxism could be viewed as problematic given their apparent commitment to emancipation as a practical concern – all 'talk' and little 'walk'.

Yet two responses need to be made here in summing up. The first is that the role of radical intellectuals is not to tell those struggling to free themselves from exploitation or oppression what to do. The assumption that it is, is of course one of the major uniting points for these otherwise disparate figures. At one level the uncoupling of theory from practice is for many of them a necessary antidote to vanguardism and substitutionism, and Post-Marxists are surely only being consistent with this view if they hold unapologetically to their stipends and prestigious posts. This uncoupling allows the 'user group', as it were, to assess for themselves the utility or veracity of Post-Marxist as well as all other recommendations, as opposed to having some 'analysis' or other thrust upon them by Party leaders.

The second response is that Marx's eleventh *Theses on Feuerbach* posits a distinction between 'interpreting the world' and 'changing it'. Such a distinction has become unhelpful in a world of plural and conflicting interpretations. Changing the world rests upon an interpretation of that world. It is interpretation that gives the world meaning, providing both the insight and the rationale for changing it. Hence theory is and will be separate from practice. The best practice is informed by theory, but also by an awareness of the limitations of theory, that what we do also impacts on the world to be theorised. But we have outlived the notion that there can be *one* true theory and *one* true movement towards emancipation. If there is an enduring theme to Post-Marxism, it is that if there is a truth at the level of theory and at the level of practice, then it is 'multiple', just as desires, needs, wants, visions are multiple. In so far as Marxism remains within the monist frame seeking to reduce this plurality to neat binaries and oppositions then of course it resists this vision of multiple interpretations, projects, emancipations.

On the other hand, Marx himself (as so often) offers a cure for the opposition between monism and pluralism, and perhaps between 'Marxism' and 'Post-Marxism'. Marx was at one level a positivist figure committed to politics as 'science', to an auto-developmental view of the historical process and the role of the individual within it, to class and collective structures as opposed to individuals and their diverse and conflicting needs and desires. But Marx himself could be a subtle and nuanced commentator concerning those very same objects of enquiry. He was committed to the self-emancipation of 'the least well-off', to a view of the historical process that was context- and condition-dependent, to a view of political action as an open field of possibility as opposed to the realisation of a utopian 'cookbook' or blueprint. If we can talk about the significance of Post-Marxism then it is to remind us of the importance of plurality, diversity, difference in understanding individual and social existence. The significance of Marx is that he showed that plurality, diversity and difference are rarely meaningfully expressed under conditions of material poverty, exploitation and oppression. Unless in this sense we address the latter we will never have the full flourishing that we associate with the former. From this point of view, just as 'Post-Marxism' represents a challenge to the reductive Marxism of 'actually existing socialism', so Marxism can surely be regarded as a kind of corrective to the wilder flights of wishful thinking displayed by many Post-Marxists. The world is still capitalist; the lives of the many are hostage to the wishes of the few. Inequality, powerlessness and oppression are, notwithstanding the heralds of the 'End of History', still with us. It is surely safe to predict that as long as they are, we will need to think about the beyond or 'outside' of this world. We will need both a theory and a practice of critical thought that offers alternatives, visions, possibilities and suggestions for betterment – and we will probably need both Marxism and its sceptical 'outside', 'Post-Marxism'.

Index